Bond
Math

The Wiley Finance series contains books written specifically for finance and investment professionals as well as sophisticated individual investors and their financial advisors. Book topics range from portfolio management to e-commerce, risk management, financial engineering, valuation and financial instrument analysis, as well as much more. For a list of available titles, visit our website at www.WileyFinance.com.

Founded in 1807, John Wiley & Sons is the oldest independent publishing company in the United States. With offices in North America, Europe, Australia, and Asia, Wiley is globally committed to developing and marketing print and electronic products and services for our customers' professional and personal knowledge and understanding.

Bond Math

The Theory Behind the Formulas

Second Edition

DONALD J. SMITH

WILEY

Cover image: abstract © aleksandarvelasevic/iStock.com
Cover design: Wiley

Published by John Wiley & Sons, Inc., Hoboken, New Jersey.

The First Edition of *Bond Math* was published by John Wiley & Sons, Inc. in 2011.

Published simultaneously in Canada.

For general information on our other products and services or for technical support, please contact our Customer Care Department within the United States at (800) 762-2974, outside the United States at (317) 572-3993, or fax (317) 572-4002.

Wiley publishes in a variety of print and electronic formats and by print-on-demand. Some material included with standard print versions of this book may not be included in e-books or in print-on-demand. If this book refers to media such as a CD or DVD that is not included in the version you purchased, you may download this material at http://booksupport.wiley.com. For more information about Wiley products, visit www.wiley.com.

Library of Congress Cataloging-in-Publication Data:

Smith, Donald J., 1947-
  Bond math : the theory behind the formulas / Donald J. Smith. — Second edition.
    pages cm. — (Wiley finance)
  Includes bibliographical references and index.
  ISBN 978-1-118-86632-0 (hardback); 978-1-118-86629-0 (ebk); 978-1-118-86636-8 (ebk)
  1. Bonds—Mathematical models.   2. Interest rates—Mathematical models.
  3. Zero coupon securities.   I. Title.
  HG4651.S57 2014
  332.63'2301519—dc23
                                                    2014018633

Printed in the United States of America.
10 9 8 7 6 5 4 3 2 1

To my students

Contents

Preface to the Second Edition

I am pleased to present the second edition of *Bond Math*. I'm sure my editors at Wiley will disagree but I'm more impressed with *who* reads the book rather than *how many*. I've been very happy with reader responses to the first edition. Best of all, based on the book, I was invited by CFA Institute to write two new readings on Fixed-Income Valuation and Risk and Return for the Chartered Financial Analyst® Level I curriculum. I was joined in that endeavor by James Adams, with whom I've been writing a series of articles on corporate finance applications of derivatives to hedge interest rate risk. One of the changes to the second edition of this book is to align the notation and terminology used in *Bond Math* with the CFA Institute readings. Also, I have added the simple model to value floating-rate notes that is used in the Fixed-Income Valuation reading.

One of my objectives is to explain the math behind numbers presented on commonly used Bloomberg pages, primarily the Yield and Spread Analysis page for bonds. Bloomberg has changed the format of this page since the first edition, so it is timely to update the examples. I like the new format—the page is less "busy," as a graphic designer might say. In Chapters 3 and 6 I show the formulas that generate the various risk and return statistics for fixed-income bonds, that is, yield to maturity, modified duration, and convexity, included on that page. But still there are some Bloomberg numbers that I think are misleading and unreliable. You see in Chapter 4 that Bloomberg makes a curious assumption for some bonds to get the projected after-tax rate of return, namely, that current U.S. tax law does not apply to the investor. Also, you see in Chapter 7 that Bloomberg shows some hard-to-understand (and therefore use) modified duration results for a floating-rate note.

Chapter 8 is significantly revised from the first edition. I now include discussion of how the financial crisis of 2007 to 2009 has changed derivatives valuation. The traditional method to value interest rate swaps, which I use in the first edition, is called LIBOR discounting. The idea is that LIBOR is a workable and reasonable proxy for the interbank "risk-free" interest rate. The financial crisis revealed the flaws in that assumption. Nowadays, OIS discounting is the standard. Rates on overnight indexed swaps are now used to generate the discount factors to value derivatives. You see that with

OIS discounting, care must be taken in valuing a swap as a combination of fixed-rate and floating-rate bonds, as you might have learned in a derivatives textbook.

A second edition of *Bond Math* has been on my wish list. Next on the list is to have it translated from American to British financial English and use examples of U.K. gilts instead of U.S. Treasuries. The title of the translation would have to be *Bond Maths*.

Preface to the First Edition

This book could be titled *Applied Bond Math* or, perhaps, *Practical Bond Math*. Those who do serious research on fixed-income securities and markets know that this subject matter goes far beyond the mathematics covered herein. Those who are interested in discussions about "pricing kernels" and "stochastic discount rates" will have to look elsewhere. My target audience is those who work in the finance industry (or aspire to), know what a Bloomberg page is, and in the course of the day might hear or use terms such as "yield to maturity," "forward curve," and "modified duration."

My objective in *Bond Math* is to explain the theory and assumptions that lie behind the commonly used statistics regarding the risk and return on bonds. I show many of the formulas that are used to calculate yield and duration statistics and, in the Technical Appendix, their formal derivations. But I do not expect a reader to actually *use* the formulas or *do* the calculations. There is much to be gained by recognizing that "there exists an equation" and becoming more comfortable using a number that is taken from a Bloomberg page, knowing that the result could have been obtained using a bond math formula.

This book is based on my 25 years of experience teaching this material to graduate students and finance professionals. For that, I thank the many deans, department chairs, and program directors at the Boston University School of Management who have allowed me to continue teaching fixed-income courses over the years. I thank Euromoney Training in New York and Hong Kong for organizing four-day intensive courses for me all over the world. I thank training coordinators at Chase Manhattan Bank (and its heritage banks, Manufacturers Hanover and Chemical), Lehman Brothers, and the Bank of Boston for paying me handsomely to teach their employees on so many occasions in so many interesting venues. Bond math has been very, very good to me.

The title of this book emanates from an eponymous two-day course I taught many years ago at the old Manny Hanny. (Okay, I admit that I have always wanted to use the word "eponymous"; now I can cross that off my bucket list.) I thank Keith Brown of the University of Texas at Austin, who co-designed and co-taught many of those executive training courses, for emphasizing the value of relating the formulas to results reported on Bloomberg. I have found that users of "black box" technologies find comfort in knowing how those bond numbers are calculated, which ones are useful, which ones are essentially meaningless, and which ones are just wrong.

Our journey through applied and practical bond math starts in the money market, where we have to deal with anachronisms like discount rates and a 360-day year. A key point in Chapter 1 is that knowing the *periodicity* of an annual interest rate (i.e., the assumed number of periods in the year) is critical. Converting from one periodicity to another—for instance, from quarterly to semiannual—is a core bond math calculation that I use throughout the book. Money market rates can be deceiving because they are not intuitive and do not follow classic time-value-of-money principles taught in introductory finance courses. You have to know what you are doing to play with T-bills, commercial paper, and bankers acceptances.

Chapters 2 and 3 go deep into calculating prices and yields, first on zero-coupon bonds to get the ideas out for a simple security like U.S. Treasury STRIPS (i.e., just two cash flows) and then on coupon bonds for which coupon reinvestment is an issue. The yield to maturity on a bond is a *summary statistic* about its cash flows—it's important to know the assumptions that underlie this widely quoted measure of an investor's rate of return and what to do when those assumptions are untenable. I decipher Bloomberg's Yield Analysis page for a typical corporate bond, showing the math behind "street convention," "U.S. government equivalent," and "true" yields. The problem is distinguishing between yields that are pure data (and can be overlooked) and those that provide information useful in making a decision about the bond.

Chapter 4 continues the exploration of rate-of-return measures on an after-tax basis for corporate, Treasury, and municipal bonds. Like all tax matters, this necessarily gets technical and complicated. Taxation, at least in the U.S., depends on when the bond was issued (there were significant changes in the 1980s and 1990s), at what issuance price (there are different rules for original issue discount bonds), and whether a bond issued at (or close to) par value is later purchased at a premium or discount. Given the inevitability of taxes, this is important stuff—and it is stuff on which Bloomberg sometimes reports a misleading result, at least for U.S. investors.

Yield curve analysis, in Chapter 5, is arguably the most important topic in the book. There are many practical applications arising from bootstrapped implied zero-coupon (or spot) rates and implied forward rates—identifying arbitrage opportunities, obtaining discount factors to get present values, calculating spreads, and pricing and valuing derivatives. However, the operative assumption in this analysis is "no arbitrage"—that is, transactions costs and counterparty credit risk are sufficiently small so that trading eliminates any arbitrage opportunity. Therefore, while mathematically elegant, yield curve analysis is best applied to Treasury securities and LIBOR-based interest rate derivatives for which the no-arbitrage assumption is reasonable.

Duration and convexity, the subject of Chapter 6, is the most mathematical topic in this book. These statistics, which in classic form measure the sensitivity of the bond price to a change in its yield to maturity, can be derived with algebra and calculus. Those details are relegated to the Technical Appendix. Another version of the risk statistics measures the sensitivity of the bond price to a shift in the entire Treasury yield curve. I call the former *yield* and the latter *curve* duration and convexity and demonstrate where and how they are presented on Bloomberg pages.

Chapters 7 and 8 examine floating-rate notes (floaters), inflation-indexed bonds (linkers), and interest rate swaps. The idea is to use the bond math toolkit—periodicity conversions, bond valuation, after-tax rates of return, implied spot rates, implied forward rates, and duration and convexity—to examine securities other than traditional fixed-rate and zero-coupon bonds. In particular, I look for circumstances of *negative duration*, meaning market value and interest rates are positively correlated. That's an obvious feature for one type of interest rate swap but a real oddity for a floater and a linker.

Understanding the risk and return characteristics for an individual bond is easy compared to a portfolio of bonds. In Chapter 9, I show different ways of getting summary statistics. One is to treat the portfolio as a big bundle of cash flow and derive its yield, duration, and convexity is if it were just a single bond with many variable payments. While that is theoretically correct, in practice portfolio statistics are calculated as weighted averages of those for the constituent bonds. Some statistics can be aggregated in this manner and provide reasonable estimates of the "true" values, depending on how the weights are calculated and on the shape of the yield curve.

Chapter 10 is on bond strategies. If your hope is that I'll show you how to get rich by trading bonds, you'll be disappointed. My focus is on how the bond math tools and the various risk and return statistics that we can calculate for individual bonds and portfolios can facilitate either aggressive or passive investment strategies. I'll discuss derivative overlays, immunization, and liability-driven investing and conclude with a request that the finance industry create target-duration bond funds.

I'd like to thank my Wiley editors for allowing me to deviate from their usual publishing standards so that I can use in this book acronyms, italics, and notation as I prefer. Now let's get started in the money market.

CHAPTER 1

Money Market Interest Rates

An interest rate is a summary statistic about the cash flows on a debt security such as a loan or a bond. As a statistic, it is a number that we calculate. An objective of this chapter is to demonstrate that there are many ways to do this calculation. Like many statistics, an interest rate can be deceiving and misleading. Nevertheless, we need interest rates to make financial decisions about borrowing and lending money and about buying and selling securities. To avoid being deceived or misled, we need to understand how interest rates are calculated.

It is useful to divide the world of debt securities into *short-term money markets* and *long-term bond markets*. The former is the home of money market instruments such as Treasury bills, commercial paper, bankers acceptances, bank certificates of deposit, and overnight and term sale-repurchase agreements (called "repos"). The latter is where we find coupon-bearing notes and bonds that are issued by the Treasury, corporations, federal agencies, and municipalities. The key reference interest rate in the U.S. money market is 3-month LIBOR (the London Interbank offer rate); the benchmark bond yield is on 10-year Treasuries.

This chapter is on money market interest rates. Although the money market usually is defined as securities maturing in one year or less, much of the activity is in short-term instruments, from overnight out to six months. The typical motivation for both issuers and investors is cash management arising from the mismatch in the timing of revenues and expenses. Therefore, primary investor concerns are liquidity and safety. The instruments themselves are straightforward and entail just two cash flows, the purchase price and a known redemption amount at maturity.

Let's start with a practical money market investment problem. A fund manager has about $1 million to invest and needs to choose between two 6-month securities: (1) commercial paper (CP) quoted at 3.80% and (2) a bank certificate of deposit (CD) quoted at 3.90%. Assuming that the credit risks are the same and any differences in liquidity and taxation are

1

immaterial, which investment offers the better rate of return, the CP at 3.80% or the CD at 3.90%? To the uninitiated, this must seem like a trick question—surely, 3.90% is higher than 3.80%. If we are correct in our assessment that the risks are the same, the CD appears to pick up an extra 10 basis points. The initiated know that first it is time for a bit of bond math.

INTEREST RATES IN TEXTBOOK THEORY

You probably were first introduced to the time value of money in college or in a job training program using equations such as these:

$$FV = PV * (1+i)^N \quad and \quad PV = \frac{FV}{(1+i)^N} \tag{1.1}$$

where FV = future value, PV = present value, i = interest rate per time period, and N = number of time periods to maturity.

The two equations are the same and merely are rearranged algebraically. The future value is the present value moved forward along a time trajectory representing compound interest over the N periods; the present value is the future value discounted back to day zero at rate i per period.

In your studies, you no doubt worked through many time-value-of-money problems, such as: How much will you accumulate after 20 years if you invest $1,000 today at an annual interest rate of 5%? How much do you need to invest today to accumulate $10,000 in 30 years assuming a rate of 6%? You likely used the time-value-of-money keys on a financial calculator, but you just as easily could have plugged the numbers into the equations in 1.1 and solved via the arithmetic functions.

$$\$1,000 * (1.05)^{20} = \$2,653 \quad and \quad \frac{\$10,000}{(1.06)^{30}} = \$1,741$$

The interest rate in standard textbook theory is well defined. It is the growth rate of money over time—it describes the trajectory that allows $1,000 to grow to $2,653 over 20 years. You can interpret an interest rate as an exchange rate across time. Usually we think of an exchange rate as a trade between two currencies (e.g., a spot or a forward foreign exchange rate between the U.S. dollar and the euro). An interest rate tells you the amounts in the same currency that you would accept at different points in time. You would be indifferent between $1,741 now and $10,000 in 30 years, assuming that 6% is the correct exchange rate for you. An interest rate also indicates the price of money. If you want or need $1,000 today, you have to pay 5% annually to get it, assuming you will make repayment in 20 years.

Despite the purity of an interest rate in time-value-of-money analysis, you cannot use the equations in 1.1 to do interest rate and cash flow calculations on money market securities. This is important: *Money market interest rate calculations do not use textbook time-value-of-money equations.* For a money manager who has $1,000,000 to invest in a bank CD paying 3.90% for half of a year, it is *wrong* to calculate the future value in this manner:

$$\$1,000,000 * (1.0390)^{0.5} = \$1,019,313$$

While it is tempting to use $N = 0.5$ in equation 1.1 for a 6-month CD, it is not the way money market instruments work in the real world.

MONEY MARKET ADD-ON RATES

There are two distinct ways that money market rates are quoted: as an *add-on rate* and as a *discount rate*. Add-on rates generally are used on commercial bank loans and deposits, including certificates of deposit, repos, and fed funds transactions. Importantly, LIBOR is quoted on an add-on rate basis. Discount rates in the U.S. are used with T-bills, commercial paper, and bankers acceptances. However, there are no hard-and-fast rules regarding rate quotation in domestic or international markets. For example, when commercial paper is issued in the Euromarkets, rates typically are on an add-on basis, not a discount rate basis. The Federal Reserve lends money to commercial banks at its official "discount rate." That interest rate, however, actually is quoted as an add-on rate, not as a discount rate. Money market rates can be confusing—when in doubt, verify!

First, let's consider rate quotation on a bank certificate of deposit. Add-on rates are logical and follow *simple interest* calculations. The interest is added on to the principal amount to get the redemption payment at maturity. Let *AOR* stand for add-on rate, *PV* the present value (the initial principal amount), *FV* the future value (the redemption payment including interest), *Days* the number of days until maturity, and *Year* the number of days in the year. The relationship between these variables is:

$$FV = PV + \left[PV * AOR * \frac{Days}{Year} \right] \tag{1.2}$$

The term in brackets is the interest earned on the bank CD—it is just the initial principal times the annual add-on rate times the fraction of the year. The expression in 1.2 can be written more succinctly as:

$$FV = PV * \left[1 + \left(AOR * \frac{Days}{Year}\right)\right] \qquad (1.3)$$

Now we can calculate accurately the future value, or the redemption amount including interest, on the $1,000,000 bank CD paying 3.90% for six months. But first we have to deal with the fraction of the year. Most money market instruments in the U.S. use an "actual/360" day-count convention. That means *Days*, the numerator, is the actual number of days between the settlement date when the CD is purchased and the date it matures. The denominator usually is 360 days in the U.S. but in many other countries a more realistic 365-day year is used. Assuming that *Days* is 180 and *Year* is 360, the future value of the CD is $1,019,500, and not $1,019,313 as incorrectly calculated using the standard time-value-of-money formulation.

$$FV = \$1,000,000 * \left[1 + \left(0.0390 * \frac{180}{360}\right)\right] = \$1,019,500$$

Once the bank CD is issued, the *FV* is a known, fixed amount. Suppose that two months go by and the investor—for example, a money market mutual fund—decides to sell. A securities dealer at that time quotes a bid rate of 3.72% and an ask (or offer) rate of 3.70% on 4-month CDs corresponding to the credit risk of the issuing bank. Note that securities in the money market trade on a *rate basis*. The bid rate is higher than the ask rate so that the security will be bought by the dealer at a lower price than it is sold. In the bond market, securities usually trade on a *price basis*.

The sale price of the CD after the two months have gone by is found by substituting *FV* = $1,019,500, *AOR* = 0.0372, and *Days* = 120 into equation 1.3.

$$\$1,019,500 = PV * \left[1 + \left(0.0372 * \frac{120}{360}\right)\right], \quad PV = \$1,007,013$$

Note that the dealer buys the CD from the mutual fund at its quoted bid rate. We assume here that there are actually 120 days between the settlement date for the transaction and the maturity date. In most markets, there is a one-day difference between the trade date and the settlement date (i.e., next-day settlement, or "T + 1").

The general pricing equation for add-on rate instruments shown in 1.3 can be rearranged algebraically to isolate the *AOR* term.

$$AOR = \left(\frac{Year}{Days}\right) * \left(\frac{FV - PV}{PV}\right) \tag{1.4}$$

This indicates that a money market add-on rate is an annual percentage rate (APR) in that it is the number of time periods in the year, the first term in parentheses, times the interest rate per period, the second term. $FV - PV$ is the interest earned; that divided by amount invested PV is the rate of return on the transaction for that time period. To annualize the periodic rate of return, we simply multiply by the number of periods in the year ($Year/Days$). I call this the *periodicity* of the interest rate. If *Year* is assumed to be 360 days and *Days* is 90, the periodicity is 4; if *Days* is 180, the periodicity is 2. Knowing the periodicity is critical to understanding an interest rate.

APRs are widely used in both money markets and bond markets. For example, the typical fixed-income bond makes semiannual coupon payments. If the payment is $3 per $100 in par value on May 15 and November 15 of each year, the coupon rate is stated to be 6%. Using an APR in the money market does require a subtle yet important assumption, however. It is assumed implicitly that the transaction can be replicated at the same rate per period. The 6-month bank CD in the example can have its *AOR* written like this:

$$AOR = \left(\frac{360}{180}\right) * \left(\frac{\$1,019,500 - \$1,000,000}{\$1,000,000}\right) = 0.0390$$

The periodicity on this CD is 2 and its rate per (6-month) time period is 1.95%. The annualized rate of 3.90% assumes replication of the 6-month transaction on the very same terms.

Equation 1.4 can be used to obtain the ex-post rate of return realized by the money market mutual fund that purchased the CD and then sold it two months later to the dealer. Substitute in $PV = \$1,000,000$, $FV = \$1,007,013$, and $Days = 60$.

$$AOR = \left(\frac{360}{60}\right) * \left(\frac{\$1,007,013 - \$1,000,000}{\$1,000,000}\right) = 0.0421$$

The 2-month holding-period rate of return turns out to be 4.21%. Notice that in this series of calculations, the meanings of PV and FV change. In one case PV is the original principal on the CD, in another it is the market value at a later date. In one case FV is the redemption amount at maturity, in another it is the sale price prior to maturity. Nevertheless, PV is always the first cash flow and FV is the second.

The mutual fund buys a 6-month CD at 3.90%, sells it as a 4-month CD at 3.72%, and realizes a 2-month holding-period rate of return of 4.21%. This statement, although accurate, contains rates that are annualized for different periodicities. Here 3.90% has a periodicity of 2; 3.72% has a periodicity of 3; and 4.21% has a periodicity of 6. Comparing interest rates that have varying periodicities can be a problem but one that can be remedied with a conversion formula. But first we need to deal with another problem—money market discount rates.

MONEY MARKET DISCOUNT RATES

Treasury bills, commercial paper, and bankers acceptances in the U.S. are quoted on a discount rate (DR) basis. The price of the security is a discount from the face value.

$$PV = FV - \left[FV * DR * \frac{Days}{Year} \right] \qquad (1.5)$$

Here, PV and FV are the two cash flows on the security; PV is the current price and FV is the amount paid at maturity. The term in brackets is the amount of the discount—it is the future (or face) value times the annual discount rate times the fraction of the year. Interest is not "added on" to the principal; instead it is included in the face value.

The pricing equation for discount rate instruments expressed more compactly is:

$$PV = FV * \left[1 - \left(DR * \frac{Days}{Year} \right) \right] \qquad (1.6)$$

Suppose that the money manager buys the 180-day CP at a discount rate of 3.80%. The face value is $1,000,000. Following market practice, the "amount" of a transaction is the face value (the FV) for instruments quoted on a discount rate basis. In contrast, the "amount" is the original principal (the *PV* at issuance) for money market securities quoted on an add-on rate basis. The purchase price for the CP is $981,000.

$$PV = \$1,000,000 * \left[1 - \left(0.0380 * \frac{180}{360} \right) \right] = \$981,000$$

What is the realized rate of return on the CP, assuming the mutual fund holds it to maturity (and there is no default by the issuer)? We can substitute the two cash flows into equation 1.4 to get the result as a 360-day *AOR* so that it is comparable to the bank CD.

$$AOR = \left(\frac{360}{180} \right) * \left(\frac{\$1,000,000 - \$981,000}{\$981,000} \right) = 0.03874$$

Notice that the discount rate of 3.80% on the CP is a misleading growth rate for the investment—the realized rate of return is higher at 3.874%.

The rather bizarre nature of a money market discount rate is revealed by rearranging the pricing equation 1.6 to isolate the *DR* term.

$$DR = \left(\frac{Year}{Days} \right) * \left(\frac{FV - PV}{FV} \right) \tag{1.7}$$

Note that the *DR*, unlike an *AOR*, is not an APR because the second term in parenthesis is not the periodic interest rate. It is the interest earned (*FV − PV*), divided by *FV*, and not by *PV*. This is not the way we think about an interest rate—the growth rate of an investment should be measured by the increase in value (*FV − PV*) given where we start (*PV*), not where we end (*FV*). The key point is that discount rates on T-bills, commercial paper, and bankers acceptances in the U.S. systematically *understate* the investor's rate of return, as well as the borrower's cost of funds.

The relationship between a discount rate and an add-on rate can be derived algebraically by equating the pricing equations 1.3 and 1.6 and assuming that the two cash flows (*PV* and *FV*) are equivalent.

$$AOR = \frac{Year * DR}{Year - (Days * DR)} \tag{1.8}$$

The derivation is in the Technical Appendix. Notice that the AOR will always be greater than the DR for the same cash flows, the more so the greater the number of days in the time period and the higher the level of interest rates. Equation 1.8 is a general conversion formula between discount rates and add-on rates when quoted for the same assumed number of days in the year.

We can now convert the CP discount rate of 3.80% to an add-on rate assuming a 360-day year.

$$AOR = \frac{360 * 0.0380}{360 - (180 * 0.0380)} = 0.03874$$

This is the same result as given earlier—there the AOR equivalent is obtained from the two cash flows; here it is obtained using the conversion formula. If the risks on the CD and the CP are deemed to be equivalent, the money manager likes the CD. Doing the bond math, the manager expects a higher return on the CD because 3.90% is greater than 3.874%, not because 3.90% is greater than 3.80%. The key point is that add-on rates and discount rates cannot be directly compared—they first must be converted to a common basis. If the CD is perceived to entail somewhat more credit or liquidity risk, the investor's compensation for bearing that relative risk is only 2.6 basis points, not 10 basis points.

Despite their limitations as measures of rates of return (and costs of borrowed funds), discount rates are used in the U.S. when T-bills, commercial paper, and bankers acceptances are traded. Assume the money market mutual fund manager has chosen to buy the $1,000,000, 180-day CP quoted at 3.80%, paying $981,000 at issuance. Now suppose that the manager seeks to sell the CP five months later when only 30 days remain until maturity, and at that time the securities dealer quotes a bid rate of 3.35% and an ask rate of 3.33% on 1-month CP. Those quotes will be on a discount rate basis. The dealer at that time would pay the mutual fund $997,208 for the security.

$$PV = \$1,000,000 * \left[1 - \left(0.0335 * \frac{30}{360} \right) \right] = \$997,208$$

How did the CP trade turn out for the investor? The 150-day holding period rate of return realized by the mutual fund can be calculated as a 360-day AOR based on the two cash flows:

$$AOR = \left(\frac{360}{150} \right) * \left(\frac{\$997,208 - \$981,000}{\$981,000} \right) = 0.03965$$

This rate of return, 3.965%, is an APR for a periodicity of 2.4. That is, it is the periodic rate for the 150-day time period (the second term in parenthesis) annualized by multiplying by 360 divided by 150.

TWO CASH FLOWS, MANY MONEY MARKET RATES

Suppose that a money market security can be purchased on January 12 for $64,000. The security matures on March 12, paying $65,000. To review the money market calculations seen so far, let's calculate the interest rate on the security to the nearest one-tenth of a basis point, given the following quotation methods and day-count conventions:

- Add-on Rate, Actual/360
- Add-on Rate, Actual/365
- Add-on Rate, 30/360
- Add-on Rate, Actual/370
- Discount Rate, Actual/360

Note first that interest rate calculations are *invariant to scale*. That means you will get the same answers if you simply use $64 and $65 for the two cash flows. However, if you work for a major financial institution and are used to dealing with large transactions, you can work with $64 million and $65 million to make the exercise seem more relevant. Interest rate calculations are also *invariant to currency*. These could be U.S. or Canadian dollars. If you prefer, you can designate the currencies to be the euro, British pound sterling, Japanese yen, Swedish krona, Korean won, Mexican peso, or South African rand.

Add-On Rate, Actual/360

Actual/360 means that the fraction of the year is the actual number of days between settlement and maturity divided by 360. There are actually 59 days between January 12 and March 12 in non–leap years and 60 days during a leap year. A key word here is "between." The relevant time period in most financial markets is based on the number of days between the starting and ending dates. In other words, "parking lot rules" (whereby both the starting and ending dates count) do not apply.

Assume we are doing the calculation for 2015.

$$AOR = \left(\frac{360}{59}\right) * \left(\frac{\$65,000 - \$64,000}{\$64,000}\right) = 0.09534, \quad AOR = 9.534\%$$

Note that the periodicity for this add-on rate is 360/59, the reciprocal of the fraction of the year. If we do the calculation for 2016, the rate is a bit lower.

$$AOR = \left(\frac{360}{60}\right) * \left(\frac{\$65,000 - \$64,000}{\$64,000}\right) = 0.09375, \quad AOR = 9.375\%$$

Add-On Rate, Actual/365

Many money markets use actual/365 for the fraction of the year, in particular those markets that have followed British conventions. The add-on rates for 2015 and 2016 are:

$$AOR = \frac{365}{59} * \left(\frac{\$65,000 - \$64,000}{\$64,000}\right) = 0.09666, \quad AOR = 9.666\%$$

$$AOR = \frac{365}{60} * \left(\frac{\$65,000 - \$64,000}{\$64,000}\right) = 0.09505, \quad AOR = 9.505\%$$

In some markets, the number of days in the year switches to 366 for leap years. This day-count convention is known as actual/actual instead of actual/365. The interest rate would be a little higher.

$$AOR = \frac{366}{60} * \left(\frac{\$65,000 - \$64,000}{\$64,000}\right) = 0.09531, \quad AOR = 9.531\%$$

Add-On Rate, 30/360

An easier way of counting the number of days between dates is to use the 30/360 day-count convention. Rather than work with an actual calendar (or use a computer), we simply assume that each month has 30 days. Therefore, there are *assumed* to be 30 days from January 12 to February 12 and another 30 days between February 12 and March 12. That makes 60 days for the time period and 360 days for the year. We get the same rate for both 2015 and 2016:

$$AOR = \frac{360}{60} * \left(\frac{\$65,000 - \$64,000}{\$64,000}\right) = 0.09375, \quad AOR = 9.375\%$$

This day-count convention is rare in money markets but commonly is used for calculating the accrued interest on fixed-income bonds.

Add-On Rate, Actual/370

Okay, actual/370 does not really exist—but it could. After all, 370 days represents on average a year more accurately than does 360 days. Importantly, the calculated interest rate to the investor goes up. Assume 59 days in the time period.

$$AOR = \frac{370}{59} * \left(\frac{\$65,000 - \$64,000}{\$64,000} \right) = 0.09799, \quad AOR = 9.799\%$$

Think of the marketing possibilities for a commercial bank that uses 370 days in the year for quoting its deposit rates: "We give you five extra days in the year to earn interest!" The cash flows have not changed. The future cash flow (the *FV*) is the initial amount (the *PV*) multiplied by one plus the annual interest rate times the fraction of the year. For the same cash flows and number of days in the time period, raising the assumed number of days in the year lowers the fraction and "allows" the quoted annual interest rate to be higher. Why hasn't a bank thought of this?

Discount Rate, Actual/360

Discount rates by design always understate the investor's rate of return and the borrower's cost of funds. Assume again that the year is 2015.

$$DR = \frac{360}{59} * \left(\frac{\$65,000 - \$64,000}{\$65,000} \right) = 0.09387, \quad DR = 9.387\%$$

Note that this discount rate can be restated as an equivalent 360-day add-on rate using the conversion equation 1.8, matching the earlier result.

$$AOR = \frac{360 * 0.09387}{360 - (59 * 0.09387)} = 0.09534, \quad AOR = 9.534\%$$

It is critically important to know the rate quotation and day-count convention when working with money market interest rates. This example demonstrates that many different money market interest rates can be used to summarize the two cash flows on the transaction. It is also important to know when one rate needs to be converted for comparison to another. For example, to convert a money market rate quoted on an actual/360 add-on basis to a full-year or 365-day basis, simply multiply by 365/360. However, a rate quoted on a 30/360 basis already is stated for a full year. It is a mistake to gross it up by multiplying by 365/360.

A HISTORY LESSON ON MONEY MARKET CERTIFICATES

One of the big problems facing U.S. commercial banks back in the 1970s was *disintermediation* caused by the Federal Reserve's Regulation Q. Reg Q limited the interest rates that banks could pay on their savings accounts and time deposits. The problem was that from time to time interest rates climbed above the Reg Q ceilings, usually because of increasing rates of inflation. Depositors naturally transferred their savings out of the banks and into money market mutual funds, which were not constrained by a rate ceiling.

The banks finally got regulatory relief. In June 1980, commercial banks were allowed to issue 6-month money market certificates (MMCs) that paid the 6-month T-bill auction rate *plus* 25 basis points. On Monday, August 25, 1980, the T-bill auction rate was 10.25%. Would an investor rather have put $50,000 into a T-bill that paid 10.25% or an MMC that paid 10.50%? Let's assume there was no difference in credit risk because the MMC was covered fully by government deposit insurance.

Obviously, the naïve person (one who has not studied bond math) thought that 10.50% on the MMC was a better deal than 10.25% on the T-bill. What the commercial banks did not advertise was that their 10.50% was an *add-on rate* set by adding 25 basis points to the T-bill auction rate, which in turn was quoted on a *discount rate* basis. To make an apples-to-apples comparison, it is essential to convert the 10.25% discount rate to an add-on basis. Assume that the number of days was 182 and that both rates were for a 360-day year. Using the conversion formula 1.8, the equivalent add-on rate for the T-bill was 10.81%.

$$AOR = \frac{360 * 0.1025}{360 - (182 * 0.1025)} = 0.1081$$

The investor clearly should have chosen the T-bill. Not only was the rate of return significantly higher (10.81% compared to 10.50%), the interest income on the T-bill was exempt from state taxes while the MMC was taxed.

The Monetary Control Act of 1980 officially phased out Reg Q for traditional savings accounts over the following six years, but the constraint effectively was gone because of the newly authorized types of deposits, such as MMCs, which paid going market rates. Also, the T-bill auction rate back then was the weighted average of the accepted competitive bid rates submitted by securities dealers. Successful bidders paid different prices based on their own bid (discount) rates. That created a problem known as the "winner's curse"—those who bid more aggressively paid higher prices for the very same security. In 1998, the Treasury adopted a single-price auction for all maturities whereby all successful bidders pay the same price based on the highest accepted rate. You might not remember, but 1980 was a year of incredible, unprecedented swings in market rates. The 6-month T-bill auction rate was 15.70% on March 28, down to 6.66% on June 20, and back up to 15.42% on December 19. That was some serious interest rate volatility!

PERIODICITY CONVERSIONS

A commonly used bond math technique is to convert an annual percentage rate from one periodicity to another. In the bond market, the need for this conversion arises when coupon interest cash flows have different payment frequencies. For example, interest payments on most fixed-income bonds are made semiannually, but on some the payments are quarterly or annually. Identifying relative value necessitates comparing yields for a common periodicity. In the money market, the need for the conversion arises when securities have different maturities. The 1-month, 3-month, and 6-month LIBOR have periodicities of about 12, 4, and 2, respectively, depending on the actual number of days in the time period.

The general periodicity conversion formula is shown in equation 1.9.

$$\left(1 + \frac{APR_m}{m}\right)^m = \left(1 + \frac{APR_n}{n}\right)^n \tag{1.9}$$

APR_m and APR_n are annual percentage rates for periodicities of m and n. Suppose that an interest rate is quoted at 5.25% for monthly compounding. Converted to a quarterly compounding basis, the new APR turns out to be 5.273%. This entails a periodicity conversion from $m = 12$ to $n = 4$ and solving for APR_4.

$$\left(1 + \frac{0.0525}{12}\right)^{12} = \left(1 + \frac{APR_4}{4}\right)^4, \quad APR_4 = 0.05273$$

The key idea is that the total return at the end of the year is the same whether one receives 5.25% paid and compounded monthly (at that same monthly rate) or 5.273% paid and compounded quarterly (at that same quarterly rate).

Suppose that another APR is 5.30% for semiannual compounding. Converting that rate to a quarterly basis (from $m = 2$ to $n = 4$) gives a new APR of 5.265%:

$$\left(1 + \frac{0.0530}{2}\right)^2 = \left(1 + \frac{APR_4}{4}\right)^4, \quad APR_4 = 0.05265$$

The general rule is that converting an APR from more frequent to less frequent compounding per year (e.g., from a periodicity of 12 to 4) raises the annual interest rate (from 5.25% to 5.273%). Likewise, converting an APR from less to more frequent compounding (2 to 4) lowers the rate (5.30% to 5.265%). Put on a common periodicity, we see that 5.25% with monthly compounding offers a slightly higher return than 5.30% semiannually.

Another periodicity conversion you are likely to encounter is from an APR to an *effective annual rate* (EAR) basis, which implicitly assumes a periodicity of 1.

$$\left(1 + \frac{APR_m}{m}\right)^m = 1 + EAR \qquad (1.10)$$

For example, an APR of 5.25% having a periodicity of 12 converts to an EAR of 5.378% while the APR of 5.30% having a periodicity of 2 converts to 5.370%.

$$\left(1 + \frac{0.0525}{12}\right)^{12} = 1 + EAR, \quad EAR = 0.05378$$

$$\left(1 + \frac{0.0530}{2}\right)^2 = 1 + EAR, \quad EAR = 0.05370$$

Some financial calculators have the APR to EAR conversion equation already programmed (note that "EFF" is sometimes used instead of "EAR"). The APR often is called a *nominal* interest rate in contrast to the *effective* rate. This is common in textbooks and in academic presentations. The idea is that the EAR represents the total return over a year, assuming replication and interest compounding at the same rate. The APR also assumes replication but merely adds up the rates per period and neglects the impact of compounding in obtaining the annualized rate of return.

An acronym used with U.S. commercial bank deposits is APY, standing for annual percentage yield. This is just another expression for the EAR. So, if the nominal rate on a 6-month bank deposit is quoted at 4.00%, its APY is displayed to be 4.04%. The higher the level of interest rates and the greater the periodicity of the nominal rate, the larger is the difference between an APR and its APY. If the APR on a 1-month bank deposit rate is 12.00%, its APY is 12.68%. It should be no surprise that banks like to display prominently the APY on time deposits and the APR on auto loans.

TREASURY BILL AUCTION RESULTS

In early July 2008, the U.S. Treasury auctioned off a series of T-bills. The official reported results for the auctions are shown in Table 1.1. Each T-bill was issued on July 3, 2008, and uses an actual/360 day-count. The Investment Rate also is called the *bond equivalent yield* (*BEY*), the term that I use in this section. The intent is to report to investors an interest rate for the security that is more meaningful than the discount rate and that allows a comparison to Treasury note and bond yields.

The given prices are straightforward applications of pricing on a discount rate basis using equation 1.6:

$$4\text{-Week:} \quad PV = 100 * \left[1 - \left(0.01850 * \frac{28}{360}\right)\right] = 99.856111$$

$$13\text{-Week:} \quad PV = 100 * \left[1 - \left(0.01900 * \frac{91}{360}\right)\right] = 99.519722$$

$$26\text{-Week:} \quad PV = 100 * \left[1 - \left(0.02135 * \frac{183}{360}\right)\right] = 98.914708$$

$$52\text{-Week:} \quad PV = 100 * \left[1 - \left(0.02295 * \frac{364}{360}\right)\right] = 97.679500$$

TABLE 1.1 T-Bill Auction Results

Term	Maturity Date	Discount Rate	Investment Rate	Price (per $100 in par value)
4 week	07-31-2008	1.850%	1.878%	99.856111
13 week	10-02-2008	1.900%	1.936%	99.519722
26 week	01-02-2009	2.135%	2.188%	98.914708
52 week	07-03-2009	2.295%	2.368%	97.679500

The 4-week, 13-week, 26-week, and 52-week T-bills almost always have 28, 91, 182, and 364 days to maturity, respectively. They typically are issued and settled on a Thursday and mature on a Thursday. The 26-week T-bill this time had 183 days in its time period because New Year's Day got in the way.

The bond-equivalent yield for each T-bill can be calculated by working with the cash flows or with a conversion formula. First, use equation 1.4 for add-on rates, letting $Year = 365$.

$$4\text{-Week}: \quad BEY = \left(\frac{365}{28}\right) * \left(\frac{100 - 99.856111}{99.856111}\right) = 0.01878, \quad BEY = 1.878\%$$

$$13\text{-Week}: \quad BEY = \left(\frac{365}{91}\right) * \left(\frac{100 - 99.519722}{99.519722}\right) = 0.01936, \quad BEY = 1.936\%$$

$$26\text{-Week}: \quad BEY = \left(\frac{365}{183}\right) * \left(\frac{100 - 98.914708}{98.914708}\right) = 0.02188, \quad BEY = 2.188\%$$

$$52\text{-Week}: \quad BEY = \left(\frac{365}{364}\right) * \left(\frac{100 - 97.679500}{97.679500}\right) = 0.02382, \quad BEY = 2.382\%$$

The first three BEY results confirm the reported Investment Rates; the fourth is *wrong*. The "official" APR—the one reported by the Treasury—on the 52-week T-bill is 2.368% while our calculation here is 2.382%. Quips like "close enough for government work" are not acceptable in bond math.

Before resolving this discrepancy, we can attempt to confirm the reported Investment Rates using a conversion formula similar to equation 1.8.

$$BEY = \frac{365 * DR}{360 - (Days * DR)} \tag{1.11}$$

This directly converts a 360-day discount rate to a 365-day add-on rate.

$$4\text{-Week}: \quad BEY = \frac{365 * 0.01850}{360 - (28 * 0.01850)} = 0.01878, \quad BEY = 1.878\%$$

$$13\text{-Week}: \quad BEY = \frac{365 * 0.01900}{360 - (91 * 0.01900)} = 0.01936, \quad BEY = 1.936\%$$

$$26\text{-Week}: \quad BEY = \frac{365 * 0.02135}{360 - (183 * 0.02135)} = 0.02188, \quad BEY = 2.188\%$$

$$52\text{-Week}: \quad BEY = \frac{365 * 0.02295}{360 - (364 * 0.02295)} = 0.02382, \quad BEY = 2.382\%$$

Notice that identical results are obtained using either the cash flows or the conversion formula and that again we have the wrong Investment Rate for the 52-week T-bill.

The source of the discrepancy is that the U.S. Treasury uses a different method to calculate its official Investment Rate (i.e., the bond equivalent yield) when the time to maturity exceeds six months. The *BEY* for the 52-week T-bill is based on this impressive formula.

$$BEY = \frac{-\dfrac{2 * Days}{365} + 2 * \sqrt{\left(\dfrac{Days}{365}\right)^2 - \left(\dfrac{2 * Days}{365} - 1\right) * \left(1 - \dfrac{100}{PV}\right)}}{\dfrac{2 * Days}{365} - 1} \quad (1.12)$$

Enter *Days* = 364 and *PV* = 97.679500 to obtain the "correct" result that *BEY* = 2.368% for the long-dated T-bill.

$$BEY = \frac{-\dfrac{2 * 364}{365} + 2 * \sqrt{\left(\dfrac{364}{365}\right)^2 - \left(\dfrac{2 * 364}{365} - 1\right) * \left(1 - \dfrac{100}{97.679500}\right)}}{\dfrac{2 * 364}{365} - 1}$$

$$= 0.02368$$

Where does equation 1.12 come from? Mathematically, it is the solution to this expression found using the quadratic rule.

$$100 = PV * \left(1 + \frac{182.5}{365} * BEY\right) * \left(1 + \frac{Days - 182.5}{365} * BEY\right) \quad (1.13)$$

The equation is derived in the Technical Appendix. The Treasury's intent is to provide an interest rate for the T-bill that is comparable to a Treasury note or bond that would mature on the same date and that still has one more coupon payment to be made.

A problem is that the annual interest rate in equation 1.13 does not have a well-defined periodicity—and knowing the periodicity of an interest rate is critical in my opinion. The first term in parenthesis in 1.13 looks like semiannual compounding for a periodicity of 2 (the annual rate of *BEY* is divided by two periods in the year). The second term suggests compounding more frequently than semiannually. For example, if *Days* = 270, it looks like close to quarterly compounding (*BEY* is divided by about four periods in the year). Frankly, the official Investment Rates reported in financial markets on long-dated T-bills are not particularly transparent: Knowing the rate and one cash flow does not allow one to calculate easily the other cash flow. Even discount rates, despite their inadequacy as rates of return, are transparent in that sense.

Suppose that we need to construct a Treasury yield curve. The idea of any yield curve in principle is to display visually the relationship between interest rates on securities that are alike on all dimensions except maturity. Ideally, all the observations would be for securities that have the same credit risk, same liquidity, and same tax status. That is why Treasury yield curves in the financial press typically are based on the most recently auctioned instruments (these are called the "on-the-run" securities). They not only are the most liquid, they also are priced close to par value. That mitigates tax effects due to prices at a premium or a discount to par value. That said, it is common in practice to see the short end of the Treasury yield curve—that is, money market rates—display interest rates having varying periodicities.

Which T-bill rates should one include in a Treasury yield curve? Surely not the discount rates (1.850%, 1.900%, 2.135%, and 2.295%). Those understate the investor's rate of return. In my opinion, the best visual display of market conditions would report annual percentage rates having the same periodicity. A natural candidate is semiannual compounding because that is how yields to maturity on Treasury notes and bonds are calculated and presented.

Therefore, I suggest that T-bill discount rates first be converted to a 365-day add-on basis and then be converted to a *semiannual bond basis* (*SABB*). Note that $SABB = APR_2$ in equation 1.9—it is the APR for a periodicity of 2.

$$\text{4-Week}: \quad \left(1 + \frac{0.01878}{365/28}\right)^{365/28} = \left(1 + \frac{SABB}{2}\right)^2, \quad SABB = 0.01886$$

$$\text{13-Week}: \quad \left(1 + \frac{0.01936}{365/91}\right)^{365/91} = \left(1 + \frac{SABB}{2}\right)^2, \quad SABB = 0.01941$$

$$\text{26-Week}: \quad \left(1 + \frac{0.02188}{365/183}\right)^{365/183} = \left(1 + \frac{SABB}{2}\right)^2, \quad SABB = 0.02188$$

$$\text{52-Week}: \quad \left(1 + \frac{0.02382}{365/364}\right)^{365/364} = \left(1 + \frac{SABB}{2}\right)^2, \quad SABB = 0.02368$$

Each APR on the left side of each equation is the *BEY* calculated above, including the "wrong" rate for the 52-week T-bill. The conversions of the 4-week and 13-week T-bills entail more frequent to less frequent compounding, so their *SABB* rates are higher than the *BEY.* The 26-week *SABB* is the same as the *BEY* because 365/183 is so close to 2. Notice that the 52-week *SABB* is the same as the "correct" *BEY* obtained with equation 1.12. That is because when *Days* = 364, equation 1.13 effectively implies semiannual compounding.

Market practice, in any case, is to use the reported Investment Rates (1.878%, 1.936%, 2.188%, and 2.368%) at the short end of Treasury yield curves. This imparts a systematic bias for an upwardly sloping term structure because the shortest maturity rates have higher periodicities than the others. Best practice, I contend, would be to use the rates that have been converted to the *SABB* (1.886%, 1.941%, 2.188%, and 2.368%).

The differences between the *SABB* and the *BEY* results in the example are quite small because the interest rates are low. Suppose instead that money market rates in the U.S. someday are much higher than they were in 2008. If the discount rates for each of these four T-bills are 12%, the "official" Investment Rates would be 12.281%, 12.547%, 12.957%, and 13.399%. Converted as above, the corresponding *SABB* rates would be 12.605%, 12.745%, 12.956%, and 13.400%. The difference at the short end of the yield curve then would be quite significant—32.4 basis points (12.605% minus 12.281%) for the 4-week bills and 19.8 basis points (12.745% minus 12.547%) for the 13-week bills.

THE FUTURE: HOURLY INTEREST RATES?

Suppose that sometime in the not-so-distant future the fastest-growing financial institution in the world is Bank 24/7/52. Its success owes to pioneering use of *hourly* interest rates for loans and deposits, an idea borrowed from the success of the hourly car rental businesses. Its (add-on) rates on short-term large time deposits (>$1,000,000) are shown in Table 1.2. The APR quoted by Bank 24/7/52 assumes a 364-day year. For instance, 3.4944% is calculated as 0.0004% * 24 * 7 * 52.

TABLE 1.2   Hourly Interest Rates

Time Period	Rate per Hour	APR
1–8 hours	0.0004%	3.4944%
9–24 hours	0.0005%	4.3680%
25–72 hours	0.0006%	5.2416%

To see how hourly interest rates might work, suppose a corporation makes a 52-hour, $5,000,000 time deposit at Bank 24/7/52. The redemption amount on the deposit can be calculated using an hourly version of equation 1.3. The corporation will receive $5,001,560 when the deposit matures.

$$FV = \$5,000,000 * \left[1 + \left(0.052416 * \frac{52}{24 * 364}\right)\right] = \$5,001,560$$

The fraction of the year no longer is the number of days divided by the assumed number of days in the year; it becomes the number of hours for the transaction divided by the assumed number of hours in the year.

Now suppose that 30 hours after making the time deposit, the corporation has sudden need for liquidity. Bank 24/7/52's policy is to buy back time deposits as a service to its regular corporate customers. The redemption amount is fixed once the deposit is issued. The present value of the time deposit after 30 hours have passed and 22 hours remain is again based on equation 1.3 but now solving for PV.

$$\$5,001,560 = PV * \left[1 + \left(0.043680 * \frac{22}{24 * 364}\right)\right], \quad PV = \$5,001,010$$

Assuming no change in the bank's rates, the corporate customer receives $5,001,010. Notice that this neglects the bank's bid-ask spread on money market transactions. In fact, Bank 24/7/52 likely would buy the deposit at a slightly higher rate (and lower price).

How did the corporation do on its short-term investment? The realized rate of return for its 30-hour holding period can be calculated with an hourly version of equation 1.4. That turns out to be 5.8822% on a 364-day add-on basis.

$$AOR = \left(\frac{364 * 24}{30}\right) * \left(\frac{\$5,001,010 - \$5,000,000}{\$5,000,000}\right) = 0.058822$$

Suppose that, for consistency, the money manager likes to convert all rates of return to a semiannual bond basis. Equation 1.9 can be used to convert that AOR to an $SABB$, but first one additional step is needed.

In general, interest rates should be put on a full-year, 365-day basis before carrying out the periodicity conversion. That is because an $SABB$ having a periodicity of 2 implicitly assumes two *evenly spaced* periods in the

365-day year, each period having 182.5 days. (Notice that this assumption is implicit in equation 1.13.) So, first we need to convert 5.8822% to an add-on rate for 365 days in the year by multiplying by 365/364.

$$\left(\frac{365}{364}\right) * 5.8822\% = 5.8984\%$$

This rate is now an APR for 292 periods in the year: (365 * 24)/30 = 292. The holding-period rate of return converted to an *SABB* is 5.9856%.

$$\left(1 + \frac{0.058984}{292}\right)^{292} = \left(1 + \frac{SABB}{2}\right)^{2}, \quad SABB = 0.059856$$

CONCLUSION

There are a number of factors that can account for the difference between any two money market interest rates. Usually the rate spread is explained by differences in credit risk, liquidity, taxation, and time to maturity. This chapter has emphasized more technical and mathematical factors, such as the method of rate quotation, the assumed number of days in the year, and the manner in which the rate per time period has been annualized. Many interest rates reasonably summarize the two cash flows on a money market security—and a significant subset of those many rates actually are used in practice.

Money market interest rates can be misleading and confusing to those who do not know the differences between add-on rates, discount rates, and interest rates in textbook time-value-of-money theory. Some rates are relics of an era when interest rate and cash flow calculations were made without computers and use arcane assumptions such as 360 days in the year. Knowing only the quoted interest rate on a money market security is not sufficient. You must also know its quotation basis, its day-count convention, and its periodicity. Only then do you have enough information to make a meaningful decision.

CHAPTER 2

Zero-Coupon Bonds

Bonds are in many ways easier to analyze than money market instruments. There are no antiquated "discount rates" that misrepresent an investor's rate of return. The yield to maturity on the bond will reflect the growth path over time for the investment under some reasonable assumptions. But the many cash flows received on a typical coupon-bearing bond cause a problem known as *coupon reinvestment risk*. The problem is that we have to estimate the rates at which we will be able to reinvest the coupons that we receive in the future, so the total return over the time to maturity is uncertain. We ignore that for now and focus in this chapter on a simple zero-coupon bond. There are just two cash flows, one at purchase and the other at redemption more than a year into the future.

Zero-coupon bonds do exist, although they are not nearly as common as standard fixed-income bonds that pay semiannual coupons. The most developed market for "zeros" is U.S. Treasury STRIPS, the acronym for Separate Trading in Registered Interest and Principal Securities. Why and how the Treasury first created STRIPS back in the 1980s is a great illustration of the process of financial engineering.

Before getting to the STRIPS story, first consider a 10-year zero-coupon corporate bond that is priced at 60 (percent of par value). The investor pays $600 now and gets $1,000 in 10 years—simple enough. A bit of bond math covered in this chapter produces a yield to maturity of 5.174% (s.a.) for this bond. The "s.a." tag, commonly used in bond markets, means that the yield is stated on a semiannual bond basis and is an annual percentage rate that has a periodicity of 2.

This yield statistic of 5.174% is the investor's rate of return over the 10 years assuming that the investor holds the bond until maturity, there is no loss arising from default by the corporate issuer, and there are no taxes. Later in this chapter we relax the first two assumptions. What is the investor's "horizon yield" if the holding period is less than 10 years? What is the implied probability of default if an otherwise comparable risk-free government bond trades at a price higher than 60? We defer the implications of taxation until Chapter 4.

THE STORY OF TIGRS, CATS, LIONS, AND STRIPS

Financial engineering can be defined as the creation of a security having a risk-return profile that is otherwise unavailable. The creation of U.S. Treasury STRIPS is a classic example. The story starts in the early 1980s, when interest rates were high due to double-digit inflation rates. When rates later dropped, the descent was steep and dramatic. For example, yields on 10-year Treasury notes averaged 14.30% during the month of June 1982 and fell to 10.85% by June 1983. Treasury yields then rose and averaged 13.56% for June 1984 before another descent to 10.16% in June 1985 and farther down to 7.80% for June 1986. Figure 2.1 displays the monthly averages of daily 10-year Treasury yields from April 1953 through May 2010.

Savvy investors during times of decreasing inflation and lower market interest rates naturally prefer long-term, low-coupon bonds. When yields go down, these securities appreciate in value much more than shorter-term, higher-coupon bonds. In Chapter 6, we return to this idea using the concept of duration. Even buy-and-hold institutional investors see value in low-coupon debt or, better yet, zero-coupon bonds, because cash flows received prior to maturity have to be reinvested at lower and lower rates, reducing the total return over the investment horizon.

The problem in the 1980s for such savvy investors was a limited supply of Treasury zero-coupon bonds. Until 1983, the Treasury issued "bearer" bonds—investors actually would have to clip each coupon from the bond

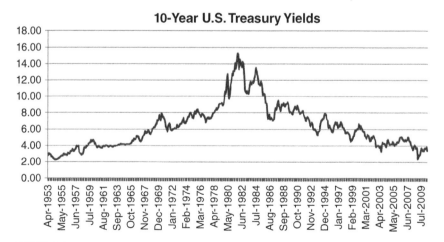

FIGURE 2.1   Monthly Averages of Daily 10-Year U.S. Treasury Note Yields from April 1953 to May 2010
Source: Federal Reserve Bank of St. Louis, FRED data series GS10

certificate and present it to the government for payment. (This usually was handled by the investor's broker and the Federal Reserve.) There was at the time a small market in zero-coupon Treasury debt created by physically clipping coupons corresponding to future payments and selling them as separate obligations. Some corporations issued zeros, but many investors seeking to benefit from lower market interest rates did not want to bear long-term corporate credit risk because the economy was just coming out of a deep recession.

This scenario provided fertile ground for financial engineering. Investment banks, notably Merrill Lynch in this story, found a way to supply the security that the market demanded. The bank would buy coupon-bearing Treasury securities—for instance, $100 million in par value of 30-year bonds having a coupon rate of 12.50%—and place them in a special-purpose entity (SPE). The SPE here is a single-purpose dedicated trust—it is empowered only to own the bonds and collect the payments; it cannot sell or lend the bonds, write options on them, or use them as collateral on loans in the repo market. The SPE then issues zero-coupon securities, which essentially are ownership rights corresponding to the coupon and principal payments. For example, the SPE could issue 0.5-year, 1.0-year, 1.5-year, out to 29.5-year zero-coupon debt having total face value of $6.25 million for each maturity and 30-year zeros having a face value of $106.25 million.

Merrill Lynch pioneered the market for "synthetic" zero-coupon Treasuries and cleverly named them Treasury Investment Growth Receipts, known by the acronym TIGRS. Selling the TIGRS for more than the purchase price of the coupon Treasuries that were placed in the SPEs became a significant source of profit for Merrill for several years in the early 1980s. Given that success, it is no surprise that other investment banks copied the design (and feline-inspired acronym)—Salomon Brothers created CATS (Certificates of Accrual on Treasury Securities), and Lehman Brothers created LIONS (Lehman Investment Opportunity Notes).

An important sales outlet for the financially engineered Treasury zeros was Individual Retirement Accounts (IRAs). Back then, all taxpayers could put up to $2,000 into an IRA and subtract that amount from pretax income. For example, Merrill priced the zero-coupon TIGRS, each of which had a face value of $1,000, to fill out the allotment. For instance, 30-year TIGRS could be priced at $50 to yield 10.239% (s.a.). The thundering herd of Merrill brokers would suggest putting 40 such TIGRS into your IRA for the year, or perhaps for older taxpayers, 8 TIGRS priced at $250 to yield 10.151% (s.a.) over 14 years. (How those yields are calculated is covered in the next section.)

At the time, this use of an SPE to create a new security was fairly new. The key legal aspect of the design was that the structure allowed the TIGRS,

CATS, and LIONS to be deemed U.S. Treasury credit risk and not a liability of the investment bank behind the process. Moreover, the SPE was "bankruptcy remote" in that default by Merrill, Salomon, or Lehman, while unthinkable at the time, would not allow their creditors to go after the underlying Treasuries. Also, the creation of synthetic zeros involved a change in tax status that had to be approved by the Internal Revenue Service—more on that in Chapter 4.

In 1985, the U.S. Treasury responded to the success (and profitability) of TIGRS, CATS, and LIONS with some clever financial engineering of its own—the STRIPS program. After 1983, Treasury securities were no longer issued in bearer form and were registered by a CUSIP (the acronym for Committee on Uniform Security Identification Procedures). Each Treasury bill, note, and bond has its own CUSIP. The innovation was to assign a CUSIP to each coupon and principal cash flow in addition to the overall security. For example, an 8%, 10-year Treasury note effectively became a portfolio of 20 separately registered coupon interest securities each with a face value of 4 (per 100 of par value) and one principal security for a face value of 100. That each security had its own CUSIP facilitated trading—the coupons could be stripped off and sold as zero-coupon *C-STRIPS*, and the principal could be sold as zero-coupon *P-STRIPS*.

C-STRIPS have a special feature in that the supply for each CUSIP increases over time, thereby enhancing the liquidity of the security. That is, coupon interest to be paid on a given date—say, February 15, 2018—has the same CUSIP regardless of which Treasury note or bond it originally comes from. The original coupon rate is irrelevant. P-STRIPS, however, always correspond to the original security and have a unique CUSIP. Their supply is fixed at issuance.

The STRIPS program has become very successful, and nowadays government securities dealers quote bid and ask prices on a full term structure of C-STRIPS and P-STRIPS. That success eliminated the profitability of TIGRS, CATS, and LIONS to the investment banks because STRIPS did not need the cumbersome SPE structure. Also, the arbitrage strategy of *bond reconstitution* emerged. This strategy is to buy the various C-STRIPS and P-STRIPS in sufficient quantity to rebuild a specific Treasury note or bond. When the purchase price for the parts is less than the sale price of the assembled whole, a profit is made.

An interesting phenomenon is that the prices on long-dated P-STRIPS typically are a bit higher than C-STRIPS that mature on the same date. For example, for trading on August 19, 2010, the *Wall Street Journal* reported that the ask prices on C-STRIPS and P-STRIPS due February 15, 2040, were 30.926 (percent of par value) and 31.422, respectively. The prices for trading on January 28, 2014, were 36.872 and 37.552. This pricing pattern has been quite persistent even though the credit risks and taxation on the zero-coupon bonds are the same.

One reason for the price difference is the greater supply, and hence liquidity, of the P-STRIPS. The coupon rate on the underlying Treasury bond is 4.625%, so for every 100 in par value of P-STRIPS, there initially are only 2.3125 of C-STRIPS. Another reason is that P-STRIPS allow the owner to carry out bond reconstitution arbitrage more easily. Suppose that STRIPS suddenly start to trade at low prices (and high yields) relative to the original Treasury bond. If a dealer or hedge fund already owns the P-STRIPS, only the sequence of C-STRIPS needs to be purchased to reconstitute and sell the T-bond. However, if the C-STRIPS are owned, the arbitrageur would have to buy a large quantity of P-STRIPS as well as the remaining C-STRIPS. So, the "option" to reconstitute when profitable is priced into the P-STRIPS. A buy-and-hold investor naturally prefers the higher yield on the C-STRIPS.

YIELDS TO MATURITY ON ZERO-COUPON BONDS

After dealing with money market interest rate calculations in Chapter 1, zero-coupon bond yields are a welcome relief and a return to classic time-value-of-money theory. A pricing formula for zeros is shown in equation 2.1,

$$PV = \frac{FV}{\left(1+\dfrac{APR_{PER}}{PER}\right)^{Years*PER}} \tag{2.1}$$

where PV = present value, or price, of the bond, FV = future value, which usually is 100 (percent of par value) at maturity, $Years$ = number of years to maturity, PER = periodicity—the number of evenly-spaced periods in the year; and APR_{PER} = yield to maturity, stated as an annual percentage rate corresponding to PER.

We can now use equation 2.1 to illustrate the yield calculations for the two TIGRS. Thirty-year TIGRS priced at $50 per $1,000 entail solving for $APR_2 = 10.239\%$, the annual yield on a semiannual bond basis for $PV = 50$, $FV = 1,000$, $Years = 30$, $PER = 2$.

$$50 = \frac{1,000}{\left(1+\dfrac{APR_2}{2}\right)^{30*2}}, \quad APR_2 = 0.10239$$

Fourteen-year TIGRS are priced at $250 to yield 10.151% (s.a.).

$$250 = \frac{1,000}{\left(1 + \dfrac{APR_2}{2}\right)^{14*2}}, \quad APR_2 = 0.10151$$

Such problems are easily solved using the time-value-of-money keys on a financial calculator or a spreadsheet program.

In this chapter, I work with a 10-year zero-coupon corporate bond that is priced at 60 (percent of par value). Its yield to maturity is 5.174% (s.a.).

$$60 = \frac{100}{\left(1 + \dfrac{APR_2}{2}\right)^{10*2}}, \quad APR_2 = 0.05174$$

The assumption of two periods in the year, while totally arbitrary, is common in financial markets because the yield on the zero then can be compared directly to yields to maturity on traditional semiannual payment fixed-income bonds. However, there is no inherent reason why the annual yield on a zero-coupon bond cannot be calculated for quarterly, monthly, daily, or even hourly compounding. Those yields turn out to be 5.141%, 5.119%, 5.109%, and 5.108% using $PER = 4, 12, 365,$ and $365 * 24$, respectively.

$$60 = \frac{100}{\left(1 + \dfrac{APR_4}{4}\right)^{10*4}}, \quad APR_4 = 0.05141$$

$$60 = \frac{100}{\left(1 + \dfrac{APR_{12}}{12}\right)^{10*12}}, \quad APR_{12} = 0.05119$$

$$60 = \frac{100}{\left(1 + \dfrac{APR_{365}}{365}\right)^{10*365}}, \quad APR_{365} = 0.05109$$

$$60 = \frac{100}{\left(1 + \dfrac{APR_{365*24}}{365*24}\right)^{10*365*24}}, \quad APR_{365*24} = 0.05108$$

Alternatively, you could convert from any one periodicity to any other using equation 1.9 from Chapter 1.

There are times in bond math when it is convenient to assume continuous compounding. That is, there are assumed to be an infinite number of compounding periods in the year. Continuous-time finance is particularly useful in interest rate term structure and option valuation models. The formula for the APR given $PER = \infty$ and the two cash flows PV and FV involves the natural logarithm (LN):

$$APR_\infty = \frac{1}{Years} * LN\left(\frac{FV}{PV}\right) \tag{2.2}$$

The 10-year zero-coupon bond priced at 60 has a yield annualized for continuous compounding equal to 5.108%, which rounded to the nearest one-tenth of a basis point is the same as hourly compounding.

$$APR_\infty = \frac{1}{10} * LN\left(\frac{100}{60}\right) = \frac{1}{10} * LN(1.6667) = \frac{1}{10} * 0.5108 = 0.05108$$

A general formula for converting from an annual rate for periodic compounding to continuous compounding is shown in equation 2.3.

$$APR_\infty = PER * LN\left(1 + \frac{APR_{PER}}{PER}\right) \tag{2.3}$$

So, instead of working with the two cash flows, you could convert 5.174% (s.a.) directly to continuous compounding.

$$APR_\infty = 2 * LN\left(1 + \frac{0.05174}{2}\right) = 2 * 0.02554 = 0.05108$$

A conversion formula to go in the other direction uses the exponential (EXP) function.

$$APR_{PER} = PER * \left[EXP\left(\frac{APR_\infty}{PER}\right) - 1\right] \tag{2.4}$$

The quarterly compounded annual yield of 5.141% can be obtained using $PER = 4$.

$$APR_4 = 4 * \left[EXP\left(\frac{0.05108}{4}\right) - 1\right] = 4 * [1.01285 - 1] = 0.05141$$

HORIZON YIELDS AND HOLDING-PERIOD RATES OF RETURN

Suppose that you buy the 10-year zero-coupon corporate bond at 60 but you have no intention of holding it all the way to maturity. Then 5.174% (s.a.) is only a reference yield—your own realized rate of return will depend on the price at which you sell the bond. We use the term *horizon yield*, or *holding-period rate of return*, for the annual rate of return when the holding period differs from the time to maturity. This can be an ex-ante yield based on a projected sale price in the future or an ex-post rate of return calculated after the fact from the actual price at the time of sale. We can even extend the idea to a holding period beyond the maturity date. Then we would need to project (or observe) the price and yield at maturity when the principal is reinvested.

A useful yardstick for assessing a horizon yield when the bond is sold prior to maturity is the *constant-yield price trajectory*. This is the path the bond price will take over the time to maturity assuming no default. Figure 2.2 shows the trajectory for the 10-year zero purchased at 60 (percent of par value). The prices for the various years are from equation 2.1. For instance, the prices at year 2 (when there are eight years remaining until maturity) and at year 7 (when there are only three years left) are 66.454 and 85.792,

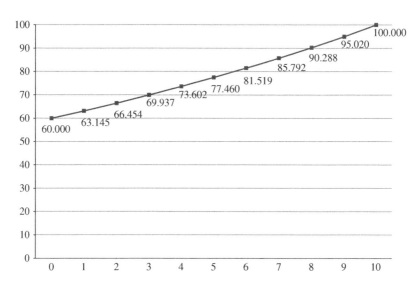

FIGURE 2.2 Constant-Yield Price Trajectory, 10-Year, Zero-Coupon Corporate Bond Priced to Yield 5.174% (s.a.)

respectively. The prices along the constant-yield trajectory also are called the *carrying values* for the bond.

$$\frac{100}{\left(1+\dfrac{0.05174}{2}\right)^{8*2}} = 66.454$$

$$\frac{100}{\left(1+\dfrac{0.05174}{2}\right)^{3*2}} = 85.792$$

When the investor is able to sell the corporate zero at a yield less than 5.174% (s.a.), the sale price will be above the trajectory and there will be a capital gain. For example, suppose that the investor sells the zero at year 2 for a price of 68 (percent of par value). At that time, the now 8-year corporate zero is trading at 4.879% (s.a.).

$$68 = \frac{100}{\left(1+\dfrac{APR_2}{2}\right)^{8*2}}, \quad APR_2 = 0.04879$$

The investor's realized 2-year holding-period rate of return turns out to be 6.357% (s.a.), which is greater than the original yield of 5.174% because the price is above the constant-yield trajectory.

$$60 = \frac{68}{\left(1+\dfrac{APR_2}{2}\right)^{2*2}}, \quad APR_2 = 0.06357$$

Notice that we set *FV* equal to 68—the redemption value of 100 is irrelevant here because the bond is sold for 68.

How much is the capital gain if the bond that is purchased at 60 is sold in year 2 at 68? Unlike equity, it should not be 8, the difference between the sale and purchase price. The movement along the constant-yield price trajectory shown in Figure 2.2 represents interest earned. So, interest income is 3.145 for the first year (= 63.145 – 60) and 3.309 for the second year (= 66.454 – 63.145). The key point is that, in principle, interest income is the change in price associated with the *passage of time*. Capital gains and losses are the changes in price related to *changes in value*—for bonds that means a change in the yield and a price above or below the carrying value. We see in Chapter 4 when we get into bond taxation how well these economic principles hold up in practice.

Now suppose that the investor does not sell after two years and instead holds on to the bond for seven years. At that time, the now 3-year corporate zero is sold for 83 because it is being priced to yield 6.308% (s.a.).

$$83 = \frac{100}{\left(1 + \dfrac{APR_2}{2}\right)^{3*2}}, \quad APR_2 = 0.06308$$

The investor's realized 7-year holding-period rate of return is 4.690% (s.a.), which is less than 5.174% because the sale price is below the trajectory.

$$60 = \frac{83}{\left(1 + \dfrac{APR_2}{2}\right)^{7*2}}, \quad APR_2 = 0.04690$$

In this case, there is a capital loss even though the investor buys at 60 and sells later at the much higher price of 83. The relevant comparison is between 83 and 85.792, the carrying value on the constant-yield price trajectory.

There in an important investment lesson in these scenarios. Suppose the buyer of the 10-year corporate zero actually has an investment horizon of 10 years and plans to hold the bond to maturity. Then the *unrealized* gain in year 2 caused by the lower yield at that time, as well as the *unrealized* loss in year 7 caused by the higher yield, has no impact on the *realized* total return. The bull market prevailing in year 2 and the bear market in year 7 are irrelevant news stories to this investor. The bond buyer achieves a locked-in yield to maturity of 5.174% (s.a.) regardless of the path that the price takes to its destination of par value—before taxes and inflation and assuming no default.

CHANGES IN BOND PRICES AND YIELDS

Bond prices change from day to day because of the passage of time. We see this in Figure 2.2, where the zero-coupon corporate bond price rises smoothly over time from 60 to 100. The other reason why bond prices change is that, in reality, the yield never is constant. Think of the yield as the investor's *required rate of return* for holding the bond to its maturity and bearing the default risk. If for some reason investors require a higher (or lower) return for the bond, the price must fall (or rise).

It is useful for analysis to break a corporate bond yield into a *benchmark* and a *spread* over (or, perhaps, under) that benchmark. Then changes in the corporate yield are due to changes in the benchmark, changes in the spread, or some combination thereof. In financial markets where there is a deep and liquid government bond market—for example, the U.S. and the U.K.—the obvious benchmark is the Treasury yield for a comparable maturity. In the euro-zone currencies, fixed rates on euro-denominated interest rate swaps are used for the benchmark because the various government bonds trade at varying yields.

Changes in benchmark yields typically reflect *macroeconomic* events, such as changes in expected inflation, foreign exchange rates, international capital flows, the business cycle, and monetary and fiscal policy. The idea is that these factors impact to varying degrees all market interest rates and all points along the yield curve. Changes in the spread, however, reflect *microeconomic* factors specific to the particular bond, for instance, its liquidity and tax status and potential losses if the issuer defaults.

Let's now revisit the example in which the investor buys the 10-year corporate zero at 60 and sells the bond two years later at 68. As we saw above, the 2-year horizon yield of 6.357% is higher than the original yield of 5.174% because at sale the 8-year bond is priced to yield only 4.879%. So, why does the yield fall? Perhaps the investor correctly anticipates lower inflation, which later reduces benchmark Treasury yields. Perhaps the investor is fortunate in buying a corporate bond that later is upgraded by the credit rating agencies, thereby reducing the spread over the benchmark. Another possibility is that Treasury yields and corporate spreads do not change at all. Maybe all that happens is that the corporate bond yield curve remains remarkably stable and upward sloping. When the bond is purchased, the 8-year and 10-year yields are 4.879% and 5.174%, and two years later the yield curve has the same shape and level.

The strategy of buying a longer-maturity bond with the intent to sell prior to maturity is known as *riding*, or *rolling down*, the yield curve. This can be very attractive when short-term rates are lower than long-term rates. The risk is that yields are higher when the bond needs be sold. To test out this strategy, let's assume that at first 2-year corporate zeros are priced at 95 to yield only 2.581% (s.a.).

$$95 = \frac{100}{\left(1 + \dfrac{APR_2}{2}\right)^{2*2}}, \quad APR_2 = 0.02581$$

The lure of buying the 10-year zero yielding 5.174% is apparent.

A *breakeven rate* is very useful in assessing the risk in the "maturity extension" strategy. We can use 2.581% to get the sale price at which trying to ride or roll down the yield curve underperforms the more direct horizon-matching alternative. That price turns out to be 63.158.

$$60 = \frac{FV}{\left(1 + \dfrac{0.02581}{2}\right)^{2*2}}, \quad FV = 63.158$$

Note that the 10-year zero would generate 6.454 in interest income over the two years because the price on the constant-yield price trajectory is 66.454. So, the strategy does well as long as the capital loss is no more than 3.296 (= 66.454 − 63.158). That price corresponds to a breakeven yield of 5.827% on 8-year corporate zeros.

$$63.158 = \frac{100}{\left(1 + \dfrac{APR_2}{2}\right)^{8*2}}, \quad APR_2 = 0.05827$$

The investor's choice so far is: Buy the 2-year zero and lock in a horizon yield of 2.581%, assuming no default, or buy the 10-year zero and achieve a higher rate of return if 8-year yields turn out to be less than the breakeven rate of 5.827%, again assuming no default. If the current 8-year yield is 4.879%, there is a cushion of 94.8 basis points: 5.827% − 4.879% = 0.948%. Obviously, the investor could consider other alternatives as well, for instance, buying the 3-year or 5-year corporate zero. The breakeven rates on those give the investor a full range of maturity choices, each having its own risk profile.

CREDIT SPREADS AND THE IMPLIED PROBABILITY OF DEFAULT

Statements about corporate bond yields inevitably include the "assuming no default" caveat. That's because the yield to maturity indicates the highest rate of return the buy-and-hold investor can expect to obtain. When there is a risk that the issuer might default, a prudent investor should *expect* to realize a return lower than the yield to maturity. If we were to draw a probability distribution for outcomes on a 10-year corporate zero-coupon bond, it would look something like Figure 2.3.

Obviously, the best outcome is that there is no default. The issuer pays the bond holder the full par value at the maturity date, and the investor's realized rate of return is 5.174% (s.a.), given the assumed purchase price of

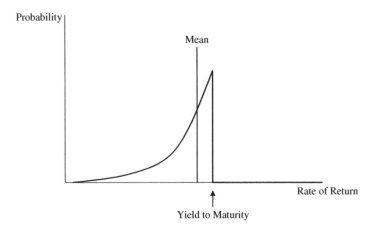

FIGURE 2.3   Probability Distribution for Rates of Return on a Corporate Bond to a Buy-and-Hold Investor

60 (percent of par value). The probability of realizing a rate of return higher than 5.174% is zero. By far the most likely outcome is no default. Fortunately for those who actually buy bonds, events of default are not all that common. But when that unfortunate event does occur, a bondholder's rate of return depends on when the default occurs and on any remaining value to the bond. Given all the possible outcomes for the realized rates of return, the mean of the probability distribution—that is, the *expected value*—will be less than 5.174%.

The key feature of Figure 2.3 is that the probability distribution is highly skewed. That's because the yield to maturity is the maximum rate the hold-to-maturity investor will ever experience. As we've seen, the horizon yield could be higher or lower if the bond is sold prior to maturity, but now we're assuming the intent is to the hold the bond for its full lifetime. Contrast this skewed distribution to a 10-year investment in equity. For it, we would likely draw a normal-looking probability distribution (i.e., a classic bell-shaped curve), perhaps adding in "fatter tails." Most of the outcomes would lie within a couple of standard deviations of the expected value. There usually is no reason to assume that higher equity returns are more or less probable than lower returns. That is, the distribution of outcomes for rates of return typically is symmetric and not highly skewed, as it is for bonds.

A nice application of bond math is to infer the probability of default given the prices on the risky zero-coupon corporate bond and an otherwise comparable risk-free security. As you might expect, some arbitrary assumptions are needed. Let's assume that a 10-year *risk-free* zero-coupon government bond is priced at 64 (percent of par value) to yield 4.513% (s.a.).

$$64 = \frac{100}{\left(1 + \dfrac{APR_2}{2}\right)^{10*2}}, \quad APR_2 = 0.04513$$

The *credit spread* on the 10-year corporate zero priced to yield 5.174% (s.a.) is 66.1 basis points: 5.174% − 4.513% = 0.661%.

The probability-of-default calculation is carried out in Table 2.1. Essentially, we build a table showing the loss if the bond were to default in any given year. We assume the probability that the bond defaults at the end of the year is Q. The third column shows the value of the corporate bond if it were risk free. This column is just the constant-yield price trajectory on the zero-coupon bond assuming the yield is 4.513% (s.a.). The price rises smoothly from 64 at day zero to 100 at maturity. For example, at the end of year 7, when three years remain, the risk-free value of the bond would be 87.469.

$$\frac{100}{\left(1 + \dfrac{0.04513}{2}\right)^{3*2}} = 87.469$$

TABLE 2.1   Calculating the Probability of Default

Year	Probability of Default	Risk-Free Value	Recovery	Default Loss	Present Value of Default Loss	Expected Loss
1	Q	66.921	26.768	40.153	38.400	38.400*Q
2	Q	69.975	27.990	41.985	38.400	38.400*Q
3	Q	73.169	29.268	43.901	38.400	38.400*Q
4	Q	76.508	30.603	45.905	38.400	38.400*Q
5	Q	80.000	32.000	48.000	38.400	38.400*Q
6	Q	83.651	33.460	50.191	38.400	38.400*Q
7	Q	87.469	34.988	52.481	38.400	38.400*Q
8	Q	91.461	36.584	54.877	38.400	38.400*Q
9	Q	95.635	38.254	57.381	38.400	38.400*Q
10	Q	100.000	40.000	60.000	38.400	38.400*Q
						384.000*Q

A particularly important and sensitive assumption is the *recovery rate*, which here is assumed arbitrarily to be 40% of the risk-free value. When events of default do occur, it's rare that bondholders are completely wiped out. Depending on the industry and the rank of the bond in the debt structure (i.e., senior versus junior), recovery rates can range widely, but assumptions of 30% to 50% are common starting places. A related term is "loss severity." If the recovery is $35 for every $100 in par value, the severity of loss is $65.

The fifth column is the loss at that time if default occurs—it is the risk-free value minus recovery. The present value of the default loss is shown in the sixth column. The risk-free rate is used to discount the losses. For example, if the bond were to default at the end of year 5, the loss would be 48.000. The present value of that loss is 38.400.

$$\frac{48.000}{\left(1 + \dfrac{0.04513}{2}\right)^{5*2}} = 38.400$$

Here the present values turn out to be the same for each year—that's because the bond is zero-coupon and the recovery rate is assumed to be a constant share of the loss. When we revisit this calculation in Chapter 3 for coupon bonds, this is not the case.

The final column in Table 2.1 shows the present value of the expected loss for each year—the present value of the default loss times the probability of that loss. For the 10 years, the sum is 384.000 * Q. The investor is compensated for the risk of those default losses by the lower price paid for the corporate bond, 60, compared to the price for a comparable risk-free bond, 64. The *implied probability of default* comes from equating the risk to the compensation: 384.000 * Q = 64 − 60 = 4, so Q = 0.0104. Therefore, the market is pricing in an annual default probability of 1.04% for this corporate zero. Technically, this is the unconditional probability of default. An alternative approach (which is harder to illustrate but more theoretically correct) is to estimate the probability of default for each year conditional on no prior default.

An important choice in this calculation is the risk-free rate. Academics often use the terms *risk-free* and *Treasury* interchangeably, but for many purposes in practical bond math, a government bond yield is probably too low. That is, the 10-year risk-free bond priced at 64 is not necessarily the 10-year Treasury STRIPS. Treasuries usually are more liquid than corporate bonds and have the benefit of being exempt from state and local income taxes. Ideally, the risk-free rate in this analysis is the yield on a bond having the same liquidity and taxation as the corporate but default risk that approaches zero.

An approximation for the implied default probability directly uses the credit spread.

$$\text{Default Probability} \approx \frac{\text{Credit Spread}}{1 - \text{Recovery Rate}} \qquad (2.5)$$

Here the credit spread is 66.1 basis points and the recovery rate is assumed to be 40%. This approximation would be an annual default probability of 1.10%, $[(0.00661/(1 - 0.40) = 0.0110]$. Although the two results are close, the advantage of the tabular method shown in Table 2.1 is its flexibility and explicit use of the time value of money. You can easily vary the recovery rate across the years, for example, if it is assumed that the current fixed assets of the issuer depreciate over time, or if there is an impending legal change that could affect creditors' rights in bankruptcy court. Also, you could introduce a term structure of risk-free rates instead of the flat yield curve assumed in the example.

CONCLUSION

In many ways a zero-coupon bond is the ultimate building block for the study of bond math because there are just two cash flows. Its yield to maturity is calculated with intuitive time-value-of-money bond math. Unlike the money market, there are no arcane conventions such as discount rates or 360-day years. Moreover, we can assume arbitrarily any compounding frequency for the annual yield, from continuous to just once a year. The price and yield calculations are straightforward and easy compared to what is coming in Chapter 3 for coupon bonds.

Prices and Yields
on Coupon Bonds

This chapter is about prices and yields on coupon bonds. The vast majority of bonds pay coupon interest regularly to investors, mostly semiannually but sometimes quarterly or just once a year. Zero-coupon bonds like Treasury STRIPS might have an interesting history, but in the study of bond math, they really are just a convenient way to introduce terminology and basic calculations—yields to maturity, horizon yields, periodicity conversions, credit spreads, and default probabilities. With all due respect to Chapter 2, Chapter 3 is much more important.

There is a which-comes-first aspect to bond prices and yields: Do prices drive yields, or do yields drive prices? If we know an investor's required rate of return for a particular bond, we can calculate the bond price. If instead we observe the price, we can calculate the yield to maturity and thereby infer the required rate of return. This chapter addresses the timing question using demand and supply diagrams. Then we work on calculating, interpreting, and critiquing the various yield statistics that are used to summarize the many cash flows on a coupon bond.

Before starting, consider a simple problem. You are looking to buy a high-yield (don't call it "junk") corporate bond for your loved one for Valentine's Day. The bond you're considering has an 8% coupon rate and semiannual payments on May 15 and November 15—that means each coupon payment is $4 per $100 of par value. Now as February 14 nears, you observe that the bond's yield to maturity is exactly 8.00% (s.a.). Given that the coupon rate and yield are the same, will the bond be trading at a discount, at par value, or at a premium? If those terms are new to you, no problem— they are covered in this chapter. Also, don't worry about accrued interest. The price I'm asking about is the "flat" price to which the accrued interest will be added. That too is covered in the chapter.

Admit it: Your answer is that the bond will be trading at par value. You no doubt were once told, or memorized for an exam, the bond price rules: When the coupon rate is less than the yield, the bond is priced at a discount; when the coupon rate is equal to the yield, the bond is priced at par value; and when the coupon rate is above the yield, the bond is priced at a premium. Your answer, of course, is wrong—not by much but wrong nevertheless. The rules you remember strictly apply only to coupon dates, and you're shopping for the high-yield corporate bond in the middle of the coupon period. After going deeper into the bond math, you'll see why the flat price will be at a slight discount, a little below par value.

MARKET DEMAND AND SUPPLY

We all learned in our economics classes that the way to think about the price of anything is through the forces of demand and supply. That's how market economies are supposed to work—at least when there are no government price controls or other impediments to the free flow of goods and services. The *market-clearing* price will be such that demand equals supply, that is, where the two curves cross in the classic economics diagram. We'll soon use those diagrams to determine the level of bond prices and yields.

Consider first Figure 3.1 illustrating a bond transaction. To force this example a bit, suppose there is only one specific bond that can be bought or sold—a 4%, annual payment, 4-year fixed-income security. On the "buy side" of the trade we have investors who are willing and able to lend money for four years. On the "sell side" there are the bond issuers who need to borrow money, such as governments that have to finance a budget deficit or businesses that are expanding production capabilities. We can include on the sell side those who already own the bond and for liquidity reasons need to divest. The two arrows describe the transaction, the exchange of money for the security.

The point of Figure 3.1 is that we can track either arrow in our analysis. The demand and supply of money in Figure 3.2a determine the equilibrium interest rate. The horizontal axis is the quantity of money; the vertical axis is the price of money (i.e., the interest rate). The bond issuers need money, so they constitute the demand curve. The curve is downward sloping because the lower the cost of borrowed funds, the more money they want. To be more technical, we could appeal to corporate finance theory and say that at

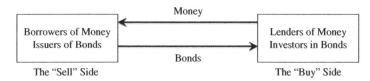

FIGURE 3.1 Exchange Diagram

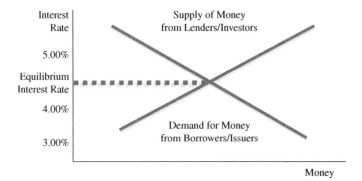

FIGURE 3.2A   The Interest Rate Diagram

a lower cost of capital, more investment projects have positive net present value. The investors' willingness to lend money, the more so the higher the rate of return, is apparent in the upward-sloping supply of money. In equilibrium, the interest rate turns out to be 4.2%.

The words "interest rate," "bond yield," and "rate of return" require some attention at this point. Often in bond math they can be used interchangeably. Sometimes "interest rate" stands for the level of market interest rates for some degree of credit risk and time to maturity. Because the graph plots money demand and supply, "interest rate" is the most natural term here, although we could use "bond yield" as well. The point is that at 4.2% lenders are willing to lend the same amount of money that borrowers want to borrow. A rate of return of 4.2% to investors, or a 4.2% cost of funds to borrowers, is the market-clearing interest rate.

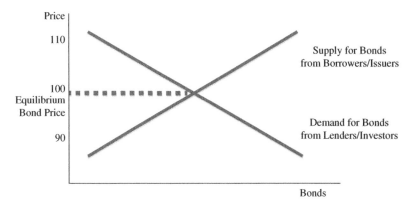

FIGURE 3.2B   The Bond Price Diagram

The same ideas are expressed in Figure 3.2b, which tracks the bond arrow in the Figure 3.1 exchange diagram. Here the horizontal axis is the quantity of 4%, 4-year bonds; the vertical axis is the bond price. The motives driving the demand for money are now represented by the supply of bonds. It's an upward-sloping line because issuers will supply more bonds when they fetch a higher price. The demand for bonds from buy-side investors slopes downward because a lower price on a fixed-coupon bond corresponds to a higher yield. The equilibrium bond price turns out to be 99.3, a small discount off par value because the 4.2% required rate of return is higher than the 4% coupon rate.

Now suppose that suddenly there is unexpected news about global commodity prices, lowering the expected *inflation rate* from 2% to 1%. If the nominal interest rate stays at 4.2%, the expected *real rate* of interest goes up from about 2.2% to 3.2%—that's good for lenders, but bad for borrowers. That statement uses the standard decomposition of a nominal interest rate into the expected real rate and the expected inflation rate.

$$(1 + \text{Nominal rate}) = (1 + \text{Expected real rate}) * (1 + \text{Expected inflation rate})$$

$$(3.1)$$

When the inflation rate is low, the cross-product term often is neglected.

$$\text{Nominal rate} \approx \text{Expected real rate} + \text{Expected inflation rate} \quad (3.2)$$

Some economists will quibble with these expressions, arguing that there should be a term for a *risk premium* on the right side of both. Their idea is that the nominal rate should include compensation for the expected real rate of return and inflation as well as uncertainty about those expectations.

In any case, when expected inflation goes down because of breaking news about global commodity prices, the nominal interest rate is not likely to remain unchanged. Instead, it typically changes because the demand and supply curves in both graphs will react. The idea is that lenders and borrowers make decisions based on the expected real rate of return and real cost of borrowed funds. Economists call this the "no money illusion."

The impact of a new level of expected inflation is illustrated in Figures 3.3a and 3.3b. In the interest rate diagram, lower inflation produces a lower equilibrium nominal interest rate, as would be expected. Given the new outlook for commodity prices, borrowers would want to borrow less and lenders would want to lend more for each nominal rate on the vertical axis because the real rate would be higher. The combination of weaker demand for funds and stronger supply pushes the nominal interest rate down to less

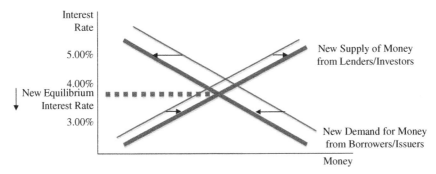

FIGURE 3.3A   The Interest Rate Diagram

than 4.00%. In the bond price diagram, the two curves shift upward so that the bond price is now at a premium above par value. In general, lower expected inflation shifts the demand for fixed-income bonds out and the supply of bonds in.

Figure 3.3a and Figure 3.3b resolve the timing issue regarding bond prices and yields. We see the inverse relation between the two visually in the diagrams without resorting to a bond pricing equation—yields go down and prices go up, and vice versa. So, which drives which? The answer is that the curves in the upper and lower panels shift simultaneously. The point is that the same market forces responding to the news about expected inflation impact both the demand and supply of money and therefore the equilibrium interest rate, and the demand and supply of bonds and therefore the equilibrium price.

That's enough economics for now; let's move to the bond math.

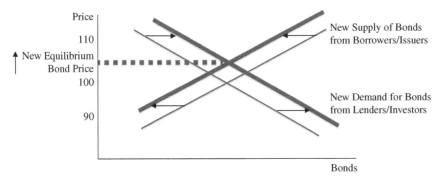

FIGURE 3.3B   The Bond Price Diagram

BOND PRICES AND YIELDS TO MATURITY IN A WORLD OF NO ARBITRAGE

Modern financial theory of bond pricing rests on the principle of *no arbitrage*. Some call this the law of one price or, even more grandly, the fundamental theorem of finance. It essentially is a theory of *relative prices*—the idea is that if we observe prices on some fundamental building blocks, for instance, zero-coupon bonds, we can deduce the fair prices on coupon bonds that promise the same future cash flows. We don't try to figure out the demand and supply for each bond in the marketplace. Instead we observe the market prices on the most actively traded securities and value the remainder assuming arbitrage opportunities are exploited and priced away.

No-arbitrage pricing is a powerful argument in developed financial markets because it does not require a lot of assumptions about information, behavior, risk aversion, and expectations. All we need are motivated and capitalized traders at hedge funds and proprietary trading desks at financial institutions. If there is an arbitrage opportunity out there, they can be trusted to find it and execute the trades to capture the profit. If you have studied the Capital Asset Pricing Model (the famous CAPM), you might recall the long list of assumptions needed to get those powerful, but theoretical, results about equity prices and the market price of risk. No-arbitrage pricing is far less ambitious—it just needs a starting place of some actively traded securities.

It's common in no-arbitrage valuation to neglect transactions costs and to assume that arbitrageurs actually can carry out the requisite trades. These assumptions hold up pretty well in the U.S. Treasury market because of the large supply of coupon bonds and zeros (i.e., C-STRIPS and P-STRIPS). In principle, arbitrageurs could use special-purpose entities to create zero-coupon corporate bonds, as in the TIGRS, CATS, and LIONS story in Chapter 2, but then the transactions costs would not be trivial.

Those caveats aside, let's now determine the no-arbitrage price for a 4-year, 4% annual coupon payment corporate bond in three different scenarios, neglecting transactions costs. First, assume that the sequence of zero-coupon bond yields is 3.500%, 3.800%, 4.100%, and 4.200%, an upward-sloping spot curve. ("Spot rate" is a commonly used synonym for zero-coupon rate.) Discounting each of the cash flows at the corresponding spot rate produces a bond price of 99.342 (percent of par value).

$$\frac{4}{(1.03500)^1} + \frac{4}{(1.03800)^2} + \frac{4}{(1.04100)^3} + \frac{104}{(1.04200)^4} = 99.342$$

TABLE 3.1 A Yield-to-Maturity and Several Zero-Coupon Curves

Date	Payment	Zero Rate (%)	PV	Zero Rate (%)	PV	Zero Rate (%)	PV	Zero Rate (%)	PV
1	4	3.500	3.865	4.920	3.812	2.130	3.917	4.182	3.839
2	4	3.800	3.712	4.690	3.650	2.820	3.784	4.182	3.685
3	4	4.100	3.546	4.300	3.525	3.650	3.592	4.182	3.537
4	104	4.200	88.219	4.160	88.355	4.250	88.050	4.182	88.280
		PRICE	99.342		99.342		99.342		99.342
		YTM	4.1820%		4.1820%		4.1820%		4.1820%

Second, assume that the zero-coupon rates instead are 4.920%, 4.690%, 4.300%, and 4.160%, a downward-sloping spot curve. It's no surprise to those who see where this is going that the bond price turns out once again to be 99.342.

$$\frac{4}{(1.04920)^1} + \frac{4}{(1.04690)^2} + \frac{4}{(1.04300)^3} + \frac{104}{(1.04160)^4} = 99.342$$

Third, to complete the example, suppose that the zero-coupon yield curve is remarkably flat at 4.182%.

$$\frac{4}{(1.04182)^1} + \frac{4}{(1.04182)^2} + \frac{4}{(1.04182)^3} + \frac{104}{(1.04182)^4} = 99.342$$

Table 3.1 shows output from the spreadsheet that I used to concoct these examples by trial and error, including a set of spot rates left out of the text. Note that the present value of each future cash flow differs but all sum to 99.342.

These examples suggest that the starting place in no-arbitrage bond valuation is the zero-coupon (or spot) yield curve and these rates are used to value coupon bonds. In practice, it goes the other way. The most actively traded securities are the newly issued coupon bonds for standard maturities—for instance, 3-month, 6-month, 1-year, 2-year, 3-year, 5-year, 7-year, 10-year, and 30-year Treasuries. Then from the prices and coupon rates on these securities, we deduce the no-arbitrage yields on zero-coupon bonds. We work through this "bootstrapping" technique in detail in Chapter 5.

Let's assume that this 4-year, 4% annual payment corporate bond is priced at 99.342 (percent of par value). Notice that if we included transaction costs for buying and selling zero-coupon bonds, we would not be able to give such an exact no-arbitrage value to the bond. Instead, we would have a range of prices, as in a typical bid-ask spread. But given a particular bond price, the yield to maturity is the *internal rate of return* (IRR) on the cash flows. An IRR is the uniform discount rate such that the sum of the present values of the future cash flows discounted at that particular interest rate for each time period equals the price of the bond. Obviously, as we can tell by the third scenario, the IRR for this bond is 4.182%.

I've come up with this example to make an important point and correct a statement that is often made about bond yields to maturity. You might read or hear that the problem with using the yield-to-maturity (YTM) statistic on a coupon bond is that it assumes a flat yield curve. But now we see that simply is not true. The first scenario has an upward-sloping zero-coupon curve and gets a no-arbitrage value of 99.342. The second has a down-sloping curve and gets the same price—a price that corresponds to the yield to maturity of 4.182% on the 4-year, 4% bond.

In my opinion, the correct way to think about a yield to maturity is as a *summary statistic* about the cash flows on the bond. It is a weighted average of the sequence of zero-coupon rates with most of the weight on the last cash flow because that one includes the principal. So, 4.182% is an "average" of 3.50%, 3.80%, 4.10%, and 4.20%, just as it is an "average" of 4.92%, 4.69%, 4.30%, and 4.16%. The quotes around "average" remind us that it is not a simple average found by adding the rates and dividing by four. Instead, it is a "present value average" of the spot rates in the sense that it obtains the same price for the bond.

The key point is that the yield-to-maturity statistic boils the many cash flows down into a single number that might be useful in making a decision regarding the bond, with emphasis on "might be." Additional inputs usually are needed to make a buy, hold, or sell decision—tax rates, expected coupon reinvestment rates, and the default probability. Remember the old quip about "a nonswimmer drowning trying to cross a river that has an *average* depth of 12 inches." Sometimes averages are insightful summary statistics (as in baseball), sometimes they are not (as in football, in my opinion). In sum, the yield to maturity on a fixed-income bond does not presume a flat yield curve.

Equation 3.3 presents the generalization of the bond pricing equation.

$$PV = \frac{PMT}{(1+z_1)^1} + \frac{PMT}{(1+z_2)^2} + \cdots + \frac{PMT+FV}{(1+z_N)^N} \tag{3.3}$$

where PV is the no-arbitrage value of the N-period bond—the sum of the present values of the cash flows, each of which is discounted using the zero-coupon rate that corresponds to the period $(z_1, z_2, \ldots, z_N)$, PMT is the coupon payment per period, and FV is the principal (usually taken to be 100 so the price can be interpreted as the percentage of par value). In Chapter 2 we used *Years* * *PER* for the time until maturity, where *PER* is the periodicity (number of periods in the year), and a discount rate of APR_{PER}/PER. Now we focus on the periodic cash flows and rates. Later in the chapter we deal with accrued interest and pricing the bond for settlement between coupon dates.

The yield to maturity (y) per period is the internal rate of return given the cash flows.

$$PV = \frac{PMT}{(1+y)^1} + \frac{PMT}{(1+y)^2} + \cdots + \frac{PMT+FV}{(1+y)^N} \qquad (3.4)$$

Comparing equations 3.3 and 3.4, we see why the bond yield can be interpreted as a "weighted average" of the zero-coupon rates—the PV, PMT, FV, and N are the same. Doing some algebra (i.e., taking the sum of the finite geometric series) allows this rearrangement. The steps are shown in the Technical Appendix.

$$PV = \frac{PMT}{y} * \left[1 - \frac{1}{(1+y)^N}\right] + \frac{FV}{(1+y)^N} \qquad (3.5)$$

Equation 3.5 is programmed into financial calculators for time-value-of-money problems. But first a couple of changes are usually made.

$$0 = +PV + \frac{PMT}{y/100} * \left[1 - \frac{1}{(1+y/100)^N}\right] + \frac{FV}{(1+y/100)^N} \qquad (3.6)$$

In equation 3.6, the interest rate per period is divided by 100 so that it can be entered as a percentage, not as a decimal. Also, the sum of the three terms is zero so that at least one of PV, PMT, or FV must be entered as a negative. That allows for the interpretation that negative inputs imply cash outflows and positive inputs are inflows. I've found that for bond math calculations, it's best to use PV as negative and PMT and FV as positive, thereby taking the perspective of the fixed-income investor.

An algebraic rearrangement of 3.5 is shown in equation 3.7.

$$\frac{PV - FV}{FV} = \frac{c - y}{y} * \left[1 - \frac{1}{(1+y)^N}\right] \qquad (3.7)$$

Here c is the coupon rate per period, PMT/FV. This expression indicates the connection between the price of the bond vis-à-vis par value and the coupon rate vis-à-vis the yield to maturity. These are the well-known (and well-remembered) rules: (1) If the bond is priced at par value ($PV = FV$), the coupon rate and the yield to maturity are equal ($c = y$); (2) if the price is a discount below par value ($PV < FV$), the coupon rate is less than the yield ($c < y$); and (3) if the price is a premium above par value ($PV > FV$), the coupon rate is greater than the yield ($c > y$). These rules apply to a coupon payment date when N is an integer. It will have to be revised slightly for settlement dates between coupon payments—more on that later in the chapter.

At this point I cannot resist relating bond pricing to assessing a person's quality of life. Think of the coupon rate as what you're promised to get in life (assuming the "issuer" doesn't default) and the yield to maturity as what you really need (to pay full par value). So, if you are getting more than you need, your life is trading at a premium. But if you are not getting what you need, your life is priced at the discount. Remember that if you have been dealt a low coupon rate, you still can have a premium life—it's a matter of keeping your needs under control. Okay, enough bond math philosophy.

SOME OTHER YIELD STATISTICS

Let's go back to the 4%, 4-year bond that is priced at 99.342. The bond's yield-to-maturity statistic, which also is called the *redemption yield*, is 4.182%. That is not the only yield statistic that can be used to describe the investor's rate of return. Another is known as the *current yield*, but I've also seen it named the *running yield* and the *income yield*. It is the annual coupon payment divided by the price of the bond. Here the current yield is 4.0265%.

$$\frac{4}{99.342} = 0.040265$$

I've always imagined that the current yield is a statistic created by a former equity trader because it is analogous to a stock's dividend yield. However, it is severely lacking as a measure of the rate of return on a bond. The numerator is the sum of the periodic coupon payments over the year and neglects the time value of money. A 4% bond that pays its coupon interest quarterly would have the same current yield as this one that pays annually if it also were priced at 99.342. Moreover, the denominator neglects the inevitable pull-to-par effect that moves the price over time toward par value, assuming no change in the probability of default. If the investor planned to sell the bond after a year, a horizon yield would provide a much better estimate of the rate of return, even though that calculation would require projecting a sale price. Assuming the price remains stable over time, while perhaps reasonable for equity, doesn't make much sense for a bond priced at a premium or a discount.

Another statistic sometimes reported for a bond is the *simple yield*. This one is also called the *Japanese* simple yield because sometimes it is used to quote JGBs (Japanese government bonds). Imagine a bond analyst (in Tokyo) looking at the current yield and thinking, "I've got to fix that numerator." To get a better projected rate of return for a buy-and-hold investor, add the straight-line amortization of the gain (from buying at a discount) or loss (from buying at a premium). The simple yield on this bond is 4.192%.

$$\frac{4 + \left(\dfrac{100 - 99.342}{4}\right)}{99.342} = 0.04192$$

Investments textbooks back in the olden days (before financial calculators and spreadsheets) used to demonstrate how to approximate the yield to maturity. Remember that an internal rate of return has no closed-form equation and needs to be obtained by trial-and-error search. Imagine another (now very old) bond analyst looking at the simple yield and thinking, "I've got to fix that denominator." To get an improved rate of return statistic, use the average of the current price and the redemption payment. The approximate yield turns out to be 4.178%.

$$\frac{4 + \left(\dfrac{100 - 99.342}{4}\right)}{\dfrac{99.342 + 100}{2}} = 0.04178$$

Although the approximate yield is not reported in practice, it is used behind the scenes—better said, under the keypad of a financial calculator or buried in the programming of a spreadsheet. It can be written generally using our notation.

$$Approximate\ Yield = \frac{PMT + \left(\dfrac{FV - PV}{N}\right)}{\dfrac{PV + FV}{2}} \qquad (3.8)$$

When you use a calculator or spreadsheet program to solve for the yield when *PV* is not equal to *FV*, the approximate yield is the starting place for the trial-and-error search process. Note that if *PV* = *FV*, the approximate yield reduces to just *PMT/FV* (i.e., the coupon rate).

Other yield statistics that might be used to summarize this 4%, 4-year bond involve converting the periodicity. Because this bond has annual coupon payments, the yield to maturity of 4.182% is an effective annual rate. Equation 1.10 can be used to convert to semiannually, quarterly, monthly, and daily compounded annual yields of 4.139%, 4.118%, 4.104%, and 4.097%, respectively. Here is the conversion from compounding annually to monthly.

$$\left(1 + \frac{APR_{12}}{12}\right)^{12} = 1.04182, \quad APR_{12} = 0.04104$$

Equation 2.3 can be used to show that there is not much difference between continuous and daily compounding. This is the conversion to compounding continuously from compounding monthly.

$$APR_{\infty} = 12 * LN\left(1 + \frac{0.04104}{12}\right) = 0.04097$$

These yield-to-maturity statistics, regardless of the periodicity, are all stated in what is called *street convention*. That means we neglect the actual timing of cash flows in terms of weekends and holidays. For example, if the 4%, 4-year bond was purchased for settlement on December 15, 2010 (a Wednesday) and matures on December 15, 2014 (a Monday), we assume the investor received the intervening coupon payments on December 15, 2011 (a Thursday), 2012 (a Saturday), and 2013 (a Sunday). In reality, those last two payments would have been made on the next Monday. Even though the timing of the payment is delayed, the payment amount represents interest accrued through December 15.

In contrast to the simplifying street convention assumptions, the *true yield* statistic solves for the internal rate of return given the specific calendar dates for cash flows, based on some schedule of bank holidays (e.g., London, New York, Tokyo). Using these assumed dates, the true yield is the solution for *true* in this equation.

$$\frac{4}{(1+true)^{365/365}} + \frac{4}{(1+true)^{733/365}} + \frac{4}{(1+true)^{1,097/365}}$$
$$+ \frac{104}{(1+true)^{1,461/365}} = 99.342$$

This calculation uses an actual/365 day-count format. For example, there actually were 733 days between purchase on Wednesday, December 15, 2010, and the second coupon payment on Monday, December 17, 2012. That includes the two additional days for delayed payment from Saturday to Monday, plus a leap day. Solving this on a spreadsheet gives a true yield of 4.179%, a little lower than the street convention yield because of the delay in the receipt of payment. In essence, the street convention yield entails solving for the internal rate of return using integers (1, 2, 3, and 4) for the exponents in the denominator whereas the true yield uses nonintegers (1, 2.008219, 3.005479, and 4.002740).

Maybe you are wondering if we really need all of these yield statistics for the bond. The answer lies in the difference between *data* and *information*. Figure 3.4 illustrates a way of differentiating these two. Think of information as a subset of data—there are lots and lots of data out there, but information is special: *Information is data that can be used in making a decision.* We're talking about bonds, so what matters is whether the yield statistic helps make a buy, hold, or sell decision. Surely this is up to each decision maker, and my perspective is that of a bond math teacher, not a bond investor or trader. But I just cannot see how the current yield, or the simple yield, or even the approximate yield help in decision making. So I classify them in Figure 3.4 as data about the bond but not as information.

On the other hand, the street convention yield to maturity can be used to compare bonds and does provide some information about the investor's possible rate of return. One of the themes of this chapter is to examine the yield-to-maturity statistic in detail and point out its limitations (for instance, if the investor does not intend to hold the bond to maturity or if the

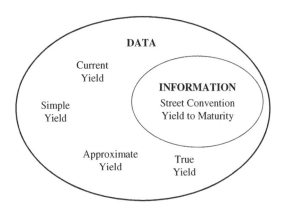

FIGURE 3.4   Data vs. Information

probability of default is not zero). All yield statistics summarize cash flows; it's just that the street convention yield to maturity does so most consistently. Plus, it has a well-defined periodicity, and that is critical in understanding and comparing interest rates.

True yields are tough to classify. In Figure 3.4, I call them data but not information, but I can see how some of you would argue that a true yield is the best datum of the lot. After all, it reflects the actual timing of cash flows rather than assumed timing. Maybe to you it is information used in decision making, but to me it is data overkill. There are so many more important things to deal with in fixed-income analysis than whether a coupon payment years into the future happens to be made on Saturday or the following Monday. For instance, at what rates will you be able to reinvest all of those coupon cash flows?

HORIZON YIELDS

The receipt of regular coupons, usually semiannually, makes horizon yield (or holding period return) analysis particularly important. With zero-coupon bonds in Chapter 2, we saw that selling prior to maturity has a dramatic impact on an investor's holding period rate of return. It depends on the yield at the time of sale, which indicates the buyer's required rate of return to hold the bond for the remainder of the time to maturity. With coupon bonds, horizon yield analysis includes all of that plus the interest rates at which coupon payments can be reinvested. This can be ex-ante analysis using projected future reinvestment rates, or ex-post analysis using actual realized rates.

We do not do justice to the issue of coupon reinvestment risk until Chapter 5 when we have a full sequence of forward interest rates to work with. So, for now assume a constant coupon reinvestment rate (CRR) for future cash flows. Also, we assume the investor holds the bond to maturity and there is no default. Given these assumptions, the holding period return (HPR) over the time to maturity depends only on the CRR. When the bond is sold prior to maturity, the HPR is a function also of the price (and yield) at the time of sale.

The objective here is to see the connection between the HPR and the traditional YTM (yield to maturity) statistic. Rather than write out a general expression relating these to the CRR, I'll just use the 4-year, 4% annual payment bond that is priced at 99.342 (percent of par value) to yield 4.182%. Note that this is the street convention yield—using the true yield would be really messy. The investor's total return on the bond investment obviously will depend on the CRR. That total return is the sum of the reinvested coupon payments plus the final coupon and principal. The first coupon is re-invested for three years, the second for two years, and the third for one year.

$$[4*(1+CRR)^3]+[4*(1+CRR)^2]+[4*(1+CRR)]+104$$

Suppose that CRR = YTM = 4.182%, so that the investor reinvests all cash flows at the original yield to maturity. The total return is 117.032 (percent of par value).

$$[4*(1.04182)^3]+[4*(1.04182)^2]+[4*(1.04182)]+104=117.032$$

You probably can guess where this is going. Now solve for the horizon yield—the annual rate of return that connects the purchase price and the total return at maturity. It is the solution for *HPR* in this expression.

$$99.342=\frac{117.032}{(1+HPR)^4}, \quad HPR=0.04182$$

This equation shows the well-known result that the yield to maturity measures the investor's rate of return only if the coupons are reinvested at that same yield. This is a standard caveat for internal rates of return in general. We can formalize this as:

$$\text{If } CRR = YTM, \quad \text{then} \quad HPR = YTM.$$

The corollaries are that:

$$\text{If } CRR > YTM, \quad \text{then} \quad HPR > YTM.$$
$$\text{If } CRR < YTM, \quad \text{then} \quad HPR < YTM.$$

This is the essence of coupon reinvestment risk—assuming no default, the buy-and-hold investor's rate of return depends on the rate at which coupons can be reinvested over the lifetime of the bond.

SOME USES OF YIELD-TO-MATURITY STATISTICS

I can think of four uses of (street convention) yields to maturity. First, yields can be used to price bonds. That means there is a one-to-one mapping, given the schedule of coupon and principal cash flows, between the price of a bond (including accrued interest, which we get to soon) and the yield to maturity. If you know the yield, you can unambiguously get the price, and vice versa. Therefore, bonds can trade on either a yield basis or a price basis. In practice, dealers usually quote just bid-and-ask prices and perhaps provide bid-and-ask yields for reference. An example of trading on a yield basis is the when-issued market before Treasury note and bond auctions. The outcome of the auction determines the particular coupon rate, so buying and selling on a when-issued basis sets the yield for the transaction. The corresponding price is calculated later once the results of the auction are known and the coupon rate is set.

Second, yields to maturity can be used to compare bonds for relative value, either as investments or as sources of borrowed funds. For this purpose, it is essential to convert securities having varying coupon payment frequencies to a common periodicity, usually a semiannual bond basis, before comparison. Issuers also should include the financing costs in their analysis to assess the *all-in* cost of funds. If the bonds that are being compared contain call or put options, their respective yields to maturity no longer matter—they are data but not information. Then additional work is needed to value those embedded options to arrive at *option-adjusted yields* and *option-adjusted spreads* (over the benchmark Treasuries).

Third, yields to maturity can be used to project the future value of investments—hopefully with careful attention to assumptions. Suppose a wealthy investor buys our 4-year, 4% corporate bond yielding 4.182% for a par value of $10,000,000, paying $9,934,200. This investment will grow to a total return of $11,703,200—if there is no default by the issuer and if each annual $400,000 interest payment is reinvested at 4.182%. But suppose the yield curve is projected to be stable and upwardly sloped over the next few years. Then how reasonable is that reinvestment assumption? Shouldn't you assume lower reinvestment rates as you slide down the yield curve and the time to maturity shortens? Suppose you are not so wealthy and are only able to buy bonds for a par value of $10,000 so that you receive just $400 in coupon interest each year. Will you be able to reinvest that amount at 4.182% if the minimum denomination for a bond is $1,000? In that case, maybe you should assume a lower, more conservative reinvestment rate, such as that available on money market securities.

Fourth, street convention yields to maturity often are used to calculate risk statistics for the bond. These risk statistics—duration and convexity in their various forms—aim to measure the sensitivity of the bond price to changes in market interest rates. This is a very important topic, which we go into in detail in Chapter 6.

IMPLIED PROBABILITY OF DEFAULT ON COUPON BONDS

In Chapter 2, we worked through the calculation of the implied probability of default on a zero-coupon corporate bond. We assumed that the amount the investor would be able to recover is a constant fraction of the risk-free value at the time of default. For a coupon bond, it is more common to set the recovery rate to be a constant fraction of the par value. But these are all arbitrary assumptions that can be changed to fit the circumstances; what matters for us is the approach to the bond math problem.

Suppose that the appropriate risk-free yield curve is flat at 3.50%. Then our 4-year, 4% annual payment corporate bond would be worth 101.837 (percent of par value) if there was no risk of default.

$$\frac{4}{(1.0350)^1} + \frac{4}{(1.0350)^2} + \frac{4}{(1.0350)^3} + \frac{104}{(1.0350)^4} = 101.837$$

As the bond is priced at 99.342, the investor's compensation for bearing the credit risk of the corporate issuer is the difference between the prices: 101.837 – 99.342 = 2.495 (percent of par value).

Table 3.2 displays the present values of the loss after recovery for each year. The annual (unconditional) probability of default is Q, and we assume default occurs only on a coupon payment date. Consider an event of default at the end of the second year just before the coupon payment. The bond would be worth 104.950 (percent of par value) at that time if it were default free.

$$\frac{4}{(1.0350)} + \frac{104}{(1.0350)^2} + 4 = 104.950$$

The loss before recovery would be the value of the remaining two years discounted at the risk-free rate plus the coupon payment due on that date.

TABLE 3.2 Calculating the Probability of Default on the 4-Year, 4% Coupon Bond

Year	Probability of Default	Risk-Free Value	Recovery	Default Loss	Present Value of Default Loss	Expected Loss
1	Q	105.401	40	65.401	63.189	63.189*Q
2	Q	104.950	40	64.950	60.632	60.632*Q
3	Q	104.483	40	64.483	58.160	58.160*Q
4	Q	104.000	40	64.000	55.772	55.772*Q
						237.753*Q

After (instantaneous) recovery of 40, the loss is 64.950. Discounted back at 3.50% to time zero, the present value of the loss is 60.632 [= 64.950/ (1.0350)²].

The sum of the expected losses for each year totals 237.753 * Q. Equating that to the compensation for default risk, 2.495, gives the result that Q = 0.010494. Our conclusion is that the market is factoring into the price of the corporate bond an annual default probability of 1.05%. That is a useful result but obviously one that is dependent on the various assumptions—the key one being the 40% recovery rate. You should appreciate the value of programming this calculation onto a spreadsheet (as I have done) so you, too, can make clever statements, such as: If the assumed recovery rate is only 10%, the implied default probability is just 0.72% per year; but if the recovery rate is much higher at 80% of par value, the annual probability of default is estimated to be 2.75%.

BOND PRICING BETWEEN COUPON DATES

It's finally time to get realistic about bond prices and yields. So far in this chapter I've conveniently assumed exactly four years to maturity on the bonds in the examples and that the next coupon payment is due one year into the future. That simplifies the calculations to draw your attention to the factors impacting yields and (pretax) rates of return—coupon reinvestment rates and the probability of default. You've probably heard the old saying "Even a broken clock gives the correct time twice a day." The analogy is that knowing how to do bond math on coupon dates for standard semiannual payment corporate and Treasury bonds makes you a valuable person— twice a year.

Extending basic bond math to between coupon dates is not hard conceptually, although some real-world accommodations are made. Suppose that the current coupon period covers T days and that the bond is being priced for settlement t days into the period. Therefore, t/T is the fraction of the period that has gone by and $1 - t/T$ is the fraction that remains. Here is a general version of equation 3.4, discounting the coupon payments (PMT) and principal redemption (FV) over the remaining N payments at the yield to maturity per period (y).

$$Flat + AI = \frac{PMT}{(1+y)^{1-t/T}} + \frac{PMT}{(1+y)^{2-t/T}} + \cdots + \frac{PMT+FV}{(1+y)^{N-t/T}} \quad (3.9)$$

On the right side of equation 3.9, the next coupon payment is discounted back over the fraction of the period ($1 - t/T$) until that cash flow is received; the following payment adds a full period to that fraction $(2 - t/T)$, and so forth. The left side is the sum of the present values of the cash flows and is the full price for the bond on the settlement date. That full price, which often is called the *dirty* or invoice price in practice, is decomposed into the flat price (*Flat*), which also is called the *clean* price, and the accrued interest (*AI*). Why dirty and clean? Surely it's not true, but I like to say it's because accrued interest in practice is impure because it's not theoretically correct.

Accrued interest is the compensation to the seller of the bond for interest income since the last coupon date. It is calculated as a straight-line share of the forthcoming payment. It is the fraction of the period that has elapsed times the amount of the payment.

$$AI = t/T * PMT \qquad (3.10)$$

Determining the fraction t/T is not an obvious matter because it depends on the day-count convention specified in the bond's documentation. Government bonds in the U.S. use actual/actual, whereas corporate, agency, and municipal bonds use 30/360. As we saw with money market instruments in Chapter 1, there are other possibilities—actual/360 and actual/365—but these are not commonly used with bonds. Also, note that there are various versions of 30/360. For instance, how many days are between April 1 and May 31 using a 30/360-day count? The answer is either 60 or 61, depending on the specification.

Multiply the numerator and denominator by $(1 + y)^{t/T}$ in equation 3.9 and substitute in equations 3.5 and 3.10 to get a general closed-form relationship between the present and future cash flows and the yield-to-maturity statistic.

$$Flat + (t/T * PMT) = \left[\frac{PMT}{y} * \left(1 - \frac{1}{(1+y)^N} \right) + \frac{FV}{(1+y)^N} \right] * (1+y)^{t/T} \qquad (3.11)$$

This equation can be used to solve for the street convention yield to maturity because the key assumption that payments are made on calendar dates without regard to weekends and holidays means that N is an integer. An important point is that the same fraction t/T is used on both sides of the equation whether the bond is a Treasury using the actual/actual day-count convention or a corporate using 30/360.

Another yield statistic you'll see quoted on corporate bonds is the *U.S. government equivalent*. The idea is to recalibrate the yield using an actual/actual day-count convention instead of 30/360. An example will clarify this. Let's assume that an 8%, semiannual payment high-yield corporate bond was being priced to yield 8.00% (s.a.) for settlement on Valentine's Day, February 14, 2011. The bond was issued at par value on November 15, 2010, and matures on November 15, 2020, a Sunday, which we'll ignore because the yield is stated in street convention. The next coupon was due on May 15, 2011, also a Sunday, which also is ignored.

Substitute into equation 3.11 $t/T = 89/180$ (the corporate bond uses a 30/360 day-count for accrued interest), $PMT = 4$ (percent of par value), $y = 0.04$ (the yield to maturity per semiannual period), $FV = 100$ (percent of par value), and $N = 20$ (semiannual periods to maturity as of the beginning of the period).

$$Flat + (89/180 * 4) = \left[\frac{4}{0.04} * \left(1 - \frac{1}{(1.04)^{20}} \right) + \frac{100}{(1.04)^{20}} \right] * (1.04)^{89/180}$$

$$Flat = 99.980394$$

The accrued interest is 1.977778 [= 89/180 * 4]; the flat (or clean) price is 99.980394; and the full (or dirty) price is 101.958172 [= 99.980394 + 1.977778], all stated as a percentage of par value. You've noticed, of course, that the price on this high-yield corporate bond is a little below par value even though the coupon rate and yield to maturity are equal.

This example breaks the bond pricing rule you no doubt remembered— "If the coupon rate equals the yield to maturity, the bond is priced at par value"—because we are now between coupon dates. Think of it this way: If you buy the bond, you need to compensate the seller for interest earned during the fraction of the period (89/180) that he or she has owned the bond. But, to be theoretically correct, you need to include in the purchase price only the *present value* of the accrued interest—that is, the present value of 1.977778. That's because the new owner of the bond will receive the next coupon payment on May 15, 2011. Market practice neglects that time-value-of-money concern, so the flat price registers that neglect. Accountants always have to balance materiality and practicality with theoretical correctness. In any case, the total price of 101.958172 (percent of par value) is correct in that it is the present value of the cash flows discounted at the yield to maturity.

The U.S. government equivalent yield for this bond turns out to be 8.0050% (s.a.), slightly above the street convention yield. It is the solution for the yield to maturity using 91/181 on the right side of the equation instead of 89/180. That's because the fraction of the period gone by on an actual/actual basis is 91/181. Notice that the left side of the equation is the same because the purchase price is what it is.

$$101.958172 = \left[\frac{4}{y} * \left(1 - \frac{1}{(1+y)^{20}} \right) + \frac{100}{(1+y)^{20}} \right] * (1+y)^{91/181},$$

$$y = 0.040025$$

Is the U.S. government equivalent yield information or just more data? I think it can be useful information if you are calculating this corporate bond's spread over a benchmark Treasury bond. Then the two yield statistics are on a fully comparable basis.

A REAL CORPORATE BOND

Let's assume that your career in fixed-income markets is moving along splendidly and now you plan to buy your loved one an investment-grade corporate bond for Valentine's Day. Figure 3.5 shows the Bloomberg Yield and Spread Analysis page for the 8 3/8% IBM bond that matures on November 1, 2019. Its flat price is 132.209 (percent of par value) for settlement on February 14, 2014. Look first at the Invoice section on the lower right side of the page. The total purchase price is shown for $1,000,000 in par value (also called the face amount—you can scale that down to a lower amount to fit your budget). The flat (or clean) price, here called the *principal*, is $1,322,090.00. The accrued interest is $23,961.81, calculated as:

$$\frac{103}{180} * \frac{0.08375}{2} * \$1,000,000 = \$23,961.81$$

The day-count convention is 30/360, giving 103 days between the last coupon on November 1 and settlement on February 14 (29 remaining days in November, 30 days in December, 30 days in January, and 14 days in February). There are assumed to be 180 days in the 6-month coupon period. The sum of the flat price and the accrued interest, $1,346,051.81, is the full (or dirty) price.

The street convention yield-to-maturity statistic for this bond is shown to be 2.322082%. That it is so much lower than the coupon rate of 8.375% explains why it is trading at such a high premium over par value. This IBM

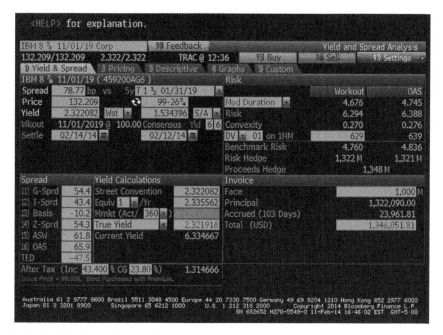

FIGURE 3.5   Bloomberg Yield and Spread Analysis Page for the IBM 8 3/8% Bond
Due 11/01/2019
Used with permission of Bloomberg.com © 2014. All rights reserved.

bond was issued in 1989 at a time of much higher market interest rates.
This yield can be confirmed using the YIELD financial function in Excel, as
shown here:

YIELD (DATE (2014,2,14), DATE (2019,11,1), 0.08375,132.209,100,2,0)

The entered items are the settlement date, maturity date, annual coupon
rate as a decimal, flat price, par value, periodicity, and the code for a 30/360
day-count. The Excel program solves for the accrued interest and then the
internal rate of return on the total cash flows.

Another way of confirming the yield to maturity is to substitute into
equation 3.11 and solve for y by trial and error. The semiannual coupon
payment (PMT) is 4.1875 per 100 of par value: 8.375%/2 * 100 = 4.1875.
There are 12 semiannual periods (N) between the last coupon payment on
November 1, 2013, and maturity on November 1, 2019. The fraction of the

period gone by is 103/180 (t/T). The left side of the equation is the full price; the right side is the present value of the coupon and principal cash flows discounted at the yield per semiannual period (y).

$$132.209 + (103/180 * 4.1875)$$

$$= \left[\frac{4.1875}{y} * \left(1 - \frac{1}{(1+y)^{12}} \right) + \frac{100}{(1+y)^{12}} \right] * (1+y)^{103/180}$$

The solution for y turns out to be 0.0116104083. Multiply that by two to annualize and round to six digits to obtain the street convention yield to maturity of 2.322082%.

Shown next is a periodicity conversion. The street convention yield of 2.322082% is on a semiannual bond basis; it converts to 2.335562% for one compounding period per year, that is, an effective annual rate.

$$\left(1 + \frac{0.02322082}{2} \right)^2 = 1.02335562$$

The true yield for this bond is 2.321916%, a bit lower than the street convention yield because three coupon dates fall on weekends (November 1, 2014, November 1, 2015, and May 1, 2016) and the payments are deferred until the following Monday. The U.S. Government and Japanese simple yields are not displayed but can be found by pulling down the menu. They are 2.324031% and 2.069000%, respectively. The former can be verified by solving this equation:

$$132.209 + (103/180 * 4.1875)$$

$$= \left[\frac{4.1875}{y} * \left(1 - \frac{1}{(1+y)^{12}} \right) + \frac{100}{(1+y)^{12}} \right] * (1+y)^{105/181}$$

The only change from the equation for street convention is to switch the day-count on the right side from 103/180 to 105/181 to reflect the actual/actual convention used on Treasuries. Here y is 0.011620153; that gives 2.324031% when annualized and rounded. I won't bother confirming the Japanese simple yield calculation—it's just a datum that I hope you never use in making a decision. The same is true for the current yield, shown to be 6.334667%. It is the sum of the coupon payments over the year divided by the flat price but how you'll use that statistic I really don't know.

$$\frac{8.375}{132.209} = 0.06334667$$

The after-tax rate of return, shown at the bottom of the page to be 1.314666%, is discussed in Chapter 4 on bond taxation. You will see that I have a problem with how Bloomberg reports after-tax yields on some bonds trading at a discount. This IBM bond is priced at a premium, and its after-tax rate is fine.

Now look at the spread calculation in the top left side of the page. The street convention yield on the IBM bond is compared to the yield on the *on-the-run* (i.e., most recently issued) 5-year Treasury note. Its coupon rate is 1.5% and it matures on January 31, 2019. Its flat price is shown to be 99–26¾ for settlement on February 12, 2014. Treasuries are quoted in 32nds, so that price means 99 + 26.75/32 = 99.8359375 per 100 of par value. Note that this Bloomberg page was taken on February 11, indicating that Treasuries settle "T+1" and corporate bonds "T+3."

The street convention yield for this T-note is 1.534396%. The same result is obtained using the YIELD function in Excel.

YIELD (DATE (2014,2,12), DATE (2019,1,31), 0.0150,99.8359375,100,2,1)

Note that the last entry item of 1 is the code for actual/actual day-count convention. The spread over this particular Treasury note for the IBM bond is 78.77 basis points: 2.322082% – 1.534396% = 0.787686%. This is not exactly an "apple-to-apple" comparison because the settlement dates and day-counts differ. The U.S. Government Equivalent yield could be used to account for the second difference, which would give a spread of 78.96 basis points: 2.324031% – 1.534396% = 0.789635%. That this is not done in practice (at least by Bloomberg) suggests that U.S. Government yields for corporate bonds are data, not information.

Several other spreads are shown in the lower left side of the Bloomberg page. The G-Spread is the street convention yield minus the yield on an interpolated Treasury curve. The idea is to find the point on the government bond yield curve that best matches the maturity on the IBM bond because there is no Treasury maturing on 11/01/19. I-spread is similar in that it is the bond yield minus the yield on an interpolated interest rate swap curve— more on swaps in Chapter 8. The Basis relates the bond spread to prices on credit default swaps—a great topic but one not covered in this book (sorry).

The Z-spread is the uniform increment over a benchmark spot (i.e., zero-coupon) curve that obtains the full price of the bond. This calculation is shown in Chapter 5. The asset swap spread (ASW) is the difference between the bond's coupon rate and a corresponding fixed rate on an interest rate swap. Finally, the option-adjusted spread (OAS) "corrects" the bond spread for the presence of embedded options. This is addressed in Chapter 6.

The duration and convexity calculations in the Risk section on the top right side of the page are very important to the study of bond math, but we have to wait until Chapter 6 for that discussion.

CONCLUSION

Owning or issuing a standard semiannual payment coupon bond entails dealing with many cash flows. A yield-to-maturity statistic is a way of summarizing these many cash flows into just one number. Of the many yield statistics that are out there, the street convention yield is probably the most informative and the most useful in making decisions. It is information and not just more data. At least it is a decent starting place to think about future coupon reinvestment rates and the probability of default. It does, however, neglect the inevitability of taxation. That no longer can be avoided.

CHAPTER 4

Bond Taxation

This chapter is about the taxation of bonds in the United States. I'm sure you already appreciate that taxes are very important in financial analysis. After all, the after-tax rate of return is what ultimately matters to an investor and the after-tax cost of funds is what matters to a borrower. But please fight the temptation to think that taxation is boring and just a matter of learning a set of rules. I hope to demonstrate that there are some interesting questions regarding taxation both in theory and in practice, as well as some very useful bond math calculations.

Discussions about taxation commonly involve four aspects of a cash flow, or accrual:

1. *Source*. Is the income/expense domestic or foreign?
2. *Timing*. Is the income/expense current or deferred?
3. *Character*. Is the cash flow ordinary income/expense or a capital gain/ loss?
4. *Exemption*. Is the ordinary income or capital gain exempt from taxation?

There are different tax rules and rates depending on the source, timing, character, and exemption status of the cash flow. I limit the discussion here to U.S. investors in U.S. bonds. Therefore, the source of the cash flow is not a factor, but the timing, character, and exemption status are in the mix.

We consider these questions: What is the difference between interest income and a capital gain for tax purposes? How and when should the implicit interest income on a zero-coupon bond be taxed? How should we compare investments in fully taxable corporate bonds and tax-exempt municipal bonds? How should projected after-tax rates of return on corporate bonds be calculated? This last question is particularly relevant. I argue that the after-tax rate on some bonds trading at a discount displayed on the widely used Bloomberg Yield and Spread Analysis page is misleading to U.S. investors, and probably has been so for the past 30 years.

Getting taxes correct is not easy, as some high-ranking U.S. government officials surely will attest. Let me be clear about this: I am not a tax attorney; I am a college professor. What I know about bond taxation comes from my reading of Internal Revenue Service (IRS) Publication 550 on Investment Income and Expenses. Some aspects of U.S. tax rules make sense to me, some make no sense at all, some are just too detailed for me to try to figure out. I aim in this chapter to target those aspects that are most relevant to the study of bond math.

BASIC BOND TAXATION

Let's start with the character of the cash flows on a standard coupon bond. Suppose that a corporation issues a 4%, annual payment, 4-year note at a price of 99.342 (percent of par value). Remember from Chapter 3 that the yield to maturity on this bond is 4.182%. Each year, the investor has taxable ordinary interest income in the amount of $40 per $1,000 of par value, and the issuer has equivalent ordinary interest expense. Importantly, that interest expense is deductible for the corporate issuer, creating the well-known tax advantage to debt financing compared to equity.

If the investor holds the bond to maturity and redeems it at par value or sells the bond prior to maturity at a price above 99.342, will there be a capital gain for tax purposes? If it is sold at a price below 99.342, will there be a capital loss? This is where bond taxation starts to get interesting. Back in the olden days (i.e., before 1984), bonds essentially were taxed like equity. Interest payments on debt securities, like dividend payments on stocks, were treated as ordinary income. The purchase price of the bond or stock was the basis for determining capital gains or losses when the security was sold or redeemed. The rule of thumb always has been that investors prefer capital gains to ordinary income because usually they are taxed at a lower rate. That is one of the motives for stock-repurchase programs in lieu of cash dividends—to return value to investors in a tax-favored manner.

The high market interest rates prevailing in the 1980s motivated the federal government to change the tax rules for bonds. Look again at Figure 2.1 in Chapter 2. Because yields had gone up, bonds that had been issued a few years earlier invariably were trading at discounts below par value. A bond newly issued at par value would require higher coupon payments, all of which would be taxed as ordinary income. Instead, the investor could buy a discount bond having a lower coupon rate. If held to maturity, that discount then would be taxed at the lower capital gains rate.

In principle, interest payments are compensation to the investor for the passage of time, scaled by the amount of credit and liquidity risk on the underlying debt obligation. Moreover, in principle, capital gains and losses arise from a change in the value of the bond as signaled by a change in its yield to maturity. The government realized that an investor who buys a bond at a discount and holds it to maturity does not necessarily merit a capital gain. The bond price is "pulled to par" as time passes, but that is not a change in value. In theory, the difference between the purchase price and the redemption amount is just interest income and should be taxed at the ordinary income rate, albeit deferred. The big change in bond taxation in 1984 had to do with character, not timing. Buying a bond issued before 1984 at a discount would generate a capital gain if held to maturity. On a bond issued after 1984, that "gain" would be taxed as ordinary income. The examples to follow should clarify this.

Our 4%, 4-year bond issued at 99.342 has an original issue discount (OID) of 0.658 (percent of par value). But the discount on this bond is so small that it qualifies as *de minimis* OID. Technically, the criterion for *de minimis* OID treatment is that the discount at issuance is less than the number of the years to maturity times 0.25. If the initial price on this 4-year bond had been less than 99 (percent of par value), it would not be designated as *de minimis* OID and instead would merit special OID tax treatment to be discussed later in the chapter. So, if the investor holds the bond to maturity, there will be a capital gain of 0.658 (percent of par value) taxable at redemption, just like in the olden days.

We can now project an after-tax rate of return for this bond. Let's assume that the investor's ordinary income tax rate over the four years is constant at 25%, the capital gains tax rate is 15%, and all taxes are paid when cash flows are received. Notice how cavalierly we make simplifying assumptions to sidestep reality. The after-tax yield (*aty*) on this bond is 3.154%, the internal rate of return on the after-tax cash flows.

$$99.342 = \frac{4*(1-0.25)}{(1+aty)^1} + \frac{4*(1-0.25)}{(1+aty)^2} + \frac{4*(1-0.25)}{(1+aty)^3} + \frac{4*(1-0.25)}{(1+aty)^4}$$
$$+ \frac{100-[(100-99.342)*0.15]}{(1+aty)^4}$$

The first four terms on the right side of the equation are straightforward— the after-tax cash flow is 3.00 (percent of par value), the pretax coupon interest payment of 4 times one minus the ordinary income tax rate of 25%. In the fifth term, the gain of 0.658 (percent of par value)—that is, 100 − 99.342 = 0.658—from purchasing the bond at a discount is taxed at the capital gains rate of 15%, and that tax obligation is subtracted from the redemption amount.

Newly issued bonds having *de minimis* OID are actually quite common in the U.S. Treasury market. That's because the auction process allows for non-competitive bids. These, mostly from retail investors and small institutions, are limited in size—currently, the maximum non competitive bid is $5 million in par value. The competitive bids submitted by government securities dealers and big financial institutions determine the stop-out, or market-clearing, yield for the Treasury notes or bonds. Then the coupon rate is set to the nearest 1/8% *below* the stop-out yield. For example, if the stop-out yield is 2.415%, the coupon rate will be set at 2 3/8%; if the stop-out rate is 2.365%, the coupon rate will be 2 1/4%. Therefore, the price at issuance will be a small discount below par value. The noncompetitive bidders, who are assured of receiving their bid amount, initially pay full par value. At settlement, they receive a payment for the amount of the discount along with their securities. If instead the coupon rate had been set above the stop-out yield, the government would need to collect the premium. It's easier to just have a *de minimis* OID.

MARKET DISCOUNT BONDS

Now consider another 4-year, annual payment corporate bond that also is priced to yield 4.182% on a pretax basis. This one has a low 1% coupon rate and trades at a much deeper discount than the 4% bond. Its price is 88.499 (percent of par value).

$$\frac{1}{(1.04182)^1} + \frac{1}{(1.04182)^2} + \frac{1}{(1.04182)^3} + \frac{101}{(1.04182)^4} = 88.499$$

Assume that this 1% bond originally was issued after 1984 at par value (or with *de minimis* OID). This is an example of buying a seasoned bond at a *market discount*. Its yield has risen and its price has fallen since issuance, perhaps due to an increase in the credit risk of the issuer or perhaps due to a higher rate of inflation.

Assuming an ordinary income tax rate of 25% and a capital gains rate of 15%, this 1% bond will have a projected after-tax yield of 3.171%. That is the internal rate of return on its after-tax cash flows.

$$88.499 = \frac{1*(1-0.25)}{(1+aty)^1} + \frac{1*(1-0.25)}{(1+aty)^2} + \frac{1*(1-0.25)}{(1+aty)^3} + \frac{1*(1-0.25)}{(1+aty)^4}$$
$$+ \frac{100-[(100-88.499)*0.25]}{(1+aty)^4}$$

The numerators in the first four terms are the interest payment multiplied by one minus the ordinary income tax rate. But notice that in the fifth term the gain from buying at a discount is taxed at the ordinary rate. Back in the olden days it would have been taxed at the capital gains rate.

These post-1984 tax rules make sense to me because the amount of the premium or discount is the present value of the "excess" or "deficiency" in the coupon rate compared to the yield to maturity. Remember that the coupon rate is what you are promised to get; the yield is what you need (in order to pay par value). For example, the 1% bond has a "deficient" coupon in the amount of 3.182 (percent of par value) per year because its yield to maturity is 4.182%. The present value of the deficiency equals the amount of the discount: 11.501 = 100 − 88.499.

$$\frac{3.182}{(1.04182)^1} + \frac{3.182}{(1.04182)^2} + \frac{3.182}{(1.04182)^3} + \frac{3.182}{(1.04182)^4} = 11.501$$

So, the discount at the time of purchase is compensation for low coupon interest income. A good portion of the investor's total return on the 1% bond is in the "capital gain." That "gain" really is just *deferred interest income*, and it is taxed appropriately at the ordinary income rate. Only a discount deemed to be *de minimis* OID at purchase generates a capital gain for tax purposes when the bond is held to maturity.

Another wrinkle in the post-1984 U.S. tax rules is that the buyer of this market discount bond can elect to report the "capital gain" as income year by year. The investor calculates the *accrued market discount* either "ratably" (i.e., using straight-line amortization), or using the constant-yield price trajectory. For example, for the 1% bond the accrual each year is 2.87525 per year [= 11.501/4] using the ratable method. That amount would be taxed annually at the ordinary income tax rate.

Usually we assume the investor would prefer to defer the tax obligation to the time of sale or redemption. Suppose the investor sells the 1% bond at 96 (percent of par value) after two years. Then the total gain of 7.501 [= 96 − 88.499] is broken down into 5.7505 taxable at the time of sale as ordinary income [= 2 * 2.87525] and the remainder of 1.7505 as a capital gain [= 7.501 − 5.7505]. In general, only gains above the accrued market discount benefit from the lower capital gains rate. If the investor holds the bond to maturity, the full accrued market discount is taxed as ordinary income at that time.

The after-tax rates of return on these two 4-year corporate bonds illustrate the usual tax advantage to discount bonds due to the timing of tax payments. The projected after-tax rate of return of 3.171% on the 1% bond is a bit higher than 3.154% on the 4% bond. That's because the tax obligation is deferred until maturity. This assumes a constant ordinary income tax rate over time, an assumption commonly made in practice. If you anticipate higher tax rates in the future, perhaps because of unending government budget deficits, you might want to amend that assumption. Notice that it would be easy to introduce an entire *term structure of tax rates* into the after-tax rate of return calculations.

A REAL MARKET DISCOUNT CORPORATE BOND

Figure 4.1 shows the Bloomberg Yield and Spread Analysis page for the 3.85% Apple Inc. (AAPL) bond that matures on May 4, 2043. Its flat price was 87.24 (percent of par value) for settlement on March 5, 2014. Its street convention yield to maturity was 4.653675%. This bond was issued on May 3, 2013, as a 30-year noncallable offering at a *de minimis* OID price of 99.418 (percent of par value). This information is shown on the Bloomberg Descriptive page; see the lower right side of Figure 4.2. The bond's price

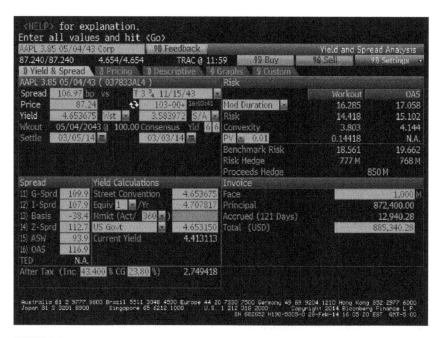

FIGURE 4.1   Bloomberg Yield and Spread Analysis Page, AAPL 3.85% Bond Due 5/04/2043, Assuming 43.40% Ordinary Income Tax Rate and 23.80% Capital Gains Rate

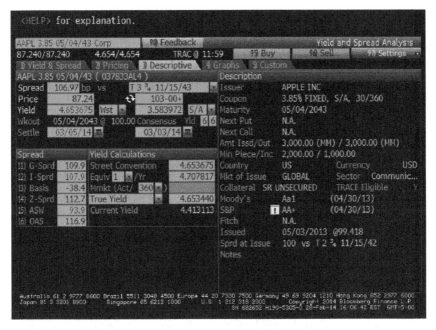

FIGURE 4.2 Bloomberg Descriptive Page, AAPL 3.85% Bond Due 5/04/2043
Used with permission of Bloomberg.com © 2014. All rights reserved.

has fallen because long-term benchmark Treasury bond yields rose in the 10 months after issuance.

First, let's confirm the pretax street convention yield to maturity of 4.653675%. This entails substituting into equation 3.11 from Chapter 3, repeated here as equation 4.1.

$$Flat + (t/T * PMT) = \left[\frac{PMT}{y} * \left(1 - \frac{1}{(1+y)^N} \right) + \frac{FV}{(1+y)^N} \right] * (1+y)^{t/T} \quad (4.1)$$

Using the 30/360 day-count convention, 121 days have elapsed since the last coupon on November 4 and there are 59 semiannual periods between November 2013 and May 2043. So, *Flat* = 87.24, *t/T* = 121/180, *PMT* = 1.925 [= 3.85/2], and *N* = 59.

$$87.24 + \left(\frac{121}{180} * 1.925 \right) = \left[\frac{1.925}{y} * \left(1 - \frac{1}{(1+y)^{59}} \right) + \frac{100}{(1+y)^{59}} \right] * (1+y)^{121/180}$$

Solving by arduous trial-and-error search (or, better, setting up the equation in an Excel spreadsheet and using Solver) obtains the result that y = 0.023268374. Annualized to a semiannual bond basis and rounded to six decimals, the yield to maturity is 4.653675%. A more direct way of confirming the Bloomberg street convention yield is to use the YIELD financial function in Excel.

YIELD(DATE(2014,3,5),DATE(2043,5,4),0.0385,87.24,100,2,0)

The inputs are the settlement date, maturity date, annual coupon rate as a decimal, flat price, par value, periodicity, and the code for the 30/360 day-count convention.

The reported after-tax rate of return of 2.749418% for this bond is troubling for two reasons. First, there is a small error in the calculation, as I demonstrate. But more important, this to me is bad bond math because it is very misleading, at least to a U.S. investor. The problem is that this is a global bond, as indicated in Figure 4.2 for the market of issue. For a reason unknown to me, Bloomberg does not use U.S. tax rules on global bonds (or on at least some private placements). Instead, the Bloomberg calculation assumes that the "gain" from buying at 87.24 and redeeming the bond at 100 (assuming no default) will be taxed at the assumed capital gains tax rate of 23.80%. Bloomberg only uses U.S. tax rules on U.S. domestic issuances. Clearly, you need to know how to do this calculation yourself.

Let's assume a U.S. investor elects to not bring the accrued market discount into income each year. That's the much easier assumption to deal with analytically. The investor's projected after-tax yield on a market discount bond is the solution for aty in this general expression.

$$Flat + AI = \frac{PMT - (PMT - AI) * tax}{(1 + aty)^{1-t/T}} + \frac{PMT * (1 - tax)}{(1 + aty)^{2-t/T}} + \cdots + \frac{PMT * (1 - tax)}{(1 + aty)^{N-t/T}}$$

$$+ \frac{FV - (FV - Flat) * tax}{(1 + aty)^{N-t/T}} \tag{4.2}$$

The left side is the purchase price, including accrued interest (AI). The first term on the right side is important to understanding this calculation. When the investor receives that first coupon payment of PMT, the accrued interest account is closed out. Only ($PMT - AI$) is taxable interest income. The ordinary income tax rate is denoted tax and is assumed to be constant. The remaining coupon payments are all reduced by the ordinary income tax payments. At redemption, tax is owed on the "gain" from buying the bond at a market discount, the difference between the par value and the flat price. Importantly, the same ordinary income tax rate on that "gain" is used because that is U.S. tax law and has been so since 1984. There is no difference to a U.S. taxpayer if the bond is designated global or domestic.

Now we can collect terms, multiply the numerator and denominator by $(1 + aty)^{t/T}$, and do the usual sum-of-a-finite-geometric-series reduction, as shown in equation 4.3.

$$
\begin{aligned}
Flat + AI = &\left[\frac{PMT * (1 - tax)}{aty} * \left(1 - \frac{1}{(1 + aty)^N} \right) \right. \\
&\left. + \frac{AI * tax}{1 + aty} + \frac{FV - (FV - Flat) * tax}{(1 + aty)^N} \right] * (1 + aty)^{t/T}
\end{aligned}
\tag{4.3}
$$

Note that $AI = t/T * PMT = 121/180 * 1.925 = 1.294028$.

$$
\begin{aligned}
87.24 + 1.294028 = &\left[\frac{1.925 * (1 - 0.434)}{aty} * \left(1 - \frac{1}{(1 + aty)^{59}} \right) + \frac{1.294028 * 0.434}{1 + aty} \right. \\
&\left. + \frac{100 - (100 - 87.24) * 0.434}{(1 + aty)^{59}} \right] * (1 + aty)^{121/180}
\end{aligned}
$$

Solving again by tedious trial-and-error search (or by using an Excel spreadsheet and Solver) obtains the result that $aty = 0.013432181$. Annualized, the projected after-tax rate of return on this bond is 2.686436%, not 2.749418% as reported on the Bloomberg Yield and Spread Analysis page.

How does Bloomberg get its after-tax rate on a market discount bond? I suspect some adjustments are made to a program equivalent to the YIELD financial function in Excel. To see this, recall the entries used above to get the before-tax, street convention yield to maturity of 4.653675%.

YIELD(DATE(2014,3,5),DATE(2043,5,4),0.0385,87.24,100,2,0)

Now multiply the third item, the annual coupon rate, by one minus the ordinary tax rate of 43.40%. Then subtract the tax on the deferred market discount from the fifth entry, the redemption amount, using the assumed capital gains tax rate of 23.80%.

YIELD(DATE(2014,3,5),DATE(2043,5,4),0.0385*(1 – 0.434),87.24,

(100 – (100 – 87.24)*0.238),2,0)

This produces an after-tax yield of 2.749418%, the same as reported on the Bloomberg Yield Analysis page.

I suggest that U.S. users of Bloomberg who would like to see a projected after-tax rate of return set the capital gains rate to whatever assumption is used for ordinary interest income. This will work for all bonds—global, domestic, private placements—because the same tax law applies to each type. Then the output will be the same as if it is done with the "tax-adjusted" YIELD function in Excel. For example, use the ordinary income tax rate of 43.40% in the fifth entry.

$$\text{YIELD(DATE(2014,3,5),DATE(2043,5,4),0.0385} * (1 - 0.434), 87.24,$$

$$(100 - (100 - 87.24) * 0.434), 2, 0)$$

This gives an after-tax yield of 2.686572%. This is virtually the same as the result calculated above, 2.686436%. But still, why is there a small difference? The (admittedly minor) problem with the "tax-adjusted" YIELD approach is that the accrued interest needed in equation 4.2 is calculated using the after-tax coupon rate. That reduces the left side of the equation. Also, the after-tax first cash flow is not corrected by the accrued interest. That reduces the right side of the equation. These two errors offset. This is no doubt a concern to only those of us who are fastidious about bond math.

PREMIUM BONDS

U.S. tax authorities were very busy in the 1980s. After fixing the taxation of market discount bonds originated after 1984, the next task was bonds purchased at a premium. In principle, the premium over par is the present value of the "excessive" coupon payments because the coupon rate is greater than the yield to maturity. You are getting more than you need (in order to pay par value). So, for tax purposes, the investor naturally would want to amortize the premium over the lifetime of the bond. That means reducing the amount of taxable interest income each year.

According to IRS Publication 550, for bonds acquired before 1985, "you can amortize the premium using any reasonable method," including straight-line amortization and something called Revenue Ruling 82-10, which the IRS does not even bother to explain. The big change was that for bonds acquired after 1985, "you must amortize the bond premium using a constant-yield method on the basis of the bond's yield to maturity." For some fun, read the torturous way that Publication 550 tries to explain to the public how to calculate the constant-yield price trajectory. It's really just basic bond math.

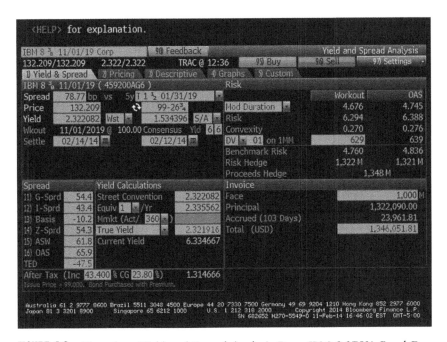

FIGURE 4.3 Bloomberg Yield and Spread Analysis Page, IBM 8.375% Bond Due 11/01/2019, Assuming 43.40% Ordinary Income Tax Rate and 23.80% Capital Gains Rate

In Chapter 3, I use the 8 3/8% IBM bond due November 1, 2019, to illustrate the various calculations on its Bloomberg Yield and Spread Analysis page; it is shown again here as Figure 4.3. This bond was priced at 132.209 flat to yield 2.322082% for settlement on February 14, 2014, Valentine's Day. Its after-tax rate is reported to be 1.314666%, assuming an ordinary income tax rate of 43.40% and a capital gains rate of 23.80%. Table 4.1 displays the spreadsheet that I used to confirm that calculation.

The first column shows the dates for the cash flows, assuming street convention for the timing of the payments. Solving for an after-tax true yield would be a lot more work. The second column is the before-tax cash flows. The full price of the bond at settlement is 134.605181, the flat price of 132.209 plus accrued interest of 2.396181 [= (103/180) * (8.375/2)]. The third column is the all-important projected after-tax cash flows. But first we need the constant-yield price trajectory shown in the fourth column. I get this using the PRICE financial function in Excel. For instance, the value of 108.8725568 for May 1, 2018, comes from:

PRICE (DATE (2018,5,1), DATE (2019,11,1),0.08375,0.02322082,100,2,0)

TABLE 4.1 After-Tax Rate Calculation on the 8 3/8% IBM Bond Due 11/01/2019

Date	Cash Flow	After-Tax Cash Flows	Constant Yield Price	Change in Price	1 – t/T	Present Value
2/14/14	134.605181	134.605181	132.2090000			
5/1/14	4.1875	3.898312	131.0840133	1.1249867	0.4278	3.887405
11/1/14	4.1875	3.526979	128.4184522	2.6655611	1.4278	3.494150
5/1/15	4.1875	3.540410	125.7219429	2.6965093	2.4278	3.484559
11/1/15	4.1875	3.553998	122.9941260	2.7278169	3.4278	3.475097
5/1/16	4.1875	3.567743	120.2346380	2.7594880	4.4278	3.465764
11/1/16	4.1875	3.581648	117.4431112	2.7915268	5.4278	3.456558
5/1/17	4.1875	3.595714	114.6191737	2.8239375	6.4278	3.447479
11/1/17	4.1875	3.609943	111.7624491	2.8567246	7.4278	3.438527
5/1/18	4.1875	3.624338	108.8725568	2.8898923	8.4278	3.429702
11/1/18	4.1875	3.638900	105.9491116	2.9234452	9.4278	3.421002
5/1/19	4.1875	3.653631	102.9917240	2.9573876	10.4278	3.412428
11/1/19	104.1875	103.668533	100.0000000	2.9917240	11.4278	96.192509
				32.2090000		134.605181

The fourth entry item is the yield to maturity, calculated using the YIELD function as in Chapter 3.

The fifth column reports the change in the constant-yield price from period to period. The sum of the column is 32.209, the premium over par value at purchase. The value of 120.2346380 on May 1, 2016, is 2.7594880 lower than the price on November 1, 2015. Now we can see the after-tax cash flow calculation for that date: 3.567743 = 4.1875 – (4.1875 – 2.7594880) * 0.4340. The amount of tax for each period is the interest payment less the amortization of the premium times the assumed ordinary tax rate. The cash flow that requires special attention is the first one on May 1, 2014, because we have to subtract the accrued interest from the interest payment: 3.898312 = 4.1875 – (4.1875 – 2.396181 – 1.1249867) * 0.4340.

The after-tax rate is the internal rate of return on the series of after-tax cash flows in column three. The sixth and seventh columns are used in getting the internal rate of return using Solver. Each after-tax cash flow is discounted at the rate per semiannual period for the time until the receipt of payment. For example, the payment on November 1, 2014, is discounted back for 1.4278 [= 2 – (103/180)] periods. The discount rate that makes the sum of the present values equal the total price of 134.605181 turns out to be 0.6571075%. Annualizing this by multiplying the two and rounding to six digits gives the after-tax rate of 1.314215%. I have no explanation for the insignificant difference between this result and that reported on the Bloomberg page, 1.314666%.

ORIGINAL ISSUE DISCOUNT BONDS

A zero-coupon bond is treated quite differently than a standard coupon bond in terms of timing but not character. In particular, zeros fall under the rules for original issue discount (OID) securities. A bond is designated OID if the issuance price is lower than the *de minimis* threshold. Therefore, a bond is deemed to be OID if the discount is more than 0.25 times the number of years to maturity. A 10-year corporate zero priced at 60 (percent of par value) easily passes that test—as would any 10-year, low-coupon bond, issued at a price below 97.5.

The key tax aspect of an OID bond is that the yearly movement along the constant-yield price trajectory is the reported ordinary interest income to the investor and interest expense to the issuer. These tax rules have been in effect since 1982; before that, straight-line amortization of the discount was allowed. That gave significant benefit to corporate issuers of zero-coupon bonds because the deductible interest expense was much more front-loaded than when the constant-yield trajectory is used.

An investor who buys and holds to maturity an OID bond will not have a capital gain because the discount will be taxed as ordinary income over the lifetime of the bond. The problem is that this is "phantom" income in that there is a tax liability each year despite the absence of a cash receipt to pay the tax. That creates a market segmentation effect—most zero-coupon bonds such as Treasury STRIPS are owned by defined benefit pension funds or by individuals in their retirement savings accounts, for example, 401(k)s. The other significant aspect to OID taxation is that capital gains and losses are measured from the constant-yield price trajectory if the bond is sold prior to maturity.

These tax rules for OID bonds match the economic fundamentals in that interest income is the price change caused purely by the passage of time. A capital gain or loss is the price movement caused by the change in value, meaning a change in the bond yield. We can see this in the 10-year zero-coupon bond issued at 60 (percent of par value) that we studied in Chapter 2. Its pretax cash flows are laid out in Figure 2.2, which shows year-by-year prices along the constant-yield trajectory. If the investor holds the bond to maturity (and there is no default), there is no capital gain for tax purposes despite buying at 60 and getting back 100. The full original issue discount of 40 is taxable ordinary interest income spread out over the 10-year life of the bond.

The investor's after-tax rate of return depends on the ordinary tax rates that prevail in each year and on the capital gains rate if the zero-coupon bond is sold prior to maturity. Let's suppose that the 10-year bond is purchased at 60 and sold two years later at 68. We calculate in Chapter 2 that this trade generates a horizon yield of 6.357% (s.a.)—but that is before OID tax consideration. Let's suppose that this investor's tax rate is 25% on ordinary income and 15% on capital gains. The OID ordinary interest incomes are 3.145 for the first year (= 63.145 − 60) and 3.309 for the second year (= 66.454 − 63.145). The annual income tax liabilities are 0.786 (= 3.145 ∗ 0.25) and 0.827 (= 3.309 ∗ 0.25), respectively.

When the bond is sold at 68, the taxable capital gain is 1.546 (= 68 − 66.454). If you remember your first financial accounting course, you'll note that the investor *credits* interest income and *debits* the bond investment by 3.145 after the first year and by 3.309 after the second year. Those entries raise the carrying book value (and the basis for taxation) of the zero-coupon bond up from 60 to 66.454. The capital gain represents the profit from selling at a price above that amount. The capital gains tax payment payable in year 2 is 0.232 (= 1.546 ∗ 0.15).

The investor's after-tax horizon yield is the internal rate of return on the after-tax cash flows. These cash flows, year by year, are −60, −0.786, +66.941, using − to indicate outflows and + for inflows. The year-0 cash flow is negative because we are taking the perspective of the buyer of the bond. The year-1 cash flow is negative because of the phantom income problem and the tax liability. The year-2 after-tax inflow of 66.941 is the sale price of 68, less the ordinary income tax of 0.827 and the capital gains tax of 0.232. The after-tax rate of return, calculated on an effective annual rate basis, is the solution for aty in this expression:

$$0 = -60 - \frac{0.786}{(1+aty)^1} + \frac{66.941}{(1+aty)^2}, \quad aty = 0.04973$$

Solving this equation requires trial-and-error search; 4.973% turns out to be the interest rate such that the net present value of all cash flows is zero. This is easily handled by a financial calculator that allows for variable cash flows or a spreadsheet program. To compare the after-tax rate of return to yields to maturity on standard bonds paying coupon interest twice a year, convert this effective annual rate to a semiannual bond basis. Using equation 1.10, it is the solution for APR_2:

$$\left(1 + \frac{APR_2}{2}\right)^2 = 1.04973, \quad APR_2 = 0.04913$$

The investor's after-tax holding period rate of return is 4.913% (s.a.).

Given these OID tax rules, we now can see what a prodigious task it was to create synthetic zero-coupon Treasury bonds such as TIGRS, CATS, and LIONS in the 1980s. The Treasury bonds that went into the special-purpose entities were taxed as traditional coupon bonds issued at par value (or *de minimis* OID). By the way, these are called non-OID bonds. So, the financial engineering involved the transformation of non-OID Treasury bonds into OID Treasury zeros. That's why the IRS back then had to approve the SPE structures and issue statements clarifying how the TIGRS, CATS, and LIONS would be taxed.

MUNICIPAL BONDS

Municipal bonds (munis) issued by state and local governments in the U.S. are an important sector in fixed-income markets because the interest income is exempt from federal taxation. Issuers are not allowed to "arbitrage" the market—that is, they are not allowed to issue debt at low yields due to the exemption and turn around and invest the funds at a higher rate. The tax-exempt status of munis appeals to wealthy individuals and some institutions as part of their tax management strategies. Investors might also be exempt from state and local income taxes if they reside in the issuer's locality. That can definitely matter to those of you living in certain high-tax East Coast cities and states.

Investors often evaluate a municipal bond based on its *equivalent taxable yield* (ETY) statistic. The intent is to be able to compare directly the yield on a tax-exempt bond to otherwise comparable fully taxable corporate offerings. This comparison is not as easy as it might sound because the bond rating agencies have different criteria for each bond type—that is, a double A-rated muni does not necessarily have the same projected probability of default (and recovery rate) as a double A-rated corporate bond. Nevertheless, let's see how to calculate an ETY both in practice and in theory.

Assume now that the 4% and 1%, annual payment, 4-year bonds priced at 99.342 and 88.499, respectively, really are tax-exempt munis and not fully taxable corporate bonds. The commonly used ETY statistic, which we can call the *street* version because it is widely used in practice, is the after-tax yield divided by one minus the assumed ordinary income tax rate. Note that the after-tax yield on the muni is not just its quoted, or pretax, yield to maturity. When the muni is purchased at a premium or discount, there still are federal tax implications. Assume the investor holds the bond to maturity (selling prior to maturity can also generate taxable capital gains and losses), the ordinary tax rate is 25%, and the capital gains rate is 15%.

The after-tax yield to maturity on the 4% muni is 4.159%, the solution for *aty*.

$$99.342 = \frac{4}{(1+aty)^1} + \frac{4}{(1+aty)^2} + \frac{4}{(1+aty)^3} + \frac{4}{(1+aty)^4}$$
$$+ \frac{100 - [(100 - 99.342) * 0.15]}{(1+aty)^4}$$

Each interest payment of 4 (percent of par value) is now exempt from federal taxes. The small gain from buying at 99.342 and redeeming at 100 is taxed at the capital gains rate because the *de minimis* OID rule applies. The street ETY for this bond is 5.545%.

$$Street\ ETY = \frac{4.159\%}{(1 - 0.25)} = 5.545\%$$

If the 1% muni bond priced at 88.499 is newly issued, it would be classified as OID. Then the movement along the constant-yield trajectory would be reported each year as tax-exempt interest income. Assume that this muni instead is a seasoned offering originally issued at par value (or *de minimis* OID) and so it is now purchased at a market discount. Its after-tax yield to maturity is 3.444%, the internal rate of return on the after-tax cash flows.

$$88.499 = \frac{1}{(1+aty)^1} + \frac{1}{(1+aty)^2} + \frac{1}{(1+aty)^3} + \frac{1}{(1+aty)^4}$$
$$+ \frac{100 - [(100 - 88.499) * 0.25]}{(1+aty)^4}$$

Notice that the market discount of 11.501 is taxed at the assumed ordinary income rate. This reflects tax rules since 1993. If this muni had been purchased before 1993, the market discount on the held-to-maturity bond would be taxed at the capital gains rate. If purchased after that date, it is taxed as ordinary income.

If this tax treatment seems odd to you, I agree completely. I'm really disappointed with the federal government because these tax rules do not make economic sense. In principle, the "gain" from buying at a market discount is just deferred interest income and should be tax exempt in my opinion. Suppose these two bonds were issued by the same state government—they mature on the same date and entail the same credit risk. Their after-tax yields to maturity should be very similar (perhaps differing due to liquidity). But the 1% market discount bond is penalized significantly because the "gain" is taxed as ordinary income—not as tax-exempt interest income. Its street ETY is only 4.592%.

$$Street\ ETY = \frac{3.444\%}{(1-0.25)} = 4.592\%$$

Let's now return to the intellectual safety of theoretical bond math. There is another way to think about calculating the ETY on a tax-exempt bond. This is to solve for the internal rate of return on a taxable offering that generates the same after-tax cash flows as the muni. Let's do this first for the 4% tax-exempt bond priced at 99.432. We need to solve this equation for ETY:

$$99.342 = \frac{4/(1-0.25)}{(1+ETY)^1} + \frac{4/(1-0.25)}{(1+ETY)^2} + \frac{4/(1-0.25)}{(1+ETY)^3}$$
$$+ \frac{4/(1-0.25)}{(1+ETY)^4} + \frac{100}{(1+ETY)^4}$$

The pretax coupon payments would have to be 5.333 [= 4/(1 − 0.25)] to equal 4 on a tax-exempt basis. The redemption amount of 100 does not need to be adjusted because both the taxable corporate and the "tax-exempt" muni face capital gains taxation on the *de minimis* OID. This ETY turns out to be 5.521%, just a bit lower than the street ETY of 5.545%.

The difference between the commonly used street ETY and what I suggest to be a better version becomes more relevant when we work through the deeper discount 1% muni bond priced at 88.499.

$$88.499 = \frac{1/(1-0.25)}{(1+ETY)^1} + \frac{1/(1-0.25)}{(1+ETY)^2} + \frac{1/(1-0.25)}{(1+ETY)^3}$$
$$+ \frac{1/(1-0.25)}{(1+ETY)^4} + \frac{100}{(1+ETY)^4}$$

The annual coupon payment on the taxable corporate bond would be 1.333 [= 1/(1 − 0.25)] to give the same after-tax cash flow as the 1% muni bond. Again the principal does not need adjustment because the market discount on both bonds is taxed at the ordinary income rate. This "better" ETY is 4.542%, 5 basis points lower than the street ETY of 4.592%.

Why is this version of ETY better than the street ETY, which is commonly used in practice? First, it is the more natural formulation of the bond math problem in my opinion. But more important, it allows the analyst to include a *term structure of tax rates*. Suppose that there is a scheduled increase in ordinary income tax rates for the wealthy investor, going up from 25% to 35% in the third year and 40% in the fourth. The "more theoretically correct" ETY on the 4% muni becomes 6.027%, the solution for *ETY* in this expression.

$$99.342 = \frac{4/(1-0.25)}{(1 + ETY)^1} + \frac{4/(1-0.25)}{(1 + ETY)^2} + \frac{4/(1-0.35)}{(1 + ETY)^3}$$
$$+ \frac{4/(1-0.40)}{(1 + ETY)^4} + \frac{100}{(1 + ETY)^4}$$

It's not obvious how to handle that assumption in the street ETY calculation (divide by some weighted average of the tax rates?). I suppose a street ETY is relevant information, and need not be relegated to "data" status, but better bond math should give us better information leading to better decisions.

CONCLUSION

I recall being told many years ago that everything interesting in finance boils down to either options or taxes. Like most overstatements, there is no doubt some truth there. But in my experience, bond taxation is often given short shrift in investments and fixed-income textbooks. Perhaps an indication of this reluctance to deal carefully with taxation is that the widely used Bloomberg Yield and Spread Analysis page reports misleading results for the projected after-tax rates of return on some market discount bonds, at least for U.S. investors.

Now on to yield curve analysis, where we predictably neglect tax effects.

CHAPTER 5

Yield Curves

A yield curve is a visual display of current conditions in some particular fixed-income bond market. It's a snapshot of interest rates in that market—a simple yet often informative graph that plots yields to maturity on the vertical axis and times to maturity on the horizontal axis for a homogeneous set of securities. A yield curve also is called the *term structure of interest rates*. Some academics distinguish the two, preserving one for zero-coupon bonds and the other for standard coupon bonds, but I use them as synonyms and specifically identify the type of securities being discussed.

Yield curves are great for the study of bond math. We see in this chapter how we can move seamlessly, albeit with some assumptions, between the commonly observed yield curve on coupon bonds and related curves that we derive—the implied spot curve and the implied forward curve. These two are hugely important in fixed-income analysis. It's no doubt an exaggeration, but I think that the implied forward curve is the single most useful line in fixed-income markets—and the implied spot curve is not far behind.

Most yield curves are based on government securities. That's so we can hold constant all the factors other than time to maturity that impact investors' required rates of return—in particular, credit risk, liquidity, and taxation. Obviously, all yields should be stated for the same periodicity. We saw in Chapter 1 that this is a problem in practice at the short-term end of the yield curve (i.e., the money market), but it can be rectified with some basic bond math. Also, the yields to maturity ideally would be for zero-coupon securities so that coupon reinvestment risk is not a factor.

In reality, there is no perfect data set for term structure analysis. Typically seen yield curves are plots of street convention yields on coupon-bearing Treasury notes and bonds instead of yields on Treasury STRIPS. In particular, the yields displayed usually are for on-the-run issues (i.e., the most recently auctioned Treasury securities). These are actively traded and typically are priced close to par value, thereby minimizing the effects of the deferral for tax purposes of the gains and losses from buying at a discount or a premium that we saw in Chapter 4. The problem is that there are gaps in the times to maturity, so some yields have to be interpolated.

We start with an intuitive look at implied forward rates in order to pay some respect to the traditional theories of the yield curve.

AN INTUITIVE FORWARD CURVE

Suppose that yields to maturity on 1-year, 2-year, and 3-year zero-coupon government bonds are 1.00%, 2.00%, and 2.50%, respectively. To preserve a bit of realism, these yields are quoted on a semiannual bond basis, meaning annual percentage rates for two periods per year. The periodicity assumption is totally arbitrary on zeros, but semiannual compounding is the norm in practice. I call these rates the 0×1, 0×2, and 0×3. These bonds presumably trade in the cash market, so the first number is the starting date and the second is the ending date. The difference is the time frame, or *tenor*, of the bond. So, 2.50% is the 0×3 yield (usually said "zero by three")—the yield on a 3-year zero-coupon bond starting today.

We can use this simple yield curve to infer the 1×2 and 2×3 forward rates. These are the implied yields on 1-year bonds starting one and two years into the future (i.e., forward in time). An implied forward rate (IFR) is the answer to this question: At what rate must one be able to reinvest the proceeds of an investment in a shorter-term bond to equal the proceeds of an investment in a longer-term bond? Intuitively, the 1×2 IFR has to be about 3.00% and the 2×3 about 3.50%. We need "about" here because we're neglecting compounding for the time being—that will be added later in the chapter.

The idea is that if an investor can buy a 1-year bond to yield 1.00% and reinvest for the second year at 3.00%, the total return matches that of 2.00% per year on the 2-year bond. Likewise, if an investor can buy the 2-year at 2.00% and reinvest for the third year at 3.50%, the same total return is obtained as on buying the 3-year bond at 2.50%. Another IFR that we can deduce from this yield curve is the 1×3. That is the annual rate on a 2-year bond starting in year 1 and ending in year 3. It has to be about 3.25%. Suppose the investor buys the 1-year earning 1.00% for the first year and then reinvests for the next two years at 3.25% per year. That strategy produces the same return over the three years as buying the 3-year at an annual yield of 2.50%.

These calculations, of course, can be formalized into official bond math equations. Let $Rate_{0 \times A}$ be the shorter-term rate for the $0 \times A$ time period, $Rate_{0 \times B}$ the longer-term rate for the $0 \times B$ period, and $Rate_{A \times B}$ the implied forward rate between years A and B. The two time periods are *A Years* and *B Years*. Equation 5.1 captures the idea of the same total return (neglecting compounding).

$$Rate_{0 \times B} \approx \left(\frac{A\,Years}{B\,Years} * Rate_{0 \times A} \right) + \left(\frac{B\,Years - A\,Years}{B\,Years} * Rate_{A \times B} \right) \quad (5.1)$$

The longer-term rate is a weighted average of the shorter-term rate and the implied forward rate, whereby the weights are the shares of the overall time frame.

A direct equation for the A × B IFR comes from rearranging equation 5.1.

$$Rate_{A \times B} \approx \frac{B\,Years * Rate_{0 \times B} - A\,Years * Rate_{0 \times A}}{B\,Years - A\,Years} \quad (5.2)$$

The 1 × 2, 2 × 3, and 1 × 3 IFRs can be estimated by substituting into equation 5.2.

$$Rate_{1 \times 2} \approx \frac{2 * 2.00\% - 1 * 1.00\%}{2 - 1} = 3.00\%$$

$$Rate_{2 \times 3} \approx \frac{3 * 2.50\% - 2 * 2.00\%}{3 - 2} = 3.50\%$$

$$Rate_{1 \times 3} \approx \frac{3 * 2.50\% - 1 * 1.00\%}{3 - 1} = 3.25\%$$

We'll see that this formula provides an excellent approximation for the more accurate result once we include compounding and the periodicity of the quoted rates.

A few words on notation are needed at this point. I really like the notation for the forward rates that I'm using, that is, the 1 × 2, 2 × 3, 1 × 3, and so on. You can visualize the time frames easily, I think. But, alas, what I like in theory is not always used in practice. A friend who works for a major bank tells me that he often sees these forward rates written as the 1y1y, 2y1y, and 1y2y, respectively. The first part is the forward time period and the second is the tenor of the underlying security. An advantage to this notation is that you can mix months and years. For instance, what is the 3m5y forward rate? It's the rate on a 5-year bond (or interest rate swap), 3 months into the future. My notation would be a bit awkward; it would have to be the 0.25 × 5.25. Anyway, I use my favored notation and avoid the awkward time frames.

The averaging implicit in equations 5.1 and 5.2 suggests an analogy to textbook microeconomic theory. Remember marginal cost and average cost? Average cost is total cost divided by the quantity (usually of widgets) produced. The average cost curve is U-shaped with increasing returns to scale at first, then later with diminishing returns. Marginal cost is the incremental cost for increasing production by one unit. The marginal cost curve crosses the average cost curve at its lowest point.

The analogy is that the forward curve is like marginal cost and the yield curve is like average cost. The buyer of a 2-year bond at 2.00% obtains an incremental, or marginal, return of 3.00% for the second year after earning 1.00% for the first year. The buyer of the 3-year at 2.50% gets a marginal return of 3.50% for the third year after earning 2.00% for the first two years (or a 1-year rate of 1.00% followed by 3.00%). This leads naturally to using the implied forward rate in maturity choice decisions. The issue will be how one's own expectation for a future rate compares to that priced into the forward curve.

Consider an investor who has a known, certain 2-year horizon and can buy any of these three zero-coupon government bonds. The obvious strategy is to buy the 2-year zero at 2.00% and lock in the rate of return (barring default on the government bond and neglecting inflation). But our investor might consider "riding the yield curve" and buy the 3-year at 2.50%. The hope is that the yield at the time of sale is "low" (and the sale price is "high"). How low? Lower than 3.50%, the 2 × 3 IFR. The companion fear is that the yield is above 3.50%. Our investor might also consider buying the 1-year at 1.00% and hope that rates rise for the second year. How high? Higher than 3.00%, the 1 × 2 implied forward rate. The risk is that the reinvestment rate is less than 3.00%. The forward curve is the benchmark for your hopes and fears.

The key point is that the investor's maturity choice decision depends, in part at least, on the held view on future cash market rates vis-à-vis the implied forward rates. Other factors undoubtedly matter as well—the risk of underperforming the obvious maturity-matching strategy, the cost of reinvesting cash, the cost and risk of having to sell the bond at the horizon date. In any case, implied forward rates provide information useful in making the decision.

While our investor is choosing an investment strategy, what is the market thinking about future government bond yields? Does the market (somehow defined) expect the 1-year yield to rise from 1.00% to 3.00% and then to 3.50%? Said differently, is the implied forward curve that we can calculate from currently observed zero-coupon market rates a reasonable forecast for future rates? The classic textbook theories of the term structure of interest rates offer different answers that question.

CLASSIC THEORIES OF THE TERM STRUCTURE OF INTEREST RATES

The best-known theory regarding yield curves is based on bond investors' and issuers' expectations about future short-term interest rates. The idea is that market participants choose maturities to maximize outcomes over some known time horizon—investors maximize their expected rate of return (i.e., the horizon yield) and issuers minimize their expected cost of borrowed funds.

The conclusions of this *expectations theory* are quite significant: Yield curves are upward-sloping (or flat, or downward-sloping) when market participants generally expect short-term rates to be rising (or steady, or falling). In particular, the implied forward rate is an unbiased market consensus forecast for the future spot rate that will be available in the market.

$$Expectations\,Theory:\,IFR_{A\times B} = E(Rate_{A\times B})$$

That is, the calculated IFR between years A and B is equal to the expected market rate for the A × B time period. Therefore, the shape of the current yield curve tells you what bond buyers and sellers in general are expecting about future market interest rates. That's valuable information—if you can rely on it.

The problem with the expectations theory is that it rests on two very strong assumptions: Bond investors and issuers are *risk neutral*, and they can buy or sell bonds at any point on the yield curve. The first assumption means that decisions are made based only on the expected rates of return (and costs of borrowed funds). In sum, they care only about the mean of the probability distribution of possible outcomes and not about the standard deviation (or variance). There is no *risk aversion* in the expectations theory.

The second assumption means that bond buyers and sellers can move freely along the term structure, buying or issuing at whatever maturity they choose. All investors can "ride the yield curve" if that strategy maximizes the expected horizon yield. All corporate bond issuers consider rolling over commercial paper to finance a major construction project if that strategy minimizes the expected long-term cost of funds.

The *segmented markets theory* goes to the other extreme. Investors and issuers are assumed to be so risk averse that they buy and sell bonds only for maturities that match their underlying time horizons. Corporate treasurers managing funds until a tax payment date in three months are interested only in 3-month money market instruments. Individual investors building a fixed-income retirement portfolio buy only long-term bonds. Corporations financing the purchase of new computers issue only intermediate-term notes and never short-term commercial paper. The idea is that risk aversion becomes a *barrier to entry* to other maturity segments, no matter how attractive interest rates might be at those points on the yield curve.

According to the segmented markets theory, an observed yield curve is simply a collection of equilibrium interest rates based on the demand for, and supply of, money as we saw in Chapter 3. Drawing the yield curve in this theory is not a work of art; it's just connecting the dots from separate, segmented markets where in each demand and supply rule. The conclusion of this theory is that the implied forward rate that we can calculate is unrelated to the expected future short-term rate.

Segmented Markets Theory: $IFR_{A \times B}$ *is unrelated to* $E(Rate_{A \times B})$

What about future interest rates? Proponents of this theory would contend that the best forecast for the shape and level of the future yield curve is the shape and level of the current yield curve—unless there is some reason to expect that demand and supply conditions at particular points along the curve will be changing.

The third classic theory introduces the obvious and realistic assumption that both risk and return matter to market participants. The *liquidity preference theory* starts with the recognition that expectations of holding-period rates of return for bond buyers and costs of borrowed funds for issuers determine what we can call the *core* yield curve. Then a "liquidity premium" is added to that core to capture the idea that investors, who are assumed to be risk averse, require extra compensation for longer-maturity bonds compared to shorter-maturity bonds. They know that in general longer-term bonds fall in value more if yields jump up, for example, due to higher expected inflation. Hence, there is a premium (or higher price) paid for safer, short-term bonds. Alternatively, we could say that there is an "illiquidity premium" built into yields on longer-term bonds.

An implication of the liquidity preference theory is that an implied forward rate is an upwardly biased estimate of the future short-term rate.

Liquidity Preference Theory: $IFR_{A \times B} > E(Rate_{A \times B})$

This bias arises because the longer-term yield (the $0 \times B$) contains a higher risk premium than the shorter-term yield (the $0 \times A$). If somehow we could extract each risk premium, we would have the core yield curve based only on expectations. That leads back to the conclusion of the expectations theory. Without that extraction, the observed yields are too high and the IFR overstates the expected market rate.

Which theory is correct? In economics, theories often are tested on their ability to explain observed data, summarized by a set of "stylized facts." For example, yield curves are usually upwardly sloped, so much so that it is "normal" that short-term rates are lower than long-term rates. Occasionally yield curves take on other forms—flat, inverted, humped, or U-shaped—but eventually they return to the normal shape, which is upward sloping and leveling off at long maturities. The liquidity preference theory has the easiest time explaining this—it's simply because investors require a higher rate of return on longer-term bonds as compensation for greater risk.

The segmented markets theory needs the *demand* for long-term funds to be strong relative to short-term funds and the *supply* of short-term funds to be strong relative to long-term funds. That seems reasonable—borrowers prefer to lock up the source of funds for an extended time period while lenders prefer the flexibility of shorter-term investments. The expectations theory struggles with the normal shape to the yield curve because market participants would have to be expecting higher future short-term rates most of the time, presumably reflecting persistent concerns over inflation.

A second stylized fact about the term structure is that short-term yields usually are more volatile than long-term yields. That means the range of historical yields at the short-term end of the curve is greater than for longer maturities. Another way of saying this is that the *term structure of volatility* is downward sloping. The last few years since the financial crisis of 2007 to 2009 have reversed the usual pattern. The Fed has kept short-term money market rates persistently low. Therefore, there has been more volatility in longer-term yields. Hopefully, the traditional pattern will return one of these years.

In any case, the expectations theory explains the downward-sloping term structure of volatility by appealing to the idea that the long-term rate is an average of expected future short-term rates. Averages should have less volatility as the number of data points increases. The liquidity preference theory gets to the same conclusion after adding the risk premium to the core based on expectations.

The segmented markets theory needs more shifting in the demand and supply of short-term funds and greater stability in the curves in the long-term market. That's not at all unreasonable, given that investors often park funds in the money market while reallocating assets across sectors and currencies. That could lead to wider swings in the supply of short-term funds and greater volatility than for longer maturities that likely attract more buy-and-hold investors. For example, institutional investors, such as life insurance companies and pension funds, receive steady cash inflows that regularly are invested in long-term bonds.

Another observed pattern in yield curve data is that short-term and long-term yields usually change in the same direction, although not always in a parallel (or shape-preserving) manner. Sometimes the yield curve steepens and sometimes it flattens, but, in general, yield changes along the curve are positively correlated. Therefore, most shifts to the term structure of interest rates are more or less parallel. Factors that raise or lower expected future short-term rates—for instance, expected inflation, the business cycle and monetary policy actions, trade balances and foreign exchange rates, tax rates and fiscal policy actions—should impact the demand for and supply of long-term funds in a similar manner. All three theories are consistent with the observed pattern.

The problem with these classic term structure theories is that there is no one compelling winner among them. Perhaps the best way of assessing the theories is to look at some real data—for instance, the "hair chart" shown in Figure 5.1 produced by JP Morgan analysts. This is great visual presentation of financial data. The solid line shows the path of 6-month LIBOR between 1988 and 2004 and the corresponding LIBOR forward curve (the hair) for each date.

In the early 1990s and again in the early 2000s, the LIBOR forward curve was quite steep and upwardly sloped. Proponents of the expectations theory, who by the way are well represented among market commentators,

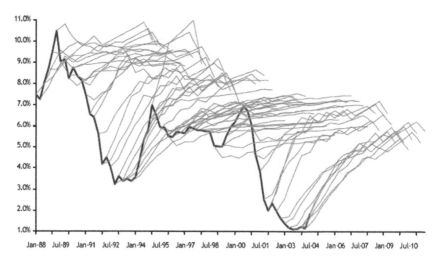

FIGURE 5.1   The LIBOR Hair Chart
Source: Guy Coughlan and Nikolaos Panigirtzoglou, "Interest Rate Term Premia and the Shape of the Yield Curve over the Long Run," JP Morgan Securities London, September 28, 2004.

would have said at the time that the market expects rates to be rising. Yet LIBOR continued to fall for several years. For a while in the late 1990s, LIBOR stabilized in the 6% range, and the forward curve flattened. Overall, there is no consistent pattern between the shape of the forward curve and subsequent market rates.

You might be asking yourself why we still care about the classical term structure theories and still teach them in academic finance courses and why I include them in a bond math book. My answer is that every finance professional making decisions about bonds relies to some extent on a forecast for future interest rates. If nothing more, these theories serve to steer us to think about what drives the shape and level of the yield curve—market participants' expectations and attitudes toward risk certainly matter, as do demand and supply factors in varying maturity segments.

Now we can move on to some bond math and topics that do have answers. Most important, we focus on applications of yield curve analysis that are theory-free. That is, these applications will not depend on the correctness of the expectations, segmented markets, or the liquidity preference theories. But first, we need to be able to get implied forward rates without continuing to commit a cardinal sin in finance—neglecting compounding.

ACCURATE IMPLIED FORWARD RATES

Equation 5.2 provides an excellent, and easy-to-calculate approximation for the implied forward rate ($Rate_{A\times B}$) that connects a shorter-term rate ($Rate_{0\times A}$) to a longer-term rate ($Rate_{0\times B}$). For now, we'll stay with bond yields so the relevant time periods continue to be *AYears* and *BYears*. Money market rates will require some special attention because of the unique manner in which they are quoted—recall the add-on rates and discount rates and 360-day years in Chapter 1.

An accurate formula for an implied forward rate that includes compounding and the specific periodicity (*PER*) for the yields is based on the expression shown in equation 5.3.

$$\left(1 + \frac{Rate_{0\times A}}{PER}\right)^{AYears*PER} * \left(1 + \frac{Rate_{A\times B}}{PER}\right)^{(BYears-AYears)*PER}$$
$$= \left(1 + \frac{Rate_{0\times B}}{PER}\right)^{BYears*PER} \tag{5.3}$$

The first term is the proceeds per unit invested for *AYears* assuming that the 0 × A rate is an APR quoted for *PER* periods per year. That amount is reinvested for the remaining time period out to year B (i.e., for *B Years* minus *A Years*, at the A × B implied forward rate). The compounded total return equals the proceeds per unit invested for *B Years* at the 0 × B rate. It is important that all three rates are annualized for the same periodicity.

The accurate implied forward rate formula comes from rearranging equation 5.3 to isolate the $Rate_{A\times B}$ term.

$$Rate_{A\times B} = \left(\frac{\left(1 + \dfrac{Rate_{0\times B}}{PER}\right)^{B\,Years/(B\,Years - A\,Years)}}{\left(1 + \dfrac{Rate_{0\times A}}{PER}\right)^{A\,Years/(B\,Years - A\,Years)}} - 1 \right) * PER \qquad (5.4)$$

Let's return to the example of 1-year, 2-year, and 3-year rates of 1.00%, 2.00%, and 2.50% quoted on a semiannual bond basis for zero-coupon government bonds. The 1 × 2 IFR, which we approximated to be 3.00%, more accurately is 3.0050%.

$$Rate_{1\times 2} = \left(\frac{\left(1 + \dfrac{0.0200}{2}\right)^{2/(2-1)}}{\left(1 + \dfrac{0.0100}{2}\right)^{1/(2-1)}} - 1 \right) * 2 = 0.030050$$

Similarly, the 2 × 3 and 1 × 3 IFRs, approximated earlier at 3.50% and 3.25%, are really 3.5037% and 3.2542%, respectively.

$$Rate_{2\times 3} = \left(\frac{\left(1 + \dfrac{0.0250}{2}\right)^{3/(3-2)}}{\left(1 + \dfrac{0.0200}{2}\right)^{2/(3-2)}} - 1 \right) * 2 = 0.035037$$

$$Rate_{1\times 3} = \left(\frac{\left(1 + \dfrac{0.0250}{2}\right)^{3/(3-1)}}{\left(1 + \dfrac{0.0100}{2}\right)^{1/(3-1)}} - 1 \right) * 2 = 0.032542$$

These examples indicate that the simple weighted averages are excellent approximations. In fact, the difference between IFRs calculated with equations 5.2 and 5.4 diminish with increasing periodicity. When the rates are quoted for continuous compounding, the approximation formula produces exact results. In general, approximations are fine for back-of-the-envelope calculations, but there is no reason not to use the accurate formula when building a spreadsheet program. Still, these formulas are for zero-coupon rates having the same periodicity. If you care only about U.S. Treasury STRIPS, you're fine. If you care about the rest of the debt market, you need more bond math.

MONEY MARKET IMPLIED FORWARD RATES

Suppose that 90-day LIBOR is 1.00% and 180-day LIBOR is 2.00%. What rate would a true believer in the expectations theory of the yield curve anticipate for 90-day LIBOR, 90 days into the future? That is, what's the 90 × 180 day forward LIBOR—3.00%, calculated as a simple average? Unfortunately, you cannot use the approximation formula or even the accurate formula with money market instruments because their rates have different periodicities; 90-day LIBOR has a periodicity of 4 and 180-day LIBOR a periodicity of 2, assuming a 360-day year. Equations 5.2 and 5.4 simply do not apply.

Our true believer could delve back into Chapters 1 and 2 and retrieve the correct procedures to deal with the periodicity problem. First, the rates are converted to a 365-day year, and then the periodicities are converted to a common basis. For instance, if they are restated for a semiannual bond basis, the IFR can be obtained using equation 5.4. If they are restated to continuous compounding, equation 5.2 will suffice. But, for good reasons discussed below, that is not typically done in practice. Instead it is more useful to calculate the IFR given the manner in which the rates are quoted and traded in the money market.

For rates quoted on an *add-on* basis (e.g., bank CDs, LIBOR, repos), equation 5.5 parallels equation 5.3.

$$\left[1+\left(AOR_{0\times A} * \frac{ADays}{Year}\right)\right] * \left[1+\left(AOR_{A\times B} * \frac{BDays-ADays}{Year}\right)\right] = \left[1+\left(AOR_{0\times B} * \frac{BDays}{Year}\right)\right] \tag{5.5}$$

We are in the money market so the relevant time periods are $ADays$ and $BDays$; $Year$ is 360 in the U.S. but 365 in many other countries. The idea is that same total return is obtained from investing in the shorter-term security at $AOR_{0\times A}$ and rolling over the proceeds at the implied forward rate for the A × B time period as is obtained when investing directly in the longer-term instrument earning $AOR_{0\times B}$.

The next step is to rearrange equation 5.5 algebraically to isolate the $AOR_{A \times B}$ term, which is the implied forward add-on money market rate between days A and B.

$$AOR_{A \times B} = \left[\frac{BDays * AOR_{0 \times B} - ADays * AOR_{0 \times A}}{BDays - ADays} \right] * \left[\frac{1}{1 + \left(AOR_{0 \times A} * \dfrac{ADays}{Year} \right)} \right]$$

(5.6)

Notice that the first term in brackets is essentially the approximation formula in equation 5.2. The second term "adjusts" that approximation downward, the more so the higher the rate and the greater the number of days.

Now we can solve for the true believer's expectation. Let $Year = 360$, $ADays = 90$, and $BDays = 180$. The 90 × 180 day (or 3 × 6 month) implied forward LIBOR turns out to be 2.9925%.

$$AOR_{A \times B} = \left[\frac{180 * 0.0200 - 90 * 0.0100}{180 - 90} \right] * \left[\frac{1}{1 + \left(0.0100 * \dfrac{90}{360} \right)} \right]$$

$$= 0.029925$$

One of the annoying realities of very low market interest rates is that some interesting bond math calculations turn out to be numerically insignificant (i.e., 3.00% versus 2.9925%). Imagine a world of much higher inflation. If 6-month LIBOR is 10% and 12-month LIBOR 20%, then the 6 × 12 implied forward LIBOR would be 28.57%—a more impressive departure from the simple approximation of 30%.

Money market rates quoted on a *discount rate* basis (e.g., commercial paper, bankers acceptances, and Treasury bills in the U.S.) are even more problematic for yield curve analysis than add-on rates. We saw in Chapter 1 that discount rates understate the investor's rate of return and are not even APRs in the traditional sense. It is very tempting to prescribe converting the discount rates to add-on rates so that equation 5.6 can be used. However, calculating the IFR on a discount rate basis can have its advantages.

Equation 5.7 is similar in structure to equation 5.3 for bond yields and to equation 5.5 for add-on rates but differs because it applies to money market discount rates.

$$\left[1-\left(DR_{0\times A} * \frac{ADays}{Year}\right)\right] * \left[1-\left(DR_{A\times B} * \frac{BDays-ADays}{Year}\right)\right]$$

$$=\left[1-\left(DR_{0\times B} * \frac{BDays}{Year}\right)\right] \tag{5.7}$$

The right side of the equation is the day-0 price per one unit of face value received *BDays* later given a discount rate of $DR_{0\times B}$. This is based on the discount rate pricing formula 1.6 in Chapter 1. The left side obtains the same day-0 price per one unit of face value. It is first discounted back from day B to day A using the rate $DR_{A\times B}$. That amount is then discounted back from day A to day 0 at rate $DR_{0\times A}$.

Rearranging equation 5.7 gives us a formula for the implied forward discount rate between days A and B.

$$DR_{A\times B} = \left[\frac{BDays * DR_{0\times B} - ADays * DR_{0\times A}}{BDays - ADays}\right] * \left[\frac{1}{1-\left(DR_{0\times A} * \frac{ADays}{Year}\right)}\right]$$

$$\tag{5.8}$$

Once again, the first term is the simple average and the second term "adjusts" the approximation. Now the presence of the minus sign in the denominator of the adjustment factor raises the IFR above the simple average. Suppose that 90-day and 180-day bankers acceptance (BA) rates are 1.00% and 2.00%. The 90 × 180 day implied forward BA discount rate turns out to be 3.0075%, above the simple average of 3.00%, albeit by a very small amount.

$$DR_{90\times 180} = \left[\frac{180 * 0.0200 - 90 * 0.0100}{180 - 90}\right] * \left[\frac{1}{1-\left(0.0100 * \frac{90}{360}\right)}\right]$$

$$= 0.030075$$

If 6-month and 12-month BA discount rates are 10% and 20%, the IFR is 31.58%. That's substantially more than the 30% approximation.

Why calculate implied forward money market rates on an add-on or discount rate basis? Why not just convert them to continuously compounded bond yields, as we would do in academia? The answer is in how the IFRs are used in practice. Typically, an IFR is compared to quoted market rates or to one's own expectation for future market rates. It simply is easier to keep all the rates on the same basis than to convert them. For instance, suppose you ask a money market trader for his or her view on the next T-bill auction. The response will be in terms of a T-bill discount rate—that is how the money market instrument trades and how the trader thinks about that market.

We soon get to some applications of IFRs, but first we have to deal with the reality that other than in the money market and with Treasury STRIPS, we just do not see very many zero-coupon bond yields.

CALCULATING AND USING IMPLIED SPOT (ZERO-COUPON) RATES

The implied spot curve is arguably the second most important calculation in yield curve analysis after the forward curve. This curve will be the sequence of spot (or zero-coupon) rates that are consistent with the prices and yields on coupon bonds. Building the implied spot curve is a great example of "bootstrapping" in that the result of one calculation is used in the subsequent one. This is not going to involve a specific formula; instead it is a process best learned by working through an example.

Suppose that we observe price and yield data on four actively traded benchmark securities for the same risk class, for instance, government bonds (see Table 5.1).

We need some simplifying assumptions to illustrate bootstrapping. We require a starting place in the money market where we observe the pricing on a short-term zero-coupon bond. Here the 1-year represents the starter zero. But keep in mind that in practice we would use the price on a T-bill or commercial paper or a time deposit that pays LIBOR. The 1-year bond is priced at 97.0625 to yield 3.0264%.

$$97.0625 = \frac{100}{1+y}, \qquad y = 0.030264$$

TABLE 5.1   Example of Observed Prices and Yields

Maturity (Years)	Coupon Rate	Price (% of Par Value)	Yield to Maturity
1	0%	97.0625	3.0264%
2	3.25%	100.8750	2.7941%
3	4.50%	102.7500	3.5181%
4	4.00%	99.3125	4.1902%

The 2-year, 3-year, and 4-year bonds are assumed make annual coupon payments to simplify the example. Assume that we are on a coupon date and the payment has just been made so that there is no accrued interest. Based on these coupon rates and the prices, we observe an interesting U-shaped yield curve because the lowest yield is on the 2-year bond. The internal rates of return follow equation 3.4 from Chapter 3 and are street convention yields for a periodicity of 1 (i.e., they are effective annual rates).

$$100.8750 = \frac{3.25}{1+y} + \frac{103.25}{(1+y)^2}, \quad y = 0.027941$$

$$102.7500 = \frac{4.50}{1+y} + \frac{4.50}{(1+y)^2} + \frac{104.50}{(1+y)^3}, \quad y = 0.035181$$

$$99.3125 = \frac{4}{1+y} + \frac{4}{(1+y)^2} + \frac{4}{(1+y)^3} + \frac{4}{(1+y)^4}, \quad y = 0.041902$$

The implied 2-year spot rate (the 0×2) turns out to be 2.7903%; it is the solution for z in this expression.

$$100.8750 = \frac{3.25}{1.030264} + \frac{103.25}{(1+z)^2}, \quad z = 0.027903$$

The first cash flow is discounted by the 0×1 spot rate of 3.0264%. That's why we need a starter zero taken from the money market. The algebra problem is to find the 2-year spot rate such that when the second cash flow is discounted by that rate, the sum is the price of the bond.

The implied 3-year spot rate (the 0×3) is 3.5476%.

$$102.7500 = \frac{4.50}{1.030264} + \frac{4.50}{(1.027903)^2} + \frac{104.50}{(1+z)^3}, \quad z = 0.035476$$

Our 0×2 result is now an input into the equation and is used to discount the second cash flow. This is what is meant by bootstrapping the curve. Note that later calculations will be susceptible to any errors made earlier in the process.

We continue working our way out the yield curve to get the implied 0×4 spot rate. This uses the initial 0×1 starter zero and the 0×2 and 0×3 implied rates.

$$99.3125 = \frac{4}{1.030264} + \frac{4}{(1.027903)^2} + \frac{4}{(1.035476)^3} + \frac{104}{(1+z)^4},$$
$$z = 0.042525$$

Clearly, this repetitive sequence of calculations is suited perfectly for a computer. You probably can see how you would build that spreadsheet, given the dates and amounts of the scheduled future cash flows on the underlying benchmark bonds. In general, you would need to use the total current market value including accrued interest on the left side of the equation.

These equations demonstrate why a yield-to-maturity statistic can be interpreted as a "present value average" of the zero-coupon rates, as we saw in Chapter 3. Consider the 4-year bond in this example. Its price is the sum of the discounted cash flows using either the yield to maturity or the sequence of spot rates.

$$\frac{4}{1.041902} + \frac{4}{(1.041902)^2} + \frac{4}{(1.041902)^3} + \frac{104}{(1.041902)^4} = 99.3125$$

$$\frac{4}{1.030264} + \frac{4}{(1.027903)^2} + \frac{4}{(1.035476)^3} + \frac{104}{(1.042525)^4} = 99.3125$$

Here 4.1902% is a "weighted average" of 3.0264%, 2.7903%, 3.5476%, and 4.2525%, with most of the weight on the last spot rate because it corresponds to the largest cash flow.

The implied spot curve can be used to derive a related description of the market, again assuming no arbitrage. This is the *par curve*—the sequence of yields such that the bond for each time to maturity trades at par value. For example, the 4-year par yield comes from the solution for *PMT*:

$$100 = \frac{PMT}{1.030264} + \frac{PMT}{(1.027903)^2} + \frac{PMT}{(1.035476)^3} + \frac{PMT+100}{(1.042525)^4},$$

$$PMT = 4.1876$$

Each cash flow is discounted using the corresponding implied spot rate. So, while the actual 4%, 4-year bond is trading at a small discount to yield 4.1902%, we now deduce that a hypothetical 4.1876%, 4-year bond would be priced at par value.

Another clever application of the implied spot curve is in calculating the credit spread over benchmark bonds. Suppose we are analyzing a 4-year, level-payment, fully amortizing bank loan. The bank loan is priced at par value and makes an annual payment of 28.2 (percent of par value), including both principal and interest. Its yield to maturity is 4.9982%.

$$100 = \frac{28.2}{1+y} + \frac{28.2}{(1+y)^2} + \frac{28.2}{(1+y)^3} + \frac{28.2}{(1+y)^4}, \quad y = 0.049982$$

What is the credit spread, assuming the four bonds in this section are Treasuries? Using the 4-year par yield, it is 81.06 basis points: 4.9982% − 4.1876% = 0.8106%. Using the actual 4-year bond, the spread is 80.80 basis points: 4.9982% − 4.1902% = 0.8080%. The problem with these is that the "average life" of this amortizing bank loan is less than four years— the 4-year Treasury yield is not the right benchmark.

A better way to assess the compensation for the credit risk (as well as any difference in liquidity and taxation) is to calculate the *static spread*, also known as the *zero-volatility spread* or just *Z-spread*. It is the uniform (hence, static) spread over the benchmark implied spot rates. It is the solution for the static spread, denoted *ss*, in this expression:

$$100 = \frac{28.2}{(1+0.030264+ss)} + \frac{28.2}{(1+0.027903+ss)^2} + \frac{28.2}{(1+0.035476+ss)^3}$$
$$+ \frac{28.2}{(1+0.042525+ss)^4}$$

Here you need trial-and-error search (or Excel and Solver) to find that *ss* = 0.014048. The static spread for this fully amortizing bank loan is 140.48 basis points.

MORE APPLICATIONS FOR THE IMPLIED SPOT AND FORWARD CURVES

Implied spot and forward rates need to be useful in making financial decisions to qualify as information and not just create more data. Fortunately, they really can be quite informative. An obvious application for bootstrapping the implied spot curve is to get the zero-coupon rates needed to derive the implied forward curve. That is, the implied spot curve can be just an intermediate step to get to get the information we need to help make a maturity choice decision.

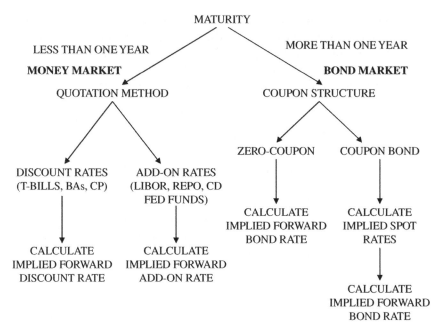

FIGURE 5.2　Summary of Implied Forward Rate Calculations

Figure 5.2 summarizes the various paths to the implied forward rate formulas. You first have to know if you are in the money market or the bond market. The time frame for the rates is a good clue—days or months versus years. If you are in the money market, you next need to know if the rates are quoted on an add-on or on a discount basis. Then you can use equation 5.6 or 5.8 to get the comparably quoted IFR. If you are in the bond market, you need to know if the observed yields are on zero-coupon bonds or, more likely, on coupon bonds. If the latter, you first have to bootstrap the implied spot rates and then calculate the IFR using equation 5.2 or 5.4, depending on your need for precision.

Suppose you have a 4-year investment horizon and can buy any of the four government bonds in the preceding example. You are deciding whether to buy the 1-year zero and reinvest at higher yields in each future year, you hope, or to buy the 4%, 4-year bond. How high would rates have to be to prefer the rollover strategy? The answer, of course, is higher than the IFRs. But you cannot just plug the yields to maturity into equation 5.2 or 5.4. Respecting bond math protocol, you need to use the implied spot rates.

$$Rate_{1\times2} = \frac{(1.027903)^2}{(1.030264)} - 1 = 0.025547$$

$$Rate_{2\times3} = \frac{(1.035476)^3}{(1.027903)^2} - 1 = 0.050790$$

$$Rate_{3\times4} = \frac{(1.042525)^4}{(1.035476)^3} - 1 = 0.063961$$

To expect a higher total return after four years by buying and rolling over 1-year bonds, you project the 1-year yield to track a path, on average, above 2.55%, 5.08%, and 6.40%.

Now suppose that you are a commercial banker working with a middle market business customer on a 12-month loan to build up working capital. The loan rate will be tied to 6-month or 12-month LIBOR. If the customer chooses 12-month LIBOR (currently 4.00%), the cost of funds is set. But if the customer chooses 6-month LIBOR (currently 3.50%), there is interest rate risk at the reset date in six months. Your customer asks for your recommendation. You know that the maturity-choice decision depends on the rate view (i.e., where 6-month LIBOR is expected to be vis-à-vis the implied forward rate). You also know that the 6 × 12 IFR is not 4.50% because of the periodicity problem. You use equation 5.6 to get a breakeven level for LIBOR of 4.42% (assuming 180 and 360 days).

$$AOR_{180\times360} = \left[\frac{360 * 0.0400 - 180 * 0.0350}{360 - 180}\right] * \left[\frac{1}{1 + \left(0.0350 * \frac{180}{360}\right)}\right]$$

$$= 0.044226$$

The customer's decision turns on whether 6-month LIBOR is expected to be above or below 4.42% in six months. That might or might not be the rate that market participants in general are expecting. That does not matter—what matters is the decision maker's own rate view. The commercial banker here can help the process by providing some historical data, the bank economist's view on monetary policy and economic conditions, and the like. The advantage of the IFR is that as a breakeven rate it provides a framework for the above-or-below decision.

Another application of the implied spot curve is bond valuation. In the example, the 4-year actively traded benchmark bond has a coupon rate of 4% and is priced at 99.3125 to yield 4.1902% on an annually compounded street convention basis. Now suppose that we want to calculate the fair value on another 4-year bond, this one having a 9% coupon rate. We neglect taxation and assume that this bond has the same liquidity and default risk as the four benchmark securities. The key point is that in a world of no arbitrage, this bond will not be priced to yield 4.1902%. Instead, its (no-arbitrage) price is the present value of the cash flows discounted at the implied spot rates.

$$\frac{9}{1.030264} + \frac{9}{(1.027903)^2} + \frac{9}{(1.035476)^3} + \frac{109}{(1.042525)^4} = 117.6342$$

Based on that price, the yield-to-maturity statistic is 4.1274%.

$$117.6342 = \frac{9}{1+y} + \frac{9}{(1+y)^2} + \frac{9}{(1+y)^3} + \frac{109}{(1+y)^4}, \quad y = 0.041274$$

The usual candidates to explain why the yields on any two bonds differ are time to maturity (the shape of the yield curve), credit risk (the probability of default and the assumed recovery rate), liquidity risk, and taxation. This example reveals another reason—coupon structure. We have three 4-year bonds for the same risk class: one yielding 4.2525% (the implied 0% coupon bond), another yielding 4.1902% (the benchmark 4% coupon bond), and this one yielding 4.1274% (the 9% coupon bond). The yield differences are entirely due to coupon structure. The more "weight" that is placed on the first few cash flows (i.e., the higher the coupon rate), the lower the yield to maturity. Of course, that conclusion depends on the shape of the curve.

Implied zero-coupon rates can be used in valuation problems beyond just bonds having different coupon rates. They have applications in corporate finance as well. Let's suppose now that the four benchmark bonds are corporate securities for a specific bond rating, say, single A. Better yet, we could assume that they are unsecured liabilities of the same A-rated issuer. Even though there might be no market for zero-coupon corporate bonds, we still can carry out the implied spot rate bootstrapping calculations. The idea is that if such corporate zeros did exist, they would have to trade at those spot yields if there were to be no arbitrage opportunities (and assuming no transactions costs to exploit those opportunities).

Now suppose that we need to value some project that has credit risk deemed to be equivalent to these corporate bonds. Clearly, this is a valuation problem begging for discounted cash flow (DCF) analysis. Assume first that our analyst does the obvious—this is a 4-year project, so he or she uses the

4-year yield to maturity of 4.1902% to do the discounting. I have always wondered why DCF corporate finance problems, at least in the textbooks I've seen, invariably use a single discount rate or cost of capital for all time periods. Coming from a bond market perspective, I see the usually upward slope to the yield curve instructing us to discount year-1 cash flow at a lower rate than year-2 cash flow.

Better analysis, in my opinion, is to use the implied spot rates (i.e., 3.0264%, 2.7903%, 3.5476%, and 4.2525%) instead of the yield on the maturity-matching coupon bond. These implied spot rates correspond to the timing of the specific cash flows, which are no different than the face values on four zero-coupon bonds. Depending on the amount and timing of the projected cash flows, this DCF calculation could produce a higher valuation for the project. All we have done to get the more appropriate discount rates is reconfigure data from the underlying yield curve and add the assumption of no arbitrage.

To be fair, the source of error in most corporate finance valuation problems is not the lack of precision in the discount rates in the denominators. Instead, the difficulty is uncertainty regarding the expected cash flows in the numerators. Often those numbers are just best-guess projections of future sales and operating costs. Then our "laser-sharp" implied spot rates represent bond math overkill. In those circumstances, we should use appropriate technology and discount all cash flows at some reasonable rate. However, there are situations when the numerators are scheduled amounts on scheduled dates—for instance, with financial contracts such as lease agreements or interest rate swaps. Then the implied spots could produce a better valuation.

For hedge funds and proprietary trading desks at financial institutions, the implied spot curve is used to identify arbitrage opportunities. The two strategies we first saw in Chapter 2 are: (1) *coupon stripping*—buy the coupon bond and sell the cash flows separately as zero-coupon coupon bonds (e.g., TIGRS, CATS, LIONS back in the early 1980s and Treasury STRIPS since 1985), and (2) *bond reconstitution*—buy the zero-coupon bonds in sufficient quantity to build and sell a coupon bond. The implied spot curve identifies when one of these arbitrage strategies might be profitable.

By design, the implied spot curve is the sequence of zero-coupon rates such that those trading two strategies break even. If actual zero-coupon bonds are trading at yields above those implied rates, a bond reconstitution strategy might work. Actual zeros would have "high yields" and therefore "low prices" relative to breakeven. The arbitrageur buys the zeros, builds the coupon bond, and sells it for a profit. To be sure, the profit would have to cover transactions costs. Those could be included directly, but then we would not have an implied spot *curve*; instead we would have an implied spot *cone*. An arbitrage opportunity arises when actual zeros are trading outside the cone. If actual zero-coupon bonds can be sold at yields below the implied spot curve (or below the cone), the arbitrageur undertakes the coupon-stripping strategy, as Merrill Lynch did in the 1980s when it created TIGRS.

A hugely important application for implied spot and forward rates is in pricing interest rate derivatives. We see this in detail in Chapter 8 on interest rate swaps. The idea is that the forward curve is a sequence of "hedge-able" future rates. They indicate the rates that can be locked in using derivatives. Once again the caveats are that there are no arbitrage opportunities and transactions costs are small enough to be neglected. Those are fine and acceptable assumptions in normal financial market conditions and active trading in derivatives. However, during a financial crisis when liquidity dries up, some arbitrage opportunities can lie there unexploited. Sad but true.

One more bond math application of the implied forward curve is worth some attention before moving on to duration and convexity. A horizon yield on a coupon bond, as we know from Chapter 3, depends critically on coupon reinvestment rates. Remember that one of the assumptions in using the yield to maturity as a measure of an investor's total return is that all coupons are reinvested at that same yield. Obviously, future rates are random. But suppose we can hedge that interest rate risk using costless and riskless derivatives and can lock in rates along the implied forward curve.

Consider again the 4-year, 4% annual payment government bond priced at 99.3125 to yield 4.1902%. We calculated the IFRs above: The 1 × 2 is 2.5547%, the 2 × 3 is 5.0790%, and the 3 × 4 is 6.3961%. What will be the 4-year horizon yield (i.e., the total pretax return after four years assuming no default) if coupons are in fact reinvested at those specific rates? Are you guessing 4.1902%? Higher? Lower?

The total return turns out to be 117.314087 (percent of par value).

$$[4 * (1.025547) * (1.050790) * (1.063961)] + [4 * (1.050790) *$$
$$(1.063961)] + [4 * (1.063961)] + 104 = 117.314087$$

In the first term in brackets, the initial coupon is rolled over at the 1 × 2, then the 2 × 3 and 3 × 4 IFRs. The second coupon is reinvested at the 2 × 3 and 3 × 4, while the third is rolled over only once at the 3 × 4 IFR. The last coupon is received at maturity along with the principal.

The 4-year horizon yield, or holding-period rate of return, is the solution for *HPR*, the annual rate connecting the purchase price to the total return.

$$99.3125 = \frac{117.314087}{(1 + HPR)^4}, \quad HPR = 0.042525$$

Notice that 4.2525% is the 0 × 4 *implied spot rate*. Derivatives (in particular, costless and riskless derivatives) lock in for the investor the 4-year spot rate, not the 4.1902% yield to maturity on the 4-year bond.

That is not a coincidence. Suppose that the bond buyer has only a 3-year investment horizon. What is the 3-year horizon yield assuming coupon reinvestment at the 1 × 2 and 2 × 3 IFRs and the ability to lock in using derivatives the sale price of the bond at the end of the third year at the 3 × 4 IFR? The total return after three years is 110.261642 (percent of par value).

$$[4 * (1.025547) * (1.050790)] + [4 * (1.050790)]$$
$$+ 4 + [104 / (1.063961)] = 110.261642$$

When the bond is sold, the proceeds are just the final coupon and principal discounted at the 3 × 4 IFR. The 3-year horizon yield is 3.5476%, which—no surprise now—is the 0 × 3 implied spot rate.

$$99.3125 = \frac{110.261642}{(1 + HPR)^3}, \quad HPR = 0.035476$$

These examples demonstrate the interconnectedness between the underlying yield curve on traded coupon bonds, the implied spot, and implied forward rates. The connection is the assumption of no arbitrage.

DISCOUNT FACTORS

Another way to calculate implied spot and forward rates is with discount factors. In fact, this is how yield curve analysis is carried out in practice using spreadsheets. A discount factor is by definition the present value of one unit of currency at some future date. A financial institution that has a multitude of loans, bonds, and derivative contracts to value needs discount factors that correspond to each future date for which cash is received or paid out. Here I keep it simple and just use the four annual payment securities in Table 5.1 to illustrate the discount factor bootstrapping process.

The 1-year bond has a coupon rate of zero and is priced at 97.0625 per 100 of par value. This one is easy: *The price of zero-coupon bond is its discount factor.* So, the 1-year discount factor, denoted DF_1, is simply

0.970625. The 2-year bond in Table 5.1 has a coupon rate of 3.25% and is priced at 100.8750. The 2-year discount factor is the solution for DF_2 in this equation.

$$100.8750 = (3.25 * 0.970625) + (103.25 * DF_2), \quad DF_2 = 0.946445$$

The bootstrapping process proceeds as in the section above where the implied spot rates are obtained. The difference is that now the algebra is much easier.

The 3-year and 4-year bonds have coupon rates of 4.50% and 4.00% and prices of 102.7500 and 99.3125, respectively. Working your way out the yield curve sequentially gets the next two annual discount factors.

$$102.75 = (4.50 * 0.970625) + (4.50 * 0.946445) + (104.50 * DF_3),$$

$$DF_3 = 0.900700$$

$$99.3125 = (4 * 0.970625) + (4 * 0.946445) + (4 * 0.900700)$$
$$+ (104 * DF_4), \quad DF_4 = 0.846552$$

The output from the previous step becomes an input in the next step.

Once you have the discount factors, valuing fixed-income bonds is straightforward. Remember the 9%, 4-year bond in the previous section? Its price turned out to be 117.6342 when each payment is discounted using the implied spot rates. Now we just need to multiply the scheduled payments by the discount factors.

$$(9 * 0.970625) + (9 * 0.946445) + (9 * 0.900700)$$
$$+ (109 * 0.846552) = 117.6341$$

Note the minor difference in the fourth decimal. This answer, 117.6341, is actually the more accurate because the spot rates entail more rounding. If both bootstrapping procedures are put on a spreadsheet, the results are identical.

Another application of the discount factors is to get the 4-year par yield, which is the coupon rate on a bond that has a (flat) price equal to par value. It's the solution for PMT in this equation.

$$100 = (PMT * 0.970625) + (PMT * 0.946445)$$
$$+ (PMT * 0.900700) + [(PMT + 100) * 0.846552], \quad PMT = 4.1876$$

The key point is that spot rates and discount factors contain the same information. Discounting with spot rates is more intuitive (and that's why I lead with it in the chapter) but using discount factors is more easily implemented on a spreadsheet.

If you start with the discount factors, you can always solve for the corresponding spot rates. Here are the calculations for the 2-year, 3-year, and 4-year zero-coupon rates, z_1, z_2, and z_3:

$$z_2 = \left(\frac{1}{0.946445} \right)^{1/2} - 1 = 0.027903$$

$$z_3 = \left(\frac{1}{0.900700} \right)^{1/3} - 1 = 0.035476$$

$$z_4 = \left(\frac{1}{0.846552} \right)^{1/4} - 1 = 0.042525$$

These are the same as above.

In addition, the implied forward rates are ratios of the discount factors. Here are the 1×2, 2×3, and 3×4 IFRs:

$$Rate_{1\times2} = \frac{0.970625}{0.946445} - 1 = 0.025548$$

$$Rate_{2\times3} = \frac{0.946445}{0.900700} - 1 = 0.050788$$

$$Rate_{3\times4} = \frac{0.900700}{0.846552} - 1 = 0.063963$$

Once again, the minor differences between these and those calculated above are due to rounding in the spot rates. These results are slightly more accurate.

To see how the *spot rates, forward rates* and *discount factors* are interrelated, think about how the 3×4 is calculated with the 3-year and 4-year spot rates.

$$Rate_{3\times4} = \frac{(1.042525)^4}{(1.035476)^3} - 1$$

This is equivalent to this equation:

$$Rate_{3 \times 4} = \frac{\dfrac{1}{(1.035476)^3}}{\dfrac{1}{(1.042525)^4}} - 1$$

The numerator is DF_3, the present value of 1 discounted back to date 0 using the 3-year spot rate; the denominator is DF_4. The ratio between the discount factors minus one is the 3 × 4 implied forward rate.

The calculations in this section are simplified because the underlying bonds make annual payments and the annual rates have a periodicity of 1. To generalize using the notation of equations 5.3 and 5.4, the discount factor for year A given the annual spot rate $Rate_{0 \times A}$ and its periodicity, PER, is:

$$DF_A = \frac{1}{\left(1 + \dfrac{Rate_{0 \times A}}{PER}\right)^{A\,Years \,*\,PER}} \qquad (5.9)$$

The spot rate given the discount factor is:

$$Rate_{0 \times A} = \left[\left(\frac{1}{DF_A}\right)^{\left(\frac{1}{A\,Years\,*\,PER}\right)} - 1\right] * PER \qquad (5.10)$$

The implied forward rate between year A and year B given the discount factors and the periodicity is:

$$Rate_{A \times B} = \left[\left(\frac{DF_A}{DF_B}\right)^{\left(\frac{1}{(B\,Years - A\,Years)\,*\,PER}\right)} - 1\right] * PER \qquad (5.11)$$

Suppose that 4-year and 5-year zero-coupon bonds are priced at 89.75 and 86.25 (percent of par value), respectively. What is the 4 × 5 implied forward rate quoted on a semiannual bond basis? Using equation 5.11 it is 4.0176% (s.a.).

$$Rate_{4\times5} = \left[\left(\frac{0.8975}{0.8625} \right)^{\frac{1}{(5-4)*2}} - 1 \right] * 2 = 0.040176$$

Another method is to solve for the 4-year and 5-year spot rates using Equation 5.10.

$$Rate_{0\times4} = \left[\left(\frac{1}{0.8975} \right)^{\left(\frac{1}{4*2} \right)} - 1 \right] * 2 = 0.027219$$

$$Rate_{0\times5} = \left[\left(\frac{1}{0.8625} \right)^{\left(\frac{1}{5*2} \right)} - 1 \right] * 2 = 0.029804$$

Equation 5.4 can be used to get the 4 × 5 implied forward using the spot rates.

$$Rate_{4\times5} = \left[\frac{\left(1 + \frac{0.029804}{2} \right)^5}{\left(1 + \frac{0.027219}{2} \right)^4} - 1 \right] * 2 = 0.040177$$

Note that *B Years − A Years* = 5 − 4 = 1. Once again there is a small difference in the fourth decimal and the result using discount factors is slightly more accurate. The main difference, however, is how much easier it is to work with discount factors, especially on a spreadsheet.

Discount rates truly are the keys to the kingdom of yield curve analysis and fixed-income valuation.

CONCLUSION

Many textbooks focus on the least important (and least interesting) aspects of yield curve analysis—the classic theories of the term structure of interest rates. Still, the expectations, segmented markets, and liquidity preference theories do serve to direct attention to the drivers of bond yields. Fortunately, there are many applications of implied spot and forward curves that are theory-free. To the extent that you believe in no-arbitrage pricing, you can move seamlessly between the observed yield curve on coupon bonds and the implied spot and forward curves.

Implied spot and forward rates are incredibly important to financial market participants. Who would not be interested in techniques that help you make maturity-choice decisions, identify arbitrage opportunities, and value debt securities and interest rate derivatives? The bond math calculations covered in this chapter are essential for fixed-income professionals (and even for amateurs).

Now we are ready to take on the other side of the trade-off between risk and return. So far we have focused mostly on measures of *return*, such as money market rates, bond yields to maturity, horizon yields, after-tax rates, and in this chapter implied spot and forward rates. Next we take a mathematical plunge into *risk* analysis—the widely heralded bond duration statistic and its not-so-famous companion, convexity.

CHAPTER 6

Duration and Convexity

Duration and convexity are statistics that estimate the sensitivity of the market value of an asset or liability to a change in interest rates. Usually the asset or liability is a fixed-income bond, but as measures of rate sensitivity, they apply to all sorts of securities and derivatives. We can ask meaningfully about the duration and convexity of a floating-rate note, an inflation-indexed bond, or an interest rate swap. That discussion will have to wait until Chapters 7 and 8. This chapter focuses on the risk statistics applicable to a typical fixed-rate or zero-coupon bond.

We start with classic *yield duration*—the sensitivity of the bond price to a change in its yield to maturity. This leads to the well-known Macaulay and modified duration statistics. *Yield convexity* is the second-order effect of that yield change. The beauty of yield duration and convexity is that they are based on fundamental mathematical properties of the bond. That means closed-form formulas can be derived for the statistics using algebra and calculus. Then we move on to other descriptions of change in interest rates—the sensitivity of the bond price to a shift in the benchmark Treasury yield curve. I call these *curve duration* and *curve convexity*.

Before diving into the bond math, let's get a sense of interest rate sensitivity using an admittedly contrived scenario. Suppose that you are the fixed-income strategist for an aggressively managed, high-yield, international bond fund. You believe that the market prices of some country's long-term bonds will rally in the next week as the market digests what you expect to be very positive news about economic conditions. In particular, two long-term sovereign bonds are trading at deeply discounted prices to yield 20%. Both bonds have an annual coupon rate of 6%, paid once a year. One bond matures in 20 years and the other in 30 years; otherwise they are identical. Which bond do you recommend, assuming that you anticipate both yields to drop by 100 basis points from 20% to 19%—the 20-year or the 30-year bond?

I've posed this problem over the last 25 years to hundreds of students, including some emerging-market, fixed-income traders. Virtually all recommend the 30-year bond; you probably do, too. Your thinking probably is that, other things being equal (meaning the coupon rate, yield to maturity, payment frequency, default risk, liquidity, taxation), the longer-term 30-year bond gains or loses more value on a percentage basis than the shorter-term 20-year bond given the same change in yield. That's true—almost all of the time. We see later in the chapter that this intuition is not always correct, and in this case, "almost always" needs to be entered into the statement. This scenario of two high-yield, deeply discounted bonds demonstrates a real bond math curiosity—the 30-year bond actually has lower sensitivity to a change in its yield to maturity than the 20-year bond. To understand this oddity, you need to explore the mathematics behind duration.

YIELD DURATION AND CONVEXITY RELATIONSHIPS

We can derive the relationship between a change in the yield to maturity and the change in the market value of a standard fixed-income bond using a bit of algebra and calculus. Equation 6.1 is a general bond pricing equation very similar to equation 3.9 in Chapter 3.

$$MV = \frac{PMT}{(1+y)^{1-t/T}} + \frac{PMT}{(1+y)^{2-t/T}} + \cdots + \frac{PMT+FV}{(1+y)^{N-t/T}} \tag{6.1}$$

The periodic coupon payments (PMT) and the principal (FV) to be redeemed in full at maturity are discounted at the yield per period (y). The settlement date is t days into the T-day period and there are N periods to maturity counting from the beginning of the current period. Here the present value of the future cash flows is the market value (MV) of the bond, that is, the full (or "dirty") price. The risk statistics for the bond are concerned with cash value, independent of how that amount is broken down for accounting into the flat (or "clean") price and accrued interest.

Yield duration and convexity entail estimating the change in market value, denoted dMV, caused by an instantaneous change in the yield to maturity per period, dy. A useful way of obtaining this estimation is with a *Taylor series expansion*. Technically, this assumes that the basic relationship in equation 6.1 is continuous and differentiable with respect to the yield. This Taylor series can go out to any number of terms depending on the required degree of precision. All we need for bond math are the first two, as shown in equation 6.2.

$$dMV \approx \left(\frac{\partial MV}{\partial y} * dy \right) + \left(\frac{1}{2} * \frac{\partial^2 MV}{\partial y^2} * (dy)^2 \right) \tag{6.2}$$

In words, the change in market value is estimated by the first partial derivative of the bond pricing formula times the change in the yield plus one-half of the second partial derivative times the change in the yield squared. The first term is the essence of yield duration; the second term is the essence of yield convexity. The partial derivatives are calculated holding the other variables (PMT, N, FV, t/T) constant when the yield changes.

At this point we can define a number of versions of the yield duration statistic.

$$Macaulay\,Duration \equiv -\frac{\partial MV}{\partial y} * \frac{1+y}{MV} \qquad (6.3)$$

This expression produces the famous statistic first described by Frederick Macaulay, a Canadian economist, in his study of U.S. railroad bond yields and stock prices between 1857 and 1936. The minus sign is part of the definition so that the duration will be a positive number. That's because the first derivative is negative due to the usual inverse relationship between the bond yield and its market value. We see some circumstances in Chapters 7 and 8 when the derivative actually is positive—we call that phenomenon *negative duration*.

Closely related and more commonly used is modified duration.

$$Modified\,Duration \equiv -\frac{\partial MV}{\partial y} * \frac{1}{MV} = \frac{Macaulay\,Duration}{1+y} \qquad (6.4)$$

We'll see that modified duration relates directly to the percentage change in the market value of the bond. Sometimes we want to estimate the change in value in terms of money, usually for a certain amount of par value.

$$Money\,Duration \equiv -\frac{\partial MV}{\partial y} = Modified\,Duration * MV \qquad (6.5)$$

In the U.S., this statistic is often called the *dollar duration*, but I prefer *money duration* because bond math is ecumenical in spirit.

The convexity statistics for the bond similarly can be defined with respect to the second partial derivative.

$$Convexity \equiv \frac{\partial^2 MV}{\partial y^2} * \frac{1}{MV} \qquad (6.6)$$

$$Money\,Convexity \equiv \frac{\partial^2 MV}{\partial y^2} = Convexity * MV \qquad (6.7)$$

These are the definitions for convexity that I like to use. Some textbooks divide them by two, thereby combining the one-half term in equation 6.2 with the second partial derivative. Also, we see later in the chapter that the convexity statistic reported on Bloomberg divides the expression in equation 6.6 by 100.

To integrate these definitions, divide both sides of equation 6.2 by MV.

$$\frac{dMV}{MV} \approx \left(\frac{\partial MV}{\partial y} * \frac{1}{MV} * dy \right) + \left(\frac{1}{2} * \frac{\partial^2 MV}{\partial y^2} * \frac{1}{MV} * (dy^2) \right) \quad (6.8)$$

This connects the *percentage change* in the market value (dMV/MV) to the change in the yield to maturity. Now substitute the definitions given in equations 6.4 and 6.6 into 6.8.

$$\frac{dMV}{MV} \approx \left(-Modified\,Duration * dy \right) + \left(\frac{1}{2} * Convexity * (dy)^2 \right) \quad (6.9)$$

The percentage change in the market value of the bond is approximated by the modified duration times the change in the yield to maturity, plus one-half the convexity statistic times the change in the yield squared. The latter is known as the *convexity adjustment* to duration. Similarly, the change in market value in money terms is approximated by the money duration and convexity statistics.

$$dMV \approx \left(-Money\,Duration * dy \right) + \left(\frac{1}{2} * Money\,Convexity * (dy)^2 \right) \quad (6.10)$$

So far we have related the instantaneous change in the yield per period, dy, to the change in market value, dMV. In practice, bond yield statistics invariably are annualized. Therefore, a more useful expression is to estimate the change in market value, either on a percentage basis or in money terms, to the change in the *annual* yield. Let Y be the annual percentage rate and PER the number of periods in the year (i.e., the APR and its periodicity). Then $Y = y * PER$, $dy = dY/PER$, and $(dy)^2 = (dY)^2/PER^2$. Substitute those into 6.9 to get an expression relating the percentage change in market value to the change in the annual yield to maturity.

$$\frac{dMV}{MV} \approx \left(-\frac{Modified\,Duration}{PER} * dY \right) + \left(\frac{1}{2} * \frac{Convexity}{PER^2} * (dY)^2 \right) \quad (6.11)$$

Modified duration divided by *PER* is the *annual modified duration* and the convexity divided by *PER* squared is the *annual convexity*.

$$\frac{dMV}{MV} \approx (-Annual\ Modified\ Duration * dY) \\ + \left(\frac{1}{2} * Annual\ Convexity * (dY)^2 \right) \tag{6.12}$$

YIELD DURATION

We can derive specific formulas for the various duration statistics by calculating carefully the first partial derivative of the bond pricing equation 6.1 with respect to a change in the yield per period. As much fun as it is to do the calculus and work though the ensuing algebra, the step-by-step process is relegated to the Technical Appendix. A general formula for the Macaulay duration statistic is shown in equation 6.13.

$$Macaulay\ Duration = \left[\frac{1+y}{y} - \frac{1+y+[N*(c-y)]}{c*[(1+y)^N - 1]+y} \right] - t/T \tag{6.13}$$

Here the coupon rate per period is denoted c, where $c = PMT/FV$.

Let's go back to the 4%, annual payment, 4-year corporate bond priced at 99.342 to yield 4.182% that we first saw in Chapter 3. Suppose that one month has transpired since then, and the bond remarkably is still yielding 4.182%. Its Macaulay duration is 3.691, found using $y = 0.04182$, $N = 4$, $c = 0.04$, and $t/T = 30/360$ assuming the 30/360 day-count convention.

$$\left[\frac{1.04182}{0.04182} - \frac{1.04182 + [4*(0.04 - 0.04182)]}{0.04 * [(1.04182)^4 - 1] + 0.04182} \right] - 30/360 = 3.774 - 0.083 = 3.691$$

That last assumption about the day-count is important—duration is the link between the change in market value and the change in yield, so how the yield is quoted matters (i.e., its periodicity and day-count convention). Change one of those assumptions and you get a slightly different duration statistic.

Now suppose that the yield on the bond increased to 4.650% during the month that has gone by instead of remaining the same. The Macaulay duration would be 3.689.

$$\left[\frac{1.04650}{0.04650} - \frac{1.04650 + [4*(0.04 - 0.04650)]}{0.04 * [(1.04650)^4 - 1] + 0.04650} \right] - 30/360 = 3.772 - 0.083 = 3.689$$

The impact from the higher yield is not much (3.691 versus 3.689) but does signal an inverse relationship between duration and yield. So, two factors are in play in reducing the duration from 3.774 one month ago (when $t/T = 0$ and $y = 0.04182$) to 3.689 now (when $t/T = 30/360$ and $y = 0.04650$). I discuss this *duration drift* due to the passage of time and the change in yield further in Chapter 10 when we consider bond portfolio strategies.

At this point you might be thinking (or recalling): "Isn't Macaulay duration the weighted average time to maturity?" In fact, it can be calculated as a weighted average of the times to receipt of cash flow, whereby the weights are the shares of market value corresponding to each payment date. This is the weighted-average formula for Macaulay duration, shown in equation 6.14—its derivation is also relegated to the Technical Appendix.

Macaulay Duration

$$
= \frac{\left(1 * \dfrac{PMT}{(1+y)^1}\right) + \left(2 * \dfrac{PMT}{(1+y)^2}\right) + \cdots + \left(N * \dfrac{PMT+FV}{(1+y)^N}\right)}{\dfrac{PMT}{(1+y)^1} + \dfrac{PMT}{(1+y)^2} + \cdots + \dfrac{PMT+FV}{(1+y)^N}} - t/T \qquad (6.14)
$$

Let's redo the last calculation to confirm that the Macaulay duration is 3.689. Enter $PMT = 4$, $FV = 100$, $y = 0.04650$, $N = 4$, and $t/T = 30/360$.

$$
\frac{\left(1 * \dfrac{4}{(1.04650)^1}\right) + \left(2 * \dfrac{4}{(1.04650)^2}\right) + \left(3 * \dfrac{4}{(1.04650)^3}\right) + \left(4 * \dfrac{104}{(1.04650)^4}\right)}{\dfrac{4}{(1.04650)^1} + \dfrac{4}{(1.04650)^2} + \dfrac{4}{(1.04650)^3} + \dfrac{104}{(1.04650)^4}} - 30/360
$$

$$
= \frac{368.443}{97.676} - 30/360 = 3.772 - 0.083 = 3.689
$$

Note that 97.676 in the denominator is the price of the bond at the beginning of the period if its yield had been 4.650%.

The modified duration for this bond is 3.525 (= 3.689/1.04650). In general, the modified duration is the Macaulay duration divided by one plus the *yield per period*, but in this case 4.650% is quoted for annual compounding. The numerical difference between the Macaulay and modified duration statistics depends on the level of interest rates and the periodicity. As rates are lower and/ or as the periodicity increases, the difference diminishes. In fact, if the yield is quoted for continuous compounding, the Macaulay and modified durations are the same. In any case, once one is known, the other is easily obtained.

These duration calculations can be confirmed on Excel. The DURATION and MDURATION financial functions deliver the annualized Macaulay and modified duration statistics. Assume arbitrarily that the 4% annual payment bond matures on December 15, 2017, and the current settlement date is January 15, 2014, one month since the last coupon date (December 15, 2013) on a 30/360 basis.

DURATION (DATE (2014, 1, 15), DATE (2017, 12, 15), 0.04, 0.0465, 1, 0)

MDURATION (DATE (2014, 1, 15), DATE (2017, 12, 15), 0.04, 0.0465, 1, 0)

The entry items are the settlement date, maturity date, annual coupon rate, annual yield to maturity, periodicity, and the code for the day-count convention (0 for 30/360, 1 for actual/actual).

The Macaulay duration of a zero-coupon bond is found by setting $c = 0$ in 6.12 or $PMT = 0$ in 6.14. In either case, it reduces to just $N - (t/T)$, the time to maturity measured in periods. The high duration on a long-term, zero-coupon bond sheds further light on the Chapter 2 story about TIGRS, CATS, and LIONS. Investment banks in the 1980s profitably transformed coupon-bearing Treasury bonds into synthetic Treasury zeros because some investors were interested in "buying duration," not yield.

Consider a 12%, semiannual payment, 28-year Treasury bond priced back then at 94 to yield 12.792% (s.a.). Its duration is 16.20 (in terms of semiannual periods), found by entering $y = 0.12792/2 = 0.06396$, $c = 0.12/2 = 0.06$, $N = 28 * 2 = 56$, and $t/T = 0$ into 6.13.

$$\left[\frac{1+0.06396}{0.06396} - \frac{1+0.06396+[56 * (0.06-0.06396)]}{0.06 * [(1+0.06396)^{56} - 1] + 0.06396} \right] = 16.20$$

The annualized Macaulay duration on this long-term 28-year coupon bond is just 8.10, which is the 16.20 semiannual periods divided by two periods in a year.

Note that I intentionally avoided saying that the duration of the bond is 8.10 *years*. There are some circumstances when it is convenient to interpret duration in terms of time, but in general it's better to think of it as the interest rate sensitivity factor. We can say that this bond will be about twice as sensitive to a shift in yield as one having duration of 4.05. I say "about" because duration alone is just the first-order approximation and neglects the convexity term. We can say that this 28-year, 12% coupon bond is the *price-risk equivalent* of an 8.10-year zero-coupon bond because their prices should respond about the same on a percentage basis given an equivalent shift in their yields to maturity.

Suppose an investment bank back in the day created a 28-year zero-coupon bond via coupon stripping and sold it to a hedge fund manager for a deeply discounted price of just 3.80 (percent of par value) to yield 12.027% (s.a.).

$$\frac{100}{\left(1+\dfrac{0.12027}{2}\right)^{56}} = 3.80$$

That yield is 76.5 basis points lower than the coupon bond, (0.12792 – 0.12027 = 0.00765). However, the zero-coupon bond has an annual Macaulay duration statistic of 28.00—that's about 3.5 times higher than 8.10. We often describe duration as a measure of risk, but it also is an opportunity statistic. In this example, the hedge fund was positioned for much greater percentage price appreciation than on the 28-year coupon bond—in fact, about 3.5 times higher if yields fall on each by the same amount. A speculative investor having a short-term horizon doesn't care about the lower yield to maturity—all the action is in the duration.

THE RELATIONSHIP BETWEEN YIELD DURATION AND MATURITY

An interesting property of Macaulay duration is revealed by letting N, the number of periods to maturity, get large and approach infinity. In equation 6.15, the general expression in equation 6.13 is simplified to apply to a coupon date (i.e., $t/T = 0$).

$$Macaulay\,Duration(t/T=0) = \frac{1+y}{y} - \frac{1+y+[N*(c-y)]}{c*[(1+y)^N - 1]+y} \quad (6.15)$$

As N approaches infinity, the denominator in the second term gets larger faster than the numerator because N is an exponent in the former and a coefficient in the latter. That whole second term goes to zero and the Macaulay duration becomes just $(1+y)/y$. Such bonds, known as perpetuities, are rare but do exist. For instance, in the U.K. bonds called *consols* paying a fixed interest payment forever have been in existence since the 18th century—and they're still out there.

Now consider bonds trading at a premium—their coupon rate is higher than the yield to maturity, $c > y$. The numerator in the second term in equation 6.15 is always positive, as is the denominator, so the Macaulay duration is less than $(1+y)/y$. For longer maturities, other things being equal, the duration increases and approaches the perpetuity threshold monotonically from below. The same pattern holds for bonds that continue to trade at par value on coupon dates because the coupon rate equals the yield, $c = y$. If we subtracted the t/T term for dates between coupon payments, we would have a "saw-tooth" pattern. As days go by during the period, the duration would decline smoothly (assuming no change in the yield) but then jump up after the coupon is paid.

Things get interesting for bonds trading at a discount—the coupon rate is less than the yield, $c < y$. When N is large enough, the numerator becomes negative. When that happens the Macaulay duration is greater than $(1 + y)/y$. But eventually for an even larger N, the duration has to approach the perpetuity threshold monotonically from above. These relationships between Macaulay duration and maturity are illustrated in Figure 6.1. For a zero-coupon bond, it's a 45-degree line because they are equal. For a perpetuity, it's a horizontal line at $(1 + y)/y$. The relationship is positive—the longer the maturity, the higher the duration—for most coupon bonds having a stated maturity, but not always.

Let's revisit the problem of the fixed-income strategist considering two 6% annual payment bonds, one maturing in 20 years and the other in 30 years. Both are priced to yield 20%, and the strategist anticipates a 100 basis point drop. The easiest way to assess the choice is to do the basic bond pricing. We're presumably on a coupon date so equation 3.5 from Chapter 3 will work fine. So will a financial calculator or Excel.

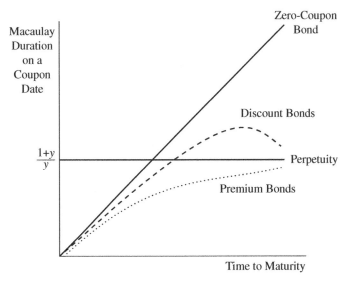

FIGURE 6.1 Relationships between Macaulay Duration and Maturity

$$20\text{-}year\,bond\,at\,20\%: \quad PV = \frac{6}{0.20} * \left[1 - \frac{1}{(1.20)^{20}}\right] + \frac{100}{(1.20)^{20}}$$

$$= 31.825884$$

$$20\text{-}year\,bond\,at\,19\%: \quad PV = \frac{6}{0.19} * \left[1 - \frac{1}{(1.19)^{20}}\right] + \frac{100}{(1.19)^{20}}$$

$$= 33.688792$$

$$Percentage\,price\,change: \quad \frac{33.688792 - 31.825884}{31.825884} = 0.0585$$

$$30\text{-}year\,bond\,at\,20\%: \quad PV = \frac{6}{0.20} * \left[1 - \frac{1}{(1.20)^{30}}\right] + \frac{100}{(1.20)^{30}}$$

$$= 30.294890$$

$$30\text{-}year\,bond\,at\,19\%: \quad PV = \frac{6}{0.19} * \left[1 - \frac{1}{(1.19)^{30}}\right] + \frac{100}{(1.19)^{30}}$$

$$= 31.949441$$

$$Percentage\,price\,change: \quad \frac{31.949441 - 30.294890}{30.294890} = 0.0546$$

It's true—given the same coupon rate and yield, the 20-year bond actually does have the higher percentage price increase for the same drop in yield, 5.85% compared to 5.46%. Try to explain this without appealing to duration. I have tried to do so but cannot. To me, it is just a bond math curiosity. It finally makes sense once we calculate the Macaulay durations using equation 6.15 (because $t/T = 0$).

$$20\text{-}year\,bond: \quad \frac{1.20}{0.20} - \frac{1.20 + [20 * (0.06 - 0.20)]}{0.06 * [(1.20)^{20} - 1] + 0.20} = 6.66$$

$$30\text{-}year\,bond: \quad \frac{1.20}{0.20} - \frac{1.20 + [30 * (0.06 - 0.20)]}{0.06 * [(1.20)^{30} - 1] + 0.20} = 6.21$$

The Macaulay duration on the 20-year bond is 6.66 but just 6.21 on the 30-year. The modified durations can be used to estimate the anticipated percentage price increase.

$$20\text{-}year\,bond: \quad \frac{dMV}{MV} \approx -\left(\frac{6.66}{1.20} * -0.0100\right) = 0.0555$$

$$30\text{-}year\,bond: \quad \frac{dMV}{MV} \approx -\left(\frac{6.21}{1.20} * -0.0100\right) = 0.0518$$

Notice that duration signals correctly the bond that has the greater price appreciation if the market responds as the strategist expects. However, the estimated changes are off by about 30 basis points compared to the actual results. By itself, duration is a conservatively biased estimate for the risk in a long position on a fixed-income bond—it overestimates the loss when the yield goes up and underestimates the gain when the yield goes down. The convexity adjustment improves the estimate in each case.

YIELD CONVEXITY

The bond convexity statistic is the second-order effect in the Taylor series expansion. Getting an equation for convexity is just a matter of more calculus and algebra; see the Technical Appendix for all the details. However, the results are complicated enough to warrant separate equations for coupon payment dates and between coupons. Equation 6.16 is the formula that applies to a coupon payment date such that $t/T = 0$.

$Convexity(t/T = 0)$

$$= \frac{\left[2 * c * (1+y)^2 * \left((1+y)^N - \frac{1+y+(y*N)}{1+y}\right)\right] + [N*(N+1)*y^2*(y-c)]}{y^2 * (1+y)^2 * (c*[(1+y)^N - 1] + y)}$$

$$(6.16)$$

Granted, there are a lot of terms in the equation, but just three variables: c, the coupon rate per period; y, the yield to maturity per period; and N, the number of periods to maturity. One simplification emerges for a zero-coupon bond for which $c = 0$. Then much of equation 6.16 drops out and the convexity reduces to $N * (N + 1)/(1 + y)^2$.

Let's work on a 4%, semiannual payment, 25-year bond priced at a discount to yield 4.40% (s.a.). First, use equation 6.13 or 6.15 to get its Macaulay duration $(t/T = 0)$, using $y = 0.0220$, $c = 0.02$, and $N = 50$.

Macaulay Duration$(t/T = 0)$

$$= \left[\frac{1.0220}{0.0220} - \frac{1.0220 + [50 * (0.02 - 0.0220)]}{0.02 * [(1.0220)^{50} - 1] + 0.0220} \right] = 31.4312$$

That's the Macaulay duration that corresponds to a change in the yield *per period*; annualized it is 15.7156 (= 31.4312/2). The annual modified duration is 15.3773 (= 15.7156/1.0220). Note that we divide by one plus the yield per period, not by the annualized yield.

Okay, now enter the same inputs for y, c, and N into equation 6.16.

Convexity$(t/T = 0) =$

$$\frac{\left[2 * 0.02 * (1.0220)^2 * \left((1.0220)^{50} - \frac{1.0220 + (0.0220 * 50)}{1.0220} \right) \right]}{(0.0220)^2 * (1.0220)^2 * \left(0.02 * \left[(1.0220)^{50} - 1 \right] + 0.0220 \right)}$$

$$= 1,281.0757$$

If you tried and got that result—congratulations! That's the convexity statistic that links the change in the yield per period to the change in market value. As in equation 6.11, it is annualized by dividing by the periodicity squared. So, this bond has an annualized yield convexity of 320.2689 (= 1,281.0757/4). Unfortunately, Excel does not have a financial function for convexity even though it uses the same inputs as duration.

Suppose three months go by and the bond is still priced to yield 4.40% (s.a.). Let $t/T = 0.50$ because we are halfway through the semiannual period. The Macaulay duration is easily calculated: 31.4312 – 0.50 = 30.9312. Annualized, it is 15.4656 (= 30.9312/2) and the modified duration is 15.1327 (= 15.4656/1.0220).

The convexity statistic between coupon payment dates is shown in equation 6.17.

Convexity = *Convexity*$(t/T = 0)$

$$- \left\{ \frac{t/T}{(1 + y)^2} * [(2 * MacDur(t/T = 0)) + (1 - t/T)] \right\} \quad (6.17)$$

The first term is the convexity that would prevail at the beginning of the period (hence $t/T = 0$) if the current yield per period y is used in the calculation in equation 6.16. Then we need to subtract the term in brackets, which contains, as a bit of a surprise, the Macaulay duration (*MacDur*) in equation 6.15 calculated for $t/T = 0$ using the yield per period y.

As time passes, yields inevitably do change, and equations 6.15 and 6.16 have to be calculated using the new yield to maturity. For convenience, I assume that the yield remains the same at 4.40% (s.a.), so we can use the already obtained results. The convexity after the three months is 1,250.7438, using *Convexity (t/T = 0)* = 1,281.0757, $t/T = 0.50$, $y = 0.0220$, and *MacDur* $(t/T = 0) = 31.4312$.

$$Convexity = 1,281.0757 - \left\{ \frac{0.50}{(1.0220)^2} * \left[(2 * 31.4312) + (1 - 0.50) \right] \right\}$$

$$= 1,250.7438$$

The annual convexity statistic is 312.6859 (= 1,250.7438/4).

In working through this convexity calculation, I have kept more precision (four decimals) than really is needed. That's because I want to illustrate how the modified duration and convexity statistics can be approximated quite accurately using *numerical methods*. The idea is to *estimate* the values for the first and second partial derivatives in equations 6.4 and 6.6. In calculus, dy is an infinitesimal change in the yield per period. I use a discrete change in this approximation, here chosen to be 20 basis points up and down.

The approximation formulas for (annual) modified yield duration and yield convexity are defined in equations 6.18 and 6.19.

$$Approximate\ Annual\ Modified\ Duration \equiv \frac{MV(down) - MV(up)}{2 * \Delta yield * MV(initial)} \quad (6.18)$$

$$Approximate\ Annual\ Convexity \equiv \frac{MV(down) + MV(up) - 2 * MV(initial)}{(\Delta yield)^2 * MV(initial)}$$

$$(6.19)$$

MV(down) and *MV(up)* are the market values calculated using a pricing model (or equation) assuming the same decrease and increase in the yield.

The initial market value for the bond, *MV(initial)*, is 94.999558 (percent of par value), using equation 3.11 from Chapter 3 and $PMT = 2$, $y = 0.0220$, $N = 50$, $FV = 100$, and $t/T = 0.50$.

$$MV(initial) = \left[\frac{2}{0.0220} * \left(1 - \frac{1}{(1.0220)^{50}} \right) + \frac{100}{(1.0220)^{50}} \right] * (1.0220)^{0.50}$$

$$= 94.999558$$

This is the combined flat price and accrued interest. You also can get this result on Excel using the financial function PRICE for the flat price and then ACCRINT to get the accrued interest. The sum of the flat price obtained with PRICE and the accrued interest from ACCRINT is the full price, 94.999558. Assume arbitrarily that the 4%, 25-year bond is issued on July 15, 2014, matures on July 15, 2039, and now on October 15, 2014 (three months into the semiannual period using a 30/360 day count), the yield is 4.40% (s.a.).

> PRICE(DATE(2014,10,15),DATE(2039,7,15),0.04,0.0440,100,2,0)
> ACCRINT(DATE(2014,7,15),DATE(2015,1,15),DATE(2014,10,15),
> 0.04,100,2,0)

If the yield goes up by 20 basis points to 4.60% (s.a.), the market value is 92.182875, found by repeating the calculation for $y = 0.0230$.

$$
MV(up) = \left[\frac{2}{0.0230} * \left(1 - \frac{1}{(1.0230)^{50}} \right) + \frac{100}{(1.0230)^{50}} \right] * (1.0230)^{0.50}
$$
$$
= 92.182875
$$

If the yield goes down to 4.20% (s.a.), the market value is 97.935084, using $y = 0.0210$.

$$
MV(down) = \left[\frac{2}{0.0210} * \left(1 - \frac{1}{(1.0210)^{50}} \right) + \frac{100}{(1.0210)^{50}} \right] * (1.0210)^{0.50}
$$
$$
= 97.935084
$$

In Excel, repeat the PRICE calculations using 0.0460 and 0.0420 for the fourth entries. The accrued interest is the same and is just 1.00 (= 90/180 * 2). Note that the general bond math formula directly uses the periodic variables—the payment per period, yield per period, and number of periods to maturity—whereas Excel (like other software programs) allows you to enter the annual variables and the periodicity that adjusts them in the formulas embedded in the programming.

Substitute these results for the MVs into equations 6.18 and 6.19 and use 0.0020 for the change in yield.

$$
Approximate\ Annual\ Modified\ Duration = \frac{97.935084 - 92.182875}{2 * 0.0020 * 94.999558}
$$
$$
= 15.1375
$$

$$Approximate\ Annual\ Convexity = \frac{97.935084 + 92.182875 - 2 * 94.999558}{(0.0020)^2 * 94.999558}$$

$$= 312.7462$$

These are really good approximations; the more accurate numbers calculated above using the mathematically derived formulas are 15.1327 and 312.6859. In fact, the approximations become even better for a smaller change in yield. In practice, the differences between the approximations and the exact results are not likely to be material. For most purposes the information content for the modified duration and convexity of this bond is 15.14 and 312.7—precision beyond that likely is just data.

Now let's look at how you probably observe bond duration and convexity statistics in practice.

BLOOMBERG YIELD DURATION AND CONVEXITY

Figure 6.2 shows the Bloomberg Yield and Spread Analysis page for the 3.85% Apple (AAPL) bond due May 4, 2043. It is priced at 87.24 for settlement on March 5, 2014. This is the market discount bond we saw in Chapter 4, where we worked through the projected after-tax rate of return calculation. Now let's confirm the (interest rate) risk numbers. This bond has a modified duration statistic of 16.285 and a convexity shown to be 3.803. I get to Bloomberg Risk, reported at 14.418, in a bit. These risk statistics are annualized and relate the total market value, 88.534028 (percent of par value, including accrued interest) to a change in the street convention yield, 4.653675%, which is quoted on a semiannual bond basis for a 30/360 day count.

Let's first get the Macaulay duration statistic for this bond. In equation 6.13, enter $y = 0.04654/2 = 0.02327$ (I'm going to round off the yield a bit), $c = 0.0385/2 = 0.01925$, $N = 59$, and $t/T = 121/180$. There are 59 semiannual coupon periods between the last payment date on November 4, 2013, and the maturity date.

$$\left[\frac{1.02327}{0.02327} - \frac{1.02327 + [59 * (0.01925 - 0.02327)]}{0.01925 * [(1.02327)^{59} - 1] + 0.02327} \right] - 121/180$$

$$= 33.9995 - 0.6722 = 33.3273$$

The annual Macaulay duration is 16.66365 (= 33.3273/2). The annual modified duration rounded to three decimals is 16.285 (= 16.66365/1.02327). The Excel function gets the same results, confirming the Bloomberg number.

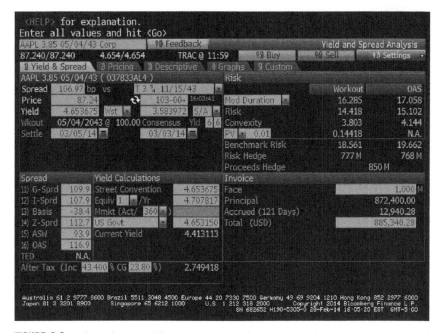

FIGURE 6.2   Bloomberg Yield and Spread Analysis Page (YA), AAPL 3.85% Bond
Due May 4, 2043
Used with permission of Bloomberg.com © 2014. All rights reserved.

MDURATION (DATE (2014, 3, 5), DATE (2043, 5, 4), 0.0385, 0.04654, 2, 0)

We need to do yield convexity in two steps. First, use the same inputs for
y, c, and N in equation 6.16.

$Convexity(t/T = 0)$

$$
= \frac{\left[2 * 0.01925 * (1.02327)^2 * \left((1.02327)^{59} - \dfrac{1.02327 + (0.02327 * 59)}{1.02327} \right) \right]}{(0.02327)^2 * (1.02327)^2 * \left(0.01925 * \left[(1.02327)^{59} - 1 \right] + 0.02327 \right)}
$$

$$
= 1,564.9865
$$

Second, substitute this result and $t/T = 121/180$ and $MacDur(t/T = 0) =$
33.9995 into equation 6.17.

$$Convexity = 1,564.9865 - \left(\frac{121/180}{(1.02327)^2} * [2 * 33.9995 + (1 - 121/180)] \right)$$

$$= 1,521.1210$$

So, the annual convexity is 380.280 (= 1,521.1210/4). Bloomberg reports the convexity to be 3.803, but that is just our result divided by 100.

Why does Bloomberg scale the yield convexity down by a factor of 100? The answer goes back to how the convexity adjustment improves the estimate of the change in market value given a change in the yield. Suppose the question at hand is how much gain in MV should we anticipate if the yield falls by 25 basis points, from 4.654% to 4.404%? We can use equation 6.12, knowing that the annual modified duration and convexity statistics are 16.285 and 380.3.

$$\frac{dMV}{MV} \approx (-16.285 * -0.0025) + \left(\frac{1}{2} * 380.3 * (-0.0025)^2 \right)$$

$$= 0.0407 + 0.0012 = 0.0419$$

We conclude that modified duration alone estimates a 4.07% increase in market value, but factoring in convexity, we get 4.19%. Duration by itself underestimates gains and overestimates losses. The convexity adjustment adds twelve basis points, bringing the estimate closer to the actual result.

Bloomberg convexity allows you to work with another version of equation 6.12. Multiply both sides by 100 to get the change in percentage terms directly.

$$100 * \frac{dMV}{MV} \approx (-Annual\ Modified\ Duration * (100 * dY))$$

$$+ \left(\frac{1}{2} * \frac{Annual\ Convexity}{100} * (100 * dY)^2 \right) \tag{6.20}$$

Because the second term of the Taylor series expansion entails the change in yield squared, the annual convexity needs to be divided by 100. Now the estimate is figured as:

$$100 * \frac{dMV}{MV} \approx (-16.285 * -0.25) + \left(\frac{1}{2} * 3.803 * (-0.25)^2 \right)$$

$$= 4.07 + 0.12 = 4.19$$

The answers are the same, of course, but in my opinion the reformulation (the convexity of 380.3 becomes 3.803) is not worth the "convenience" of using the convexity adjustment in equation 6.20 rather than equation 6.12. Frankly, Bloomberg convexity reflects the olden days when such estimates were made on the back of an envelope or with a handheld calculator; nowadays we use spreadsheets. Moreover, convexity can be used as a summary statistic for bond strategy—more on this in Chapter 10—and for that purpose, there is no advantage to scaling convexity down to such a small number.

Macaulay and modified durations are measures of percentage price sensitivity. Money duration and its variants indicate the price change. Often this is on a per-basis-point basis; that is, the change in the value of the bond for a one-basis-point change in the yield. These variants go by various names—the BPV (basis point value), the PV01 (price, or present, value of an "01" change in yield), and the DV01 (the dollar value of an "01"). Sometimes these are calculated simply by multiplying the money duration by 0.0001—that is, the modified duration times the market value, times one basis point. Bloomberg determines the PV01 and DV01 a little differently.

The Bloomberg Risk statistic is the PV01 * 100. On the Apple bond in Figure 6.2, the PV01 is 0.14418 and Risk is 14.418. If the yield goes up by 100 basis points, the flat price of the bond will go down by approximately 14.418 (per 100 of par value), from 87.24 to 72.822, (87.24 − 14.418 = 72.822). For bonds trading at a discount such as this one, Bloomberg Risk is less than modified duration. For bonds trading at a premium, Risk is greater than duration.

I demonstrate the PV01 calculation using Excel because it requires the precise street convention yield to maturity, 0.04653675. We solve for the new flat prices after changing the yield by adding and subtracting one basis point (0.0001).

PRICE (DATE (2014,3,5), DATE (2043,5,4), 0.0385, 0.04663675, 100, 2, 0)

PRICE (DATE (2014, 3, 5), DATE (2043, 5, 4), 0.0385, 0.04643675, 100, 2, 0)

The new flat prices are 87.384344 for the lower yield and 87.095987 for the higher yield. The PV01 is the difference in these prices divided by two.

$$PV01 = \frac{87.384344 - 87.095987}{2} = 0.14418$$

Notice that we could include the accrued interest in the numerator, but it just cancels out.

So, what do we know about the interest rate risk of this Apple bond? Its modified duration is 16.285 and its convexity is 3.803 (as scaled by Bloomberg). These relate to changes in the yield to maturity. We can say that if the yield jumps up suddenly by 100 basis points, the market value will fall by approximately 16.285% using duration alone. If we add in the convexity adjustment, we can say that the expected drop will be more like 14.384%. If we actually ran the experiment on a spreadsheet, we would see that the bond price actually would fall by 14.540%. Our estimate works quite well, even for a large jump in the yield.

Yield duration and convexity are impact statistics and not causation factors. The yield might have gone up because of an unexpected downgrade in the issuer's credit rating. Or it might have gone up because all bond yields increased following dramatically revised forecasts for expected inflation. We explore this further in the next chapter. There, understanding the sensitivity of floating-rate notes (floaters) requires that we ask *why* the yield changes. Let's now step beyond classic yield duration and consider how market value changes when the entire benchmark Treasury yield curve shifts up or down.

CURVE DURATION AND CONVEXITY

A number of versions of duration have been introduced since Macaulay first wrote down a formula for the statistic in the 1930s. I always wonder: Does this mean he *invented* it or *discovered* it? Anyway, another version that I'll call *spot duration* sometimes is used in academic fixed-income research (where it is called "Fisher-Weil duration").

$$Spot\,Duration = \frac{\left(1 * \dfrac{PMT}{(1+z_1)^1}\right) + \left(2 * \dfrac{PMT}{(1+z_2)^2}\right) + \cdots + \left(N * \dfrac{PMT+FV}{(1+z_N)^N}\right)}{\dfrac{PMT}{(1+z_1)^1} + \dfrac{PMT}{(1+z_2)^2} + \cdots + \dfrac{PMT+FV}{(1+z_N)^N}} - (t/T) \qquad (6.21)$$

This looks much like the weighted-average formula for Macaulay duration in equation 6.14. The difference is that instead of discounting the cash flows with the yield to maturity, the sequence of spot, or zero-coupon, rates (z_1, $z_2, \ldots, z_N$) is used. The price of the bond in the denominator is the same as in equation 6.14—recall from Chapter 3 that the yield is a "weighted average" of the spot rates. The numerator can be different, however, the more so the greater the slope to the yield curve.

An advantage to spot duration is that it implicitly includes the shape of the yield curve. One can then analyze the impact on market value following *nonparallel* shifts to the term structure, for instance, a steepening such that the increase in z_N is greater than z_1. The problem in taking this academic construct into practice is that the requisite sequence of zero-coupon rates generally is not available for corporate, agency, and municipal bonds, only for Treasury securities. Moreover, as we saw in Chapter 4, Treasury STRIPS have significantly different taxation than coupon bonds and usually are less liquid. For that reason, spot durations are not reported on data systems like Bloomberg; nor are they used in practice.

Macaulay and modified durations, however, depend only on an observable and unambiguous input: the bond price and from it the yield to maturity. You might hear the complaint made by some that "Macaulay duration assumes a flat yield curve." That is just not true, in the same way that the yield to maturity statistic does not assume a flat term structure. It's the same argument as I made in Chapter 3. The yield is a summary statistic about the cash flows on the bond; it's the internal rate of return. Yield duration and convexity estimate the change in market value associated with a change in that summary statistic. Many different shapes to the underlying spot curve can produce the same yield to maturity; many different shifts to that underlying spot curve can produce the same change in the yield. This explains why yield duration and convexity merely *estimate* the actual change in market value (along with dropping the remaining terms of the Taylor series).

A more significant problem with yield duration is that on some securities it has little meaning. That's because the yield itself is not well defined. Consider a callable bond. What is its yield? Is it the yield to maturity—that is, assuming the embedded call option is and will remain out of the money (so the bond will not be called)? Is it the yield to first call date—that is, assuming the call option is and will remain in the money (so it definitely will be called)? Often on callable bonds you will see the "yield to worst," which is the lowest of the yields to first call, second call, and so on, out to the yield to maturity. Presumably it's the most conservative measure of rate of return, but I think it's just more bond data, not information. In any case, is the duration of a callable bond its sensitivity to a change in the yield to worst?

Figure 6.3 illustrates this problem. It shows the Bloomberg Yield and Spread Analysis page for the 6% Fannie Mae bond that matures on April 18, 2036. This bond is callable at par value one time on April 18, 2016 (this is called the *workout* date on Bloomberg). The bond is priced flat at 108.625 for settlement on March 12, 2014. Its street convention yield to maturity is shown to be 1.795488%.

Suppose that you work in the back office of an investment firm, and one of your many jobs is to enter the key statistics on newly acquired bonds into the risk management tracking system. Would you enter 1.795488% for the yield? Would you enter 1.949 for the modified duration for this bond and 0.049 for the convexity (or 4.9)? I hope not! These risk and return statistics assume that the bond definitely will be called. They are calculated using April 18, 2016, as the maturity date. Although it is quite likely that Fannie Mae in fact will call the bond, which is trading at a premium above the strike price on

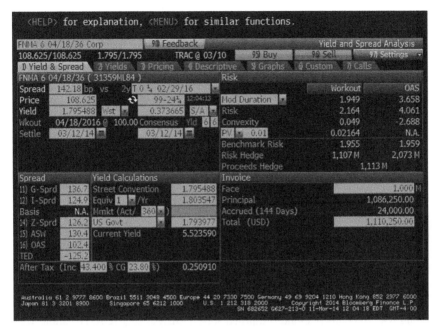

FIGURE 6.3 Bloomberg Yield and Spread Analysis Page, 6% Fannie Mae Callable Bond
Used with permission of Bloomberg.com © 2014. All rights reserved.

the option and so is in the money, there is always a chance that interest rates go up unexpectedly and bond is not called. We need to be careful in stating risk statistics based on an optimistic view of future market conditions.

For better numbers, you should go to the Bloomberg Option-Adjusted Spread Analysis page (OAS1) for the same Fannie Mae bond, shown in Figure 6.4, to get more reasonable yield, duration, and convexity statistics for this callable bond. Bloomberg uses an interest rate term structure model to value the callable bond, here a lognormal model. Starting with the underlying CMT (Constant Maturity Treasury) yield curve, shown at the right in Figure 6.4, the implied spot and forward rates are calculated in the same manner as in Chapter 5. Then around that forward curve a range of possible rates is postulated, consistent with the assumed level of interest rate volatility, in this instance, 18.96%. Those rates are then calibrated to value exactly the benchmark Treasury bonds. The principle of no arbitrage allows the model to value other securities.

Given the model and, importantly, the assumed level of rate volatility, the *option-adjusted spread* (OAS) for the Fannie Mae callable bond is determined to be 102.3 basis points. That is the spread over the chosen Treasury

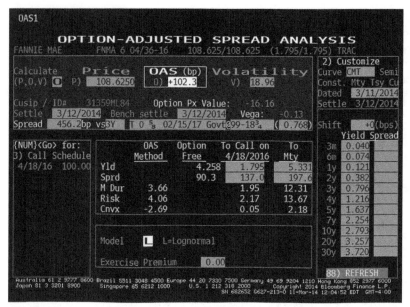

FIGURE 6.4 Bloomberg Option-Adjusted Spread Analysis Page (OAS1), Fannie Mae Callable Bond
Used with permission of Bloomberg.com © 2014. All rights reserved.

security (the 0.625% T-note due February 15, 2017) after subtracting out the value of the embedded call option. The OAS measures the compensation to the investor for the remaining risk factors—that is, default, liquidity, and taxation—and allows for direct comparison to other callable, as well as noncallable, bonds to identify relative value.

There is a lot of bond data on these two Bloomberg pages. It's up to the fixed-income analyst to identify the information. Consider first the Spread of 142.18 basis points shown in the top left of the Yield and Spread Analysis page. That's the difference between the yield to call, 1.795488%, and the yield on the indicated benchmark Treasury, the 0.25% T-Note that matures on February 29, 2016. Its yield is 0.373665%. The spread is 1.421823% (= 1.795488% − 0.373665%).

Next, look at the Spread of 456.2 basis points shown in the left side of the OAS1 page. Where does it come from? Well, the yield to maturity on the bond (i.e., assuming away the presence of the call option) is 5.330604%. It's shown in the middle of the page rounded to three digits, but you can get the full precision on Excel.

YIELD (DATE (2014, 3, 12), DATE (2036, 4, 18), 0.06, 108.625, 100, 2, 0)

The benchmark Treasury now is the 0.625% note due on February 15, 2017. It's priced at 99.5859375 (= 99 + 18.75/32) to yield 0.768116%.

YIELD (DATE (2014, 3, 12), DATE (2017, 2, 15), 0.00625, 99.5859375, 100, 2, 1)

The spread over the Treasury is 4.562488% (= 5.330604% – 0.768116%). But what is the meaning to a yield spread on bonds with such divergent times to maturity?

Fortunately, there is useful information on these pages, especially the OAS of 102.3 basis points (given that you are fine with the assumed volatility). Another is the *option-adjusted yield* (OAY), the yield after including the estimated value of the option. The value of the embedded call is determined to be 16.16 (percent of par value), shown in the Bloomberg OAS1 page as "Option Px Value." (I don't know why it is shown as a negative amount.) This is added to the flat price of the bond to get the option-adjusted flat price, 124.785 (= 108.625 + 16.16). The OAY is the yield to maturity based on that price. It's shown to be 4.258%, the "Option Free Yld" in the middle of the page. That result is easily confirmed using the Excel YIELD function.

YIELD (DATE (2014, 3, 12), DATE (2036, 4, 18), 0.06, 124.785, 100, 2, 0)

The idea of the OAY is that if the embedded call option, which has a value of 16.16, were somehow to be removed, the bond would trade at a higher price and a lower yield to maturity.

The same option-pricing model that produces the OAS and OAY is used for the interest rate risk statistics. First, all the benchmark Treasury CMT yields used to get the spot and forward rates (i.e., those shown at the right in Figure 6.4) are increased by a certain number of basis points. Then the model is run, generating a new value for the bond, *MV(up)*. Next the benchmark yields are decreased by the same amount, and the model generates *MV(down)*. *MV(initial)* on this bond is 111.025 (percent of par value, including accrued interest).

Those market values are the inputs to equations 6.22 and 6.23 for the effective duration and convexity, which are *curve* duration and convexity statistics very similar to those for approximate annual modified *yield* duration and convexity. The difference is that now in the denominator the change is to the entire benchmark yield curve rather than to the bond's own yield to maturity.

$$Effective\ Duration \equiv \frac{MV(down) - MV(up)}{2 * \Delta curve * MV(initial)} \tag{6.22}$$

$$Effective\ Convexity \equiv \frac{MV(down) + MV(up) - 2 * MV(initial)}{(\Delta curve)^2 * MV(initial)} \tag{6.23}$$

The effective duration for this callable bond is 3.66, reported in Figure 6.4 under OAS method. On Bloomberg effective duration is called *OAS duration*. The OAS convexity or effective convexity or, as I prefer, *curve convexity*, is reported to be −2.69. Once again, this is scaled by dividing by 100; I would rather see −269. Negative convexity is a common feature with callable bonds because of the limit to price appreciation as the yield falls.

Curve duration and convexity also can be calculated for bonds that do not have embedded derivatives. In fact, the contrast between yield duration and curve duration has interesting implications for bond strategy and risk management. It becomes most meaningful in assessing the rate sensitivities of long-term, low-coupon bonds. To see this, Figure 6.5 shows the Bloomberg Yield and Spread Analysis page for the zero-coupon Treasury P-STRIPS maturing on May 15, 2042. It is priced at 33.51171875 (= 33 + 16.375/32) to yield 3.918000% (s.a.) on a street convention basis for settlement on March 12, 2014. (Note how strange-looking that Japanese simple yield of 7.041% is. Do not bother looking at the after-tax rate—assuming a zero-coupon bond like this P-STRIPS is issued at par value and that it is a non–OID bond with a market discount is just wrong. Also, I don't understand why the principal is shown to be 335,111.24 in the Invoice section

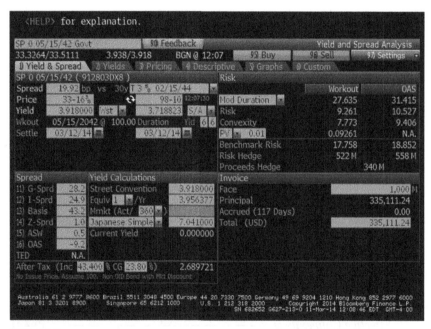

FIGURE 6.5   Bloomberg Yield Analysis Page (YA), Treasury P-STRIPS Due May 15, 2042.
Used with permission of Bloomberg.com © 2014. All rights reserved.

rather than 335,117.19 given that the bond price is shown to be 33–16 3/8. Yes, I have a love-hate relationship with some Bloomberg pages.)

Let's first confirm the reported yield modified duration and convexity numbers for the P-STRIPS reported under the "Workout" heading. Because the coupon rate is zero, its Macaulay duration (in semiannual periods) is just $N - t/T = 57 - 117/181 = 56.3536$. There are 57 semiannual periods between the start of the current period on November 15, 2013, and the maturity date. Note that the day count is actual/actual because this is a Treasury security, even though there are no coupon payments. Dividing by two gives an annual Macaulay duration of 28.1768 (= 56.3536/2). Dividing that by one plus the yield per period gives the reported annual modified duration, 27.635 [= 28.1768/(1 + 0.03918/2)]. The yield convexity entails substitution into equations 6.16 and 6.17, here combined because so many terms drop out when $c = 0$.

$$
\frac{57 * 58}{\left(1 + \dfrac{0.03918}{2}\right)^2} - \left[\frac{117/181}{\left(1 + \dfrac{0.03918}{2}\right)^2} * [2 * 57 + (1 - 117/181)]\right]
$$
$$
= 3,109.074
$$

Dividing that by the periodicity squared obtains the annual convexity, 777.2685 (= 3,109.074/4). Bloomberg scales that down and reports 7.773.

Now look at right side of the Risk section, which shows results from the Bloomberg OAS1 page for the same zero-coupon Treasury STRIPS. The modified *curve duration* is 31.415 and the *curve convexity* is 9.406 (I would prefer 940.6). These are the effective duration and convexity statistics obtained by shifting the benchmark Treasury yield curve. Those risk statistics are considerably higher than the modified *yield duration* of 27.635 and *yield convexity* of 7.773 (or 777.3).

Which numbers do you use? It depends on the circumstance. If you own the Treasury P-STRIPS and want an estimate of the change in market value given a change in its yield to maturity, yield duration and convexity provide your answer. However, if you own a portfolio of Treasury notes and bonds and want to aggregate the risk statistics—that is, calculate the *average* portfolio modified duration and convexity—you should use the curve duration and curve convexity for each. This is a very important point, to which I return in Chapter 9 on bond portfolios.

However, before wrapping up this chapter and moving on to interesting extensions such as floaters, linkers, and swaps, let's look at *why* the curve duration and convexity on this long-term, zero-coupon bond are so different from the yield duration and convexity. The answer goes to the heart of bond math and the assumption of no arbitrage in financial modeling. In brief, it's because the yield curve is so steep in this example—flat curves simply are not so interesting. Look at the benchmark Treasury CMT curve at the right of Figure 6.4. These are the yields on coupon Treasury notes and bonds for the same settlement date of March 12, 2014, as the P-STRIPS. When the underlying yield curve for coupon bonds is upward sloping, the implied spot curve as we derived in Chapter 5 will lie above it. It's no surprise at all that the 3.918% STRIPS yield is higher than coupon bonds having similar times to maturity. In Figure 6.5, the spread on the STRIPS is reported to be 19.92 basis points above the 3.718823% yield on the 3.625% Treasury bond due February 15, 2044.

The key point is that when we shift the benchmark Treasury curve up and down in the interest rate term structure model to get the effective duration and convexity, the implied spot yields shift as well but not by the same amount. That happens only when the curve is flat. In fact, the implied spot curve shifts by a larger amount because of the upward slope. Suppose the curve duration and convexity statistics are based on a 25-basis point shift to the benchmark par curve. To be consistent with the no-arbitrage assumption, the yields on long-term, zero-coupon bonds will shift by more than 25 basis points. A larger change in the yield leads to a larger change in market value—so the curve duration and convexity statistics are larger as well.

For a numerical example of this important and interesting property of bond math, suppose that 1-year and 2-year annual payment bonds are priced at par value and have coupon rates of 2% and 10%, respectively. This is an incredibly steep par curve but will make the point with minimal bootstrapping. The 0×2 implied spot rate is 10.433927%, as expected above the 10% yield on the 2-year coupon bond. The approximation formulas for duration and convexity are very sensitive to rounding so I need to display a high degree of precision.

$$100 = \frac{10}{1.02} + \frac{110}{(1+z)^2}, \quad z = 0.10433927$$

A 2-year zero-coupon bond is priced at 81.996435 (percent of par value), assuming no arbitrage and no transactions costs.

$$\frac{100}{(1.10433927)^2} = 81.996435$$

Its Macaulay duration is 2 and its modified duration is 1.8110 (= 2/1.10433927). Its convexity is 4.9198 [= $(2*3)/(1.10433927)^2$]. Those are the yield duration and convexity statistics.

To get the curve duration and convexity, first shift the underlying yield curve, which in this case is the par curve, up by 25 basis points. The new 0×2 implied spot rate is 10.694755%, an increase of 26.1 basis points $(0.10694755 - 0.10433927 = 0.00261)$.

$$100 = \frac{10.25}{1.0225} + \frac{110.25}{(1+z)^2}, \quad z = 0.10694755$$

The no-arbitrage price on the 0×2 zero-coupon bond falls to 81.610476.

$$\frac{100}{(1.10694755)^2} = 81.610476$$

Then shift the par curve down by 25 basis points. The new 2-year implied spot rate is 10.173098%, a decrease of 26.1 basis points $(0.10433927 - 0.10173098 = 0.00261)$.

$$100 = \frac{9.75}{1.0175} + \frac{109.75}{(1+z)^2}, \quad z = 0.10173098$$

The price goes up to 82.385139.

$$\frac{100}{(1.10173098)^2} = 82.385139$$

We now have the inputs for effective duration and convexity in equations 6.22 and 6.23: *MV(initial)* = 81.996435, *MV(up)* = 81.610476, *MV(down)* = 82.385139, and the change in the yield curve is 0.0025. Remember that "up" and "down" here refer to the change in the yield curve, not the price.

$$Effective\,Duration = \frac{82.385139 - 81.610476}{2 * 0.0025 * 81.996435} = 1.8895$$

$$Effective\,Convexity = \frac{82.385139 + 81.610476 - 2 * 81.996435}{(0.0025)^2 * 81.996435} = 5.3563$$

If we put 0.00261 in the denominator of each, we would get the approximations for the modified yield duration and yield convexity, but that is not the point. We want to understand the sensitivity with respect to a change in the benchmark yield curve, not with respect to the yield to maturity. Corresponding to a 25-basis point parallel shift in the yield curve, the curve duration of 1.8895 and curve convexity of 5.3563 are more relevant interest rate sensitivities than the yield duration of 1.8110 and yield convexity of 4.9198.

CONCLUSION

Duration and, to a lesser extent, convexity are core topics in the study of bond math, right up there with price and yield calculations and conversions, and yield curve analysis. These statistics are fundamentally mathematical and are derived using algebra and calculus. Duration is sometimes just a building block for more developed models of risk. For example, value-at-risk (VaR) analysis includes the effect of varying volatilities and correlations for points along the yield curve. Although VaR commonly is used for risk measurement in financial institutions and is subject to its own limitations and misapplications, it goes "beyond duration" in terms of mathematics and statistics. But to get there, you need a solid foundation in classic duration analysis.

In its primary application, duration estimates the change in market value corresponding to a change in the yield to maturity. This estimation is improved with the convexity adjustment. Most literature on this topic focuses on a single fixed-income bond. But if you owned only one bond, why would you need to *estimate* changes in market value? If you have a financial calculator and some good bond math formulas, or if you have an Excel spreadsheet and can open the financial functions, you can get the new bond price for any change in its yield to maturity.

In practice, we need to think about *portfolios* of bonds and the *average* duration and convexity statistics. Those averages will be helpful in risk management and in structuring the portfolio. How the market value of the overall portfolio, and specific holdings within it, move when the benchmark Treasury yield curve shifts becomes relevant. We need to think about the difference between classic *Macaulay and modified yield duration and convexity*, which are fine for individual securities, and *curve duration and convexity*, which are more applicable to measuring risk in portfolios of bonds.

In this chapter we worked with traditional fixed-income and zero-coupon bonds. Now we turn to other types of bonds, in particular, floating-rate and inflation-indexed bonds, and then to a very important type of derivative contract, interest rate swaps. We will have to use all of our bond math core topics to understand them.

CHAPTER 7

Floaters and Linkers

Learning bond math involves building a set of analytical tools. That is what we've been doing for the most part in the first six chapters—rate conversions, pricing and yield calculations, after-tax cash flows, implied spot and implied forward rates, duration, and convexity. The payoff ultimately comes in analyzing bond portfolios and fixed-income strategies, as we see in Chapters 9 and 10. But first we can use the toolkit to look at types of debt securities other than the traditional fixed-rate and zero-coupon bonds we've been working with so far.

Floating-rate notes (floaters or FRNs) remind us that trying to minimize interest rate risk in the bond market is rather like squeezing one end of a balloon to make it smaller. Obviously, the future cash flows on a fixed-rate bond are known in advance (barring default, of course). Therefore, interest rate volatility is realized entirely in the fluctuation of current market value. Floaters aim to minimize price volatility, but at the expense of uncertain future cash flows. Interest payments typically are tied to a money market reference rate—for instance, 3-month LIBOR. By design, the duration of a floater is very low, typically close to zero, for changes in market interest rates regardless of the time to maturity.

Inflation-indexed bonds (or linkers) adjust future coupon and/or principal cash flows for realized inflation. The idea is to maintain real value in terms of the purchasing power of future cash flows. There are two designs: (1) The coupon rate is fixed while the principal changes with the consumer price index (CPI), and (2) the principal is fixed while the coupon rate adjusts for changes in the CPI. I like to call the first type *P-Linkers* because the link is to the principal and the second type *C-Linkers* because the link is to the coupon rate. Both designs provide the investor with inflation protection— their inflation durations are zero, or at least close to zero. However, their real rate durations can be quite high, even higher than those for traditional fixed-rate bonds of comparable time to maturity.

A theme, actually a subplot, to this chapter is *negative duration*. That's an oddity for a debt security that does not contain an embedded option. The idea

139

is that the bond price goes up (or down) when interest rates go up (or down). It's the opposite reaction from the usual inverse relationship between bond price and yield. If you work with or have studied floating-rate notes, ask yourself what type of standard FRN (e.g., one paying 3-month LIBOR plus a fixed margin) might have negative duration—a floater trading at a discount or at a premium? If you know the answer to that, try this: When might an inflation-indexed bond, in particular a C-Linker, have negative inflation duration—when it's trading at a discount or at a premium? If you have no idea, read on.

FLOATING-RATE NOTES IN GENERAL

Interest payments on a standard floating-rate note adjust from period to period to reflect changes in a money market reference rate. The market for floaters started in the 1970s when interest rates began to rise due to "inflation creep," as it was called back then. Fixed-income bonds, which were seen to be boring compared to the excitement of the stock market, finally became interesting. Interest in bonds arose because conservative, buy-and-hold investors experienced losses, at least in terms of current market value, when yields to maturity went up. Floaters, first issued by commercial banks, were offered to investors as a way of "preserving capital value," meaning that they transferred interest rate risk from market value to future cash flows.

Consider a 10-year, floating-rate note making quarterly interest payments of 3-month LIBOR plus 0.50%. LIBOR is set at the beginning of each period, and the interest payment is made in arrears at the end of the period. In practice, the rate typically is set two business days prior to the start of the period. Although there might be a cap or floor on the interest rate, thereby setting a maximum or minimum payment, here we deal only with "straight floaters" that have no such embedded options. So, if 3-month LIBOR turns out to be 1.50%, the annual interest rate for the period is 2.00%. The interest payment for the quarter will be about $0.50 per $100 of par value, depending on the number of days in the period. Most FRNs use an actual/360 day-count in the U.S.; actual/365 is used in many other markets.

Notice that while the money market reference rate varies, the margin over LIBOR is fixed at 50 basis points. That's the key to understanding the market value volatility (i.e., duration) of the floater. LIBOR, the standard reference rate for U.S. dollar-denominated FRNs, captures *macroeconomic* factors (e.g., expected inflation, monetary policy, and general business conditions). Students are often surprised that one of the most important interest rates in the U.S. financial market is determined in London, not in New York. Moreover, most of the commercial banks that are surveyed each day to set LIBOR are not even headquartered in the U.S. The margin on the FRN, like the spread over the benchmark yield on a fixed-rate bond, captures *microeconomic* factors (e.g., credit risk of the issuer, liquidity, and taxation).

As long as this floater's "correct" margin continues to be 50 basis points, meaning no change in credit risk, liquidity, or taxation, the FRN will trade at par value on each coupon payment date. The 10-year floater is then the financial equivalent of rolling over a series of 40 short-term time deposits, each paying three-month LIBOR + 0.50%. Each time deposit is initially like a 3-month zero-coupon money market security having an annual Macaulay duration of about 0.25.

The usual presentation of the interest rate sensitivity of floaters makes the assumption of repricing at par value on each payment date. That is, the duration equals the time remaining in the coupon period. However, assuming no change in credit risk or liquidity severely limits our analysis. Although that assumption might be reasonable for government floaters, the U.S. Treasury has just started to issue FRNs in January of 2014. Most floating-rate notes in existence have been issued by financial institutions that can and do experience downgrades in their credit ratings (and even upgrades once upon a time). The liquidity of these FRNs can also change over time. Fortunately, we can use some bond math tools to build valuation models for floaters that do not necessarily reprice at par value. From those models, we can derive expressions for duration.

A SIMPLE FLOATER VALUATION MODEL

Remember from Chapter 3 that the reason why a fixed-rate bond trades at a premium or discount is that the coupon rate (what you are promised to receive from the issuer) is more or less than the yield to maturity (what you would need to pay par value). The same idea applies to a floating-rate note—the amount of the premium or discount is the present value of the difference between the fixed margin (the "quoted margin") over the reference rate and the required margin (which, following market terminology, is called the *discount margin*) in order for the floater to trade at par value. The quoted margin is what you get; the discount margin is what you need.

A simple model to value a floating-rate note is expressed in equation 7.1.

$$MV = \frac{\dfrac{(Index + QM) * FV}{PER}}{\left(1 + \dfrac{Index + DM}{PER}\right)^1} + \frac{\dfrac{(Index + QM) * FV}{PER}}{\left(1 + \dfrac{Index + DM}{PER}\right)^2} + \cdots + \frac{\dfrac{(Index + QM) * FV}{PER} + FV}{\left(1 + \dfrac{Index + DM}{PER}\right)^N}$$

$$(7.1)$$

Here MV = market value, *Index* = reference rate, QM = quoted margin, FV = future value, PER = periodicity, DM = discount margin, and N = number of periods to maturity. *Index*, QM, and DM are annual percentage rates. This is a simple model because: (1) MV is for a coupon reset date so that N is an integer (and there is no accrued interest), (2) it implicitly assumes a 30/360 day-count so that PER also is an integer; and (3) the same reference rate for *Index* is used for all future payments, implying that the yield curve is flat as is the forward curve. Despite these simplifications, the model can illustrate some interesting properties of FRNs.

Suppose that a 10-year floater that pays 3-month LIBOR + 0.50% quarterly is priced at 92 (percent of par value). Clearly, something has happened if the note was originally issued at par value. Probably that something is a credit rating downgrade—investors now require a higher spread over LIBOR than 50 basis points for this issuer. Assume that current 3-month LIBOR is 1.50%. We now can *estimate* the DM by substituting MV = 92, FV = 100, *Index* = 0.0150, QM = 0.0050, and N = 40 into equation 7.1.

$$92 = \frac{\dfrac{(0.0150+0.0050)*100}{4}}{\left(1+\dfrac{0.0150+DM}{4}\right)^{1}} + \frac{\dfrac{(0.0150+0.0050)*100}{4}}{\left(1+\dfrac{0.0150+DM}{4}\right)^{2}} + \cdots$$

$$+ \frac{\dfrac{(0.0150+0.0050)*100}{4}+100}{\left(1+\dfrac{0.0150+DM}{4}\right)^{40}}$$

Combining terms in the numerators, this becomes:

$$92 = \frac{0.50}{\left(1+\dfrac{0.0150+DM}{4}\right)^{1}} + \frac{0.50}{\left(1+\dfrac{0.0150+DM}{4}\right)^{2}} + \cdots$$

$$+ \frac{0.50+100}{\left(1+\dfrac{0.0150+DM}{4}\right)^{40}}$$

This is now a basic time-value-of-money problem where we can solve for the internal rate of return, y, as in equation 3.4 in Chapter 3.

$$92 = \frac{0.50}{(1+y)^1} + \frac{0.50}{(1+y)^2} + \cdots + \frac{0.50+100}{(1+y)^{40}}$$

The solution is that y is 0.7314%, or 0.007314. Therefore, $DM = 0.014256$.

$$0.007314 = \frac{0.0150 + DM}{4}, \quad DM = 0.014256$$

Because of the credit downgrade, investors now require an estimated spread of 142.56 basis points over LIBOR on the floater that is only paying 50 basis points.

Floating-rate notes require that we think differently about duration as a measure of interest rate sensitivity. On a traditional fixed-income bond, the yield duration statistic estimates the price change following a change in the yield to maturity. The cause of that yield change doesn't matter—it could be a credit rating downgrade or an increase in expected inflation. Floaters change that thinking. Now we need to assess separately the impact of a change in market interest rates, as captured by the reference rate (i.e., *Index*), and a change in the required spread (i.e., *DM*). The former is the *rate duration* and the latter the *credit duration*. These are also called the *index duration* and the *spread duration*, respectively.

The simple model can be used to estimate the rate and credit durations for the 10-year floater paying 3-month LIBOR + 0.50%. To get them, we'll use the approximate modified duration formula from Chapter 6. We could also get the rate and credit convexities, but I'll focus here only on the first-order effects (feel free to have fun with the bond math on your own!). To get the rate duration for the floater, bump the level for *Index* up and down by five basis points, from 1.50% up to 1.55% and down to 1.45%. The result for *MV(up)* is 92.019557; *MV(down)* turns out to be 91.980781. *MV(initial)* is 92.

$$MV(up) = \frac{\dfrac{(0.0155+0.0050)*100}{4}}{\left(1+\dfrac{0.0155+0.014256}{4}\right)^1} + \frac{\dfrac{(0.0155+0.0050)*100}{4}}{\left(1+\dfrac{0.0155+0.014256}{4}\right)^2} + \cdots$$

$$+ \frac{\dfrac{(0.0155+0.0050)*100}{4}}{\left(1+\dfrac{0.0155+0.014256}{4}\right)^{40}} = 92.019557$$

$$MV(down) = \frac{\frac{(0.0145+0.0050)*100}{4}}{\left(1+\frac{0.0145+0.014256}{4}\right)^1} + \frac{\frac{(0.0145+0.0050)*100}{4}}{\left(1+\frac{0.0145+0.014256}{4}\right)^2} + \cdots$$

$$+ \frac{\frac{(0.0145+0.0050)*100}{4}}{\left(1+\frac{0.0145+0.014256}{4}\right)^{40}} = 91.980781$$

Notice the QM of 0.50% and the DM of 1.4256% are held constant as the market reference rate is raised. Also, using the same rate for $Index$ for all future periods presumes a parallel shift to a flat yield curve. A key assumption implicit in the calculation of $MV(up)$ and $MV(down)$ is that the rate changes impact the next cash flow. Therefore, the shift occurs before the rate is set for the current time period.

We can now calculate the approximate rate duration for the floater, using a version of equation 6.18 for approximate annual modified duration.

$$Approximate\ Rate\ Duration \equiv \frac{MV(down) - MV(up)}{2 * \Delta Index * MV(initial)} \tag{7.2}$$

Substituting into equation 7.2 obtains the perhaps surprising result that the rate duration is negative at –0.4215.

$$Approximate\ Rate\ Duration = \frac{91.980781 - 92.019557}{2 * 0.0005 * 92} = -0.4215$$

First note that this is a small number, close to zero. That is to be expected for a floating-rate note. By design and intent, the investor should be protected from changes in benchmark interest rates. Intuitively, this is because both the numerator and denominator go up and down together as the flat yield curve shifts up and down. But the negative number implies that this FRN has a value that is positively correlated to market rates. This floater appreciates in value, albeit by a small amount, in rising-rate bear markets when virtually all other debt securities are depreciating. An interesting phenomenon!

Negative duration arises because this floater is trading at a discount. The amount of the discount is the present value of an annuity—the difference between the quoted margin and the required (or discount) margin. If credit quality deteriorates further, the annuity becomes larger and the price of the floater falls, just like a fixed-rate bond. If there is no further change in credit quality or liquidity, the size of the annuity remains the same. Then a higher benchmark rate (i.e., *Index*) reduces the present value of the annuity and the amount of the discount goes down. So, the floater's price goes up when the benchmark rate goes up—hence, negative duration. A lower benchmark yield raises the present value of the annuity, increasing the size of the discount. The price falls when the yield falls—again, negative duration. It's just the opposite when the FRN is priced at a premium. The rate duration is positive but still close to zero.

Now let's hold the benchmark rate constant and bump the discount margin to measure the impact of a change in credit quality. *Index* remains at 1.50% while *DM* is raised and lowered by five basis points, up from 1.4256% to 1.4756% and down to 1.3756%.

$$MV(up) = \frac{\frac{(0.0150 + 0.0050) * 100}{4}}{\left(1 + \frac{0.0150 + 0.014756}{4}\right)^1} + \frac{\frac{(0.0150 + 0.0050) * 100}{4}}{\left(1 + \frac{0.0150 + 0.014756}{4}\right)^2} + \cdots$$

$$+ \frac{\frac{(0.0150 + 0.0050) * 100}{4}}{\left(1 + \frac{0.0150 + 0.014756}{4}\right)^{40}} = 91.588461$$

$$MV(down) = \frac{\frac{(0.0150 + 0.0050) * 100}{4}}{\left(1 + \frac{0.0150 + 0.013756}{4}\right)^1} + \frac{\frac{(0.0150 + 0.0050) * 100}{4}}{\left(1 + \frac{0.0150 + 0.013756}{4}\right)^2} + \cdots$$

$$+ \frac{\frac{(0.0150 + 0.0050) * 100}{4}}{\left(1 + \frac{0.0150 + 0.013756}{4}\right)^{40}} = 92.413971$$

The approximate credit duration for the floater follows from equation 7.2.

$$Approximate\ Credit\ Duration \equiv \frac{MV(down) - MV(up)}{2 * \Delta DM * MV(initial)} \quad (7.3)$$

Substitute these results into equation 7.3 to get a credit duration of 8.9729.

$$Approximate\ Credit\ Duration = \frac{92.413971 - 91.588461}{2 * 0.0005 * 92} = 8.9729$$

This number should not be a surprise. From the perspective of credit risk, a 10-year floater represents the same risk as a 10-year fixed-rate bond. In the pricing equations, the numerators remain constant while the denominators go up and down. If the discount margin goes up by 1%, this floater will fall in value by about 9%, just like a fixed-rate bond having a modified duration of about 9.

The results of this section are all *estimates* based on a simple valuation model with simplifying assumptions. That is, the discount margin of 1.4256%, the rate duration of –0.4215, and the credit duration of 8.9729 are statistics conditional on the model on which they are based. Hence, there is *model risk*. If you change the assumptions to the model, you get different results. Next we'll relax some of those simplifying assumptions. This will allow for the derivation of closed-form equations for the discount margin and the rate duration.

A SOMEWHAT MORE COMPLEX FLOATER VALUATION MODEL

The simple model in the previous section valued the FRN on a coupon reset date and used the current observation of the reference rate for all future rates. Now we want to consider valuation on a date between interest payments and to allow for some shape to the yield curve. In particular, future cash flows are discounted at a long-term rate, not at the current money market rate. Relaxing these assumptions makes the model somewhat more complex and realistic, but still some accommodations need to be made to keep it tractable. Where possible, the notation follows what has been used in earlier chapters.

Consider a floating-rate note that resets its interest rate *PER* times per year. As of the beginning of the current period (date 0), the floater has Z years to maturity, or a total of $PER * Z$ periods. Let R_0 denote the reference index rate set for date 0 and QM the quoted margin that is added to the reference rate to get the interest payment. Interest is paid in arrears at the end the period, T days later. The interest payment *(INT)* is $(R_0 + QM)$ * *(T/Year)* * *FV*, where *Year* is the assumed number of days in the year and *FV* is the face (or par) value on the note.

Assume that the floater is priced for settlement on some date t in the current period. The fraction t/T of the period has gone by, and $1 - t/T$ remains. Let *DM* represent the fixed margin (i.e., the discount margin) that is required by investors as of date t for the note to trade at its par value on date 1 at the end of the current period. The total value of the FRN on date 1 is the interest payment that is determined on date 0 plus the price of the note on that date. That price is the par value plus the present value of the annuity representing the difference between DM and QM. Let y be the appropriate interest rate per period for discounting that annuity. As of date 1, there are $PER * Z - 1$ periods remaining until maturity.

The present value of the annuity as of date 1 is denoted PV_{ANN} and defined to be:

$$PV_{ANN} \equiv \left[\frac{\frac{(QM - DM) * FV}{PER}}{(1 + y)^1} + \frac{\frac{(QM - DM) * FV}{PER}}{(1 + y)^2} + \cdots + \frac{\frac{(QM - DM) * FV}{PER}}{(1 + y)^{PER*Z-1}} \right]$$

$$(7.4)$$

The annual amount of the surplus or deficient payment is $(QM - DM) * FV$. Dividing by PER to get the amount per period is a simplification because most FRNs use an actual/360 day-count. Therefore, the amount typically would vary slightly from period to period but in this case it is constant.

Equation 7.4 contains the sum of a finite geometric series and can be reduced to equation 7.5:

$$PV_{ANN} = \left(\frac{(QM - DM) * FV}{PER * y} \right) * \left[1 - \frac{1}{(1 + y)^{PER*Z-1}} \right] \quad (7.5)$$

PV_{ANN} is negative when $QM < DM$, meaning the quoted margin is deficient, most likely due to a credit rating downgrade or a loss in liquidity. Investors require a higher margin over the reference rate in order to pay par value on date 1, so the FRN trades at a discount. Similarly, PV_{ANN} is positive when $QM > DM$, so the floater trades at a premium.

The market value of the floater on date t—that is, the full price (including accrued interest)—is denoted MV. It is the forthcoming interest payment plus the price of the FRN on date 1, both discounted back over the remainder of the period at the yield per period.

$$MV = \frac{INT + FV + PV_{ANN}}{(1 + y)^{1-t/T}} \quad (7.6)$$

Here you can see that this still is a relatively simple model in that the same yield is used for all the discounted cash flows. You could argue that a better discount rate in equation 7.6 would be a short-term money market rate, but then the model is even more complicated.

Combining equations 7.5 and 7.6 provides a general valuation formula for the floater, given the discount margin.

$$MV = \frac{INT + FV + \left(\dfrac{(QM - DM) * FV}{PER * y}\right) * \left[1 - \dfrac{1}{(1+y)^{PER*Z-1}}\right]}{(1+y)^{1-t/T}} \quad (7.7)$$

A formula for DM given the current market value is obtained by rearranging equation 7.7.

$$DM = QM - \frac{MV * (1+y)^{1-t/T} - (INT + FV)}{\dfrac{FV}{PER * y} * \left[1 - \dfrac{1}{(1+y)^{PER*Z-1}}\right]} \quad (7.8)$$

A payoff from building this more complex model is to obtain a general formula for the Macaulay duration ($MacDurFRN$) of the floating-rate note for date t in the coupon period, as shown in equation 7.9. The details to the derivation are in the Technical Appendix, but in brief entail using calculus and algebra on the first derivative of MV in equation 7.7 given a change in the yield per period.

$$MacDurFRN = (1 - t/T) + \left(1 - \frac{INT + FV}{MV * (1+y)^{1-t/T}}\right) * \left(\frac{1+y}{y} - \frac{PER * Z - 1}{(1+y)^{PER*Z-1} - 1}\right) \quad (7.9)$$

We get to a numerical example of this equation in the next section, but for now let's examine the expression. Substitute equation 7.6 into equation 7.9 and rearrange the middle term.

$$MacDurFRN = (1 - t/T) + \left(\frac{PV_{ANN}}{MV * (1+y)^{1-t/T}}\right) * \left(\frac{1+y}{y} - \frac{PER * Z - 1}{(1+y)^{PER*Z-1} - 1}\right) \quad (7.10)$$

Although not obvious, the third term in parenthesis is always positive—it's the Macaulay duration of a fixed-payment annuity maturing in $PER * Z - 1$

periods. Therefore, the sign of the Macaulay duration for the FRN depends on the middle term. If $QM = DM$, $PV_{ANN} = 0$ and $MacDurFRN = 1 - t/T$. That is the standard result for a risk-free floater having no change in credit risk, liquidity, or taxation—the Macaulay duration is just the fraction of the period remaining until the next reset date. When $QM < DM$ and $PV_{ANN} < 0$, it's possible for $MacDurFRN$ to be negative, especially for long-term FRNs (so that $PER * Z$ is large) that are near a payment date (so that t/T nears 1). The corollary is that when $QM > DM$ because of a credit rating upgrade, $PV_{ANN} > 0$ and $MacDurFRN$ is greater than $1 - t/T$.

Figure 7.1 is my effort at illustrating this property of a floating-rate note. In the upper panel, $QM = DM$ so that there has been no change in the credit risk since issuance and the floater resets at par value on the next coupon payment date. Just before LIBOR is fixed for the period, the duration is 0; immediately after the fixing, the duration jumps up to 1. Then as t goes from 0 to T (moving right to left), the duration slides down the 45-degree line. When the fraction of the period gone by is t/T, for instance when there are $n + 1 - t/T$ periods remaining until maturity, the $MacDurFRN$ is $1 - t/T$. In the middle panel, $QM > DM$ and the floater will trade at a premium above par value on the next rate reset date. The key observation is the duration is above $1 - t/T$. In the lower panel, we see the possibility of negative duration when $QM < DM$. The FRN trades at a discount to par value. $MacDurFRN$ is less than $1 - t/T$ and could be below zero.

It's easy to get the modified duration for the floater from $MacDurFRN$— just divide by one plus the yield per period. The key point is that these are rate duration statistics, not credit duration. They indicate the change in value following a change in the benchmark interest rate, not in the spread over that rate. To see these equations in action, it's time to look at an actual floating-rate note.

AN ACTUAL FLOATER

On February 3, 2004, Citigroup Global Markets issued at par value a 17-year floating-rate note that pays 6-month LIBOR + 0.20%. Figure 7.2 displays its Bloomberg Description page. This is a Euro medium-term note (MTN) but is denominated in U.S. dollars. This floater resets the coupon rate semiannually and uses a 30/360 day-count. Most FRNs in the U.S. domestic issuance market reset quarterly, are tied to 3-month LIBOR, and accrue interest on an actual/360 basis.

Figure 7.3 presents the Bloomberg Yield and Spread Analysis (YAS) page for this floater for settlement on March 28, 2014. The (flat) price is

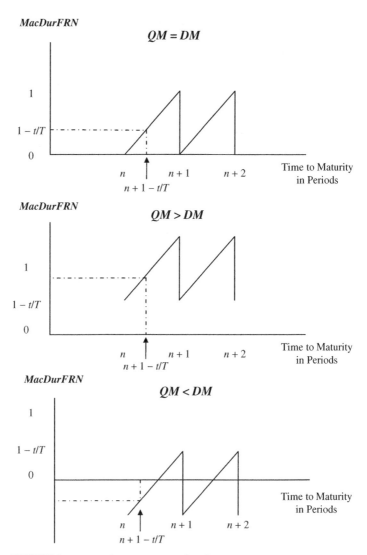

FIGURE 7.1   Macaulay Duration of a Floating-Rate Note

93.08 per 100 of par value. The FRN is trading at a discount because the quoted margin of 20 basis points is less than the discount margin, shown to be 127.372125 basis points. The settlement date is 55 days into the 180-day semiannual period.

The coupon rate for the current period is 0.537%. This rate was set at the beginning of the period on February 3, 2014 (actually it is set two

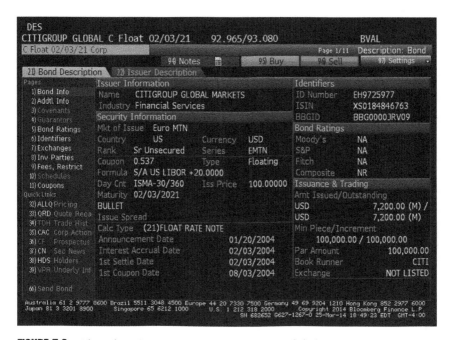

FIGURE 7.2 Bloomberg Description Page, Citigroup Global Markets Floating-Rate Note
Used with permission of Bloomberg.com © 2014. All rights reserved.

business days before). Presumably, 6-month LIBOR was 0.337%—that plus the quoted margin of 0.20% determines the interest rate for the period. The interest payment due at the end of the semiannual period is 0.2685 per 100 of par value: 0.00537 * 180/360 * 100 = 0.2685. The accrued interest is 0.082042 (= 55/180 * 0.2685). That plus the flat price of 93.08 gives a full price of 93.162042 per 100 of par value. The Bloomberg YAS page shows those amounts in the Invoice section for $1 million in face (or par) value.

Before trying to interpret some of the other numbers reported in Figure 7.3, let's use the somewhat more complex valuation model on this actual floater. The inputs to equation 7.8 to get the estimated discount margin are: $QM = 0.0020$, $MV = 93.162042$, $t/T = 55/180$, $INT = 0.2685$, $FV = 100$, $PER = 2$, $Z = 7$. The remaining parameter is y, the interest rate per period for discounting the annuity based on the difference between QM and DM. Fortunately, the Bloomberg page provides a quote for the Fixed Equivalent Yield at the bottom of the page corresponding to the maturity of the floater. That yield is determined by assuming the coupon rate on the floater is swapped to a synthetic fixed rate and then solving for the internal rate of return. It's

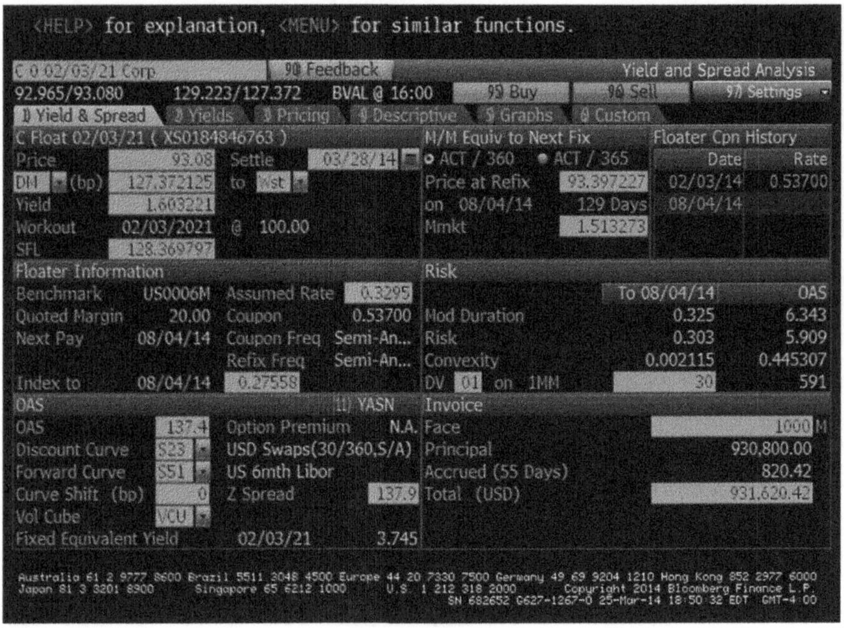

FIGURE 7.3 Bloomberg Yield and Spread Analysis Page (YAS), Citigroup Global Markets Floating-Rate Note, Settlement on March 28, 2014
Used with permission of Bloomberg.com © 2014. All rights reserved.

shown to be 3.745%. I'll presume it's on a semiannual bond basis so that $y =$ 0.018725 (= 3.745%/2).

$$DM = 0.0020 - \frac{93.162042 * (1.018725)^{1-55/180} - (0.2685 + 100)}{\frac{100}{2 * 0.018725} * \left[1 - \frac{1}{(1.018725)^{2*7-1}}\right]}$$

$$= 0.0123081$$

The model gives a discount margin of 123.081 basis points.

The same inputs can be used in equation 7.9 to estimate the Macaulay duration for the floater.

$$MacDurFRN = (1 - 55/180) + \left(1 - \frac{0.2685 + 100}{93.162042 * (1.018725)^{1-55/180}}\right)$$

$$* \left(\frac{1.018725}{0.018725} - \frac{2 * 7 - 1}{(1.018725)^{2*7-1} - 1}\right) = 0.273137$$

This is the duration in terms of semiannual periods; annualized it is 0.136569 (= 0.273137/2). The annualized modified duration is 0.134058 (= 0.136569/1.018725). This is the *rate duration* statistic—it indicates the sensitivity of the market value to changes in benchmark interest rates, in particular, to the yield used to discount future cash flows. As expected, it is close to zero.

This FRN is trading at a discount, so its duration is less than the time until the next reset date. In Figure 7.1 in the lower panel, the duration is sliding down the 45-degree line and might even become negative. As an experiment, suppose that the flat price and the Fixed Equivalent Yield remain the same as the next coupon date on August 4, 2014, nears. For instance, on July 4 there will be just one month to go so that $1 - t/T = 1 - 150/180$. The accrued interest goes up to 0.22375 (= 150/180 * 0.2685) per 100 of par value. The full price, that is, the market value, would be 93.30375.

$$MacDurFRN = (1 - 150/180) + \left(1 - \frac{0.2685 + 100}{93.30375 * (1.018725)^{1-150/180}}\right)$$

$$* \left(\frac{1.018725}{0.018725} - \frac{2 * 7 - 1}{(1.018725)^{2*7-1} - 1}\right) = -0.314124$$

Annualized, the modified duration would be –0.154175. Negative duration! Another approach to getting the risk statistics is to use the approximation formulas, as in equations 7.2 and 7.3. But first it is useful to show that the estimated discount margin of 123.081 basis points is consistent with the current market value. To do that, the inputs are substituted into equation 7.7.

$$MV = \frac{0.2685 + 100 + \left(\frac{(0.0020 - 0.0123081) * 100}{2 * 0.018725}\right) * \left[1 - \frac{1}{(1.018725)^{2*7-1}}\right]}{(1.018725)^{1-55/180}}$$

$$= 93.162042$$

This is no surprise at all because equations 7.7 and 7.8 are the same, just rearranged algebraically. This is *MV(initial)* in the approximation formulas.

Now let's raise and lower the Fixed Equivalent Yield by one basis point, up from 3.745% to 3.755% and then down to 3.735%. That entails changing y, the yield per semiannual period, to 0.018775 and to 0.018675, holding the discount margin and the other variables constant.

$$MV(up) = \frac{0.2685 + 100 + \left(\frac{(0.0020 - 0.0123081) * 100}{2 * 0.018775} \right) * \left[1 - \frac{1}{(1.018775)^{2*7-1}} \right]}{(1.018775)^{1-55/180}}$$

$$= 93.160793$$

$$MV(down) = \frac{0.2685 + 100 + \left(\frac{(0.0020 - 0.0123081) * 100}{2 * 0.018675} \right) * \left[1 - \frac{1}{(1.018675)^{2*7-1}} \right]}{(1.018675)^{1-55/180}}$$

$$= 93.163291$$

Substitute these results into equation 7.2 for the approximate rate duration.

$$Approximate\ Rate\ Duration = \frac{93.163291 - 93.160793}{2 * 0.0001 * 93.162042} = 0.134067$$

This is virtually the same number for modified duration that is obtained above starting with the closed-form formula for *MacDurFRN*.

Now we can use the same approach to estimate the credit duration. Raise and lower the discount margin by one basis point, up from 123.081 basis points to 124.081 and down to 122.081, holding all the other variables the same.

$$MV(up) = \frac{0.2685 + 100 + \left(\frac{(0.0020 - 0.0124081) * 100}{2 * 0.018725} \right) * \left[1 - \frac{1}{(1.018725)^{2*7-1}} \right]}{(1.018725)^{1-55/180}}$$

$$= 93.105553$$

$$MV(down) = \frac{0.2685 + 100 + \left(\frac{(0.0020 - 0.0122081) * 100}{2 * 0.018725} \right) * \left[1 - \frac{1}{(1.018725)^{2*7-1}} \right]}{(1.018725)^{1-55/180}}$$

$$= 93.218532$$

Substitute these into equation 7.3 for approximate credit duration.

$$Approximate\ Credit\ Duration = \frac{93.218532 - 93.105553}{2 * 0.0001 * 93.162042} = 6.063575$$

The somewhat more complex valuation model estimates these risk statistics for the Citigroup Global Markets floater: a low modified duration of 0.134 with respect to changes in market interest rates and a much higher modified duration of 6.064 with respect to changes in credit risk. The estimated discount margin is 123.081 basis points, significantly above the quoted margin of 20 basis points because the FRN is trading at a discount below par value.

Now let's see how those results compare to those on the Bloomberg YAS page. In Figure 7.3 the estimated discount margin is 127.372125 basis points. Two modified duration numbers are shown, 0.325 for the next rate reset date on August 4, 2014, and 6.343 for OAS duration. The former looks to be the sensitivity to interest rates (hence is a low number close to zero) and the latter the sensitivity to credit risk (hence a much higher number similar to a comparable maturity fixed rate bond).

Frankly, I'm disappointed with the differences between these reported results and those that I obtain. In the first edition of this book and in an earlier academic journal article where I first developed the FRN valuation model, my numbers and those reported on Bloomberg were very close and sometimes identical. I expect some variance for the discount margin because I use a single yield for discounting future cash flows and I understand that Bloomberg uses the forward curve. I have found that our DM results get closer when the yield curve gets flatter. Currently, the yield curve is rather steep, so the difference between 123 and 127 basis points is not unreasonable.

However, I cannot figure out how Bloomberg gets the reported modified duration statistics. I decided to try another settlement date for the same Citigroup Global Markets floater. Figure 7.4 shows the YAS page for settlement on April 17, 2014. The flat price is up a bit to 93.3 per 100 of par value, and the discount margin is down to 124.676965 basis points. The modified duration to the next reset date on August 4, 2014, is now 0.277. It appears to me that Bloomberg calculates this number as a small adjustment (perhaps in how days are counted) to the fraction of the year remaining in the coupon period. I suspect it will slide down toward zero as August 4 nears and then jump up after the coupon reset. It is as if its formula is the $1 - t/T$ term in equation 7.9 but does not include the terms that capture the effect of the bond being priced at a premium or discount.

The real shocker for me on this page is the OAS modified duration statistic of –0.107. How can it go from 6.343 on March 28 to –0.107 a few

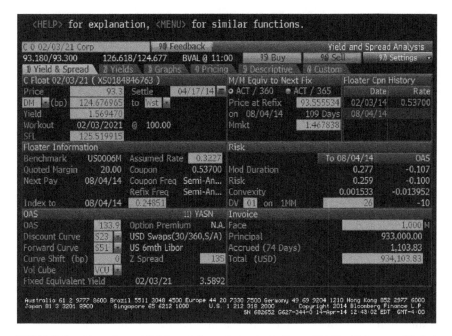

FIGURE 7.4 Bloomberg Yield and Spread Analysis Page (YAS), Citigroup Global Markets Floating-Rate Note, Settlement on April 17, 2014
Used with permission of Bloomberg.com © 2014. All rights reserved.

weeks later? We know that duration can be negative and that it changes as time passes and yields change, but not like that! I thought it reflected credit duration and was calculated by bumping the discount margin and using the approximation formula. Part of the mystery can be explained by looking at the YASN Floater Analysis page shown in Figure 7.5. Look at the Stochastic Risk section. This reports some of the Greeks (delta, gamma, vega) usually associated with options. [I've been known to tell classes with a serious face that "vega" is the new Greek letter discovered on a submerged urn recently found by some option traders while scuba diving off an island in the Aegean Sea.] It also reports the OAS modified duration to be 6.3180 and the Market modified duration to be −0.1068. Somehow the definition of OAS duration gets reversed between the YAS and YASN pages as −0.1068 is rounded to −0.107.

The moral of the story is the importance of being able to calculate these risk statistics using a simple, transparent model and not always having to rely on what is a "black box" to the user. If I owned this Citigroup floater, I'd use my own rate and credit duration numbers.

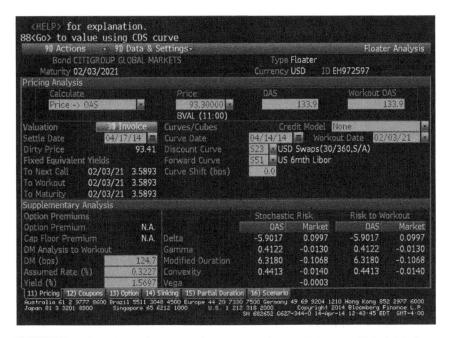

FIGURE 7.5 Bloomberg Floater Analysis Page (YASN), Citigroup Global Markets Floating-Rate Note, Settlement on April 17, 2014

INFLATION-INDEXED BONDS: C-LINKERS AND P-LINKERS

The market for inflation-indexed bonds (linkers) has grown enormously in the past 30 years. P-Linkers, for which the coupon rate is fixed and the principal is linked to changes in the consumer price index (ΔCPI), are usually issued by governments. These include U.S. Treasury TIPS (Treasury Inflation-Protected Securities), which have been available since 1997 and borrowed their design from linkers issued in the United Kingdom (1981), Australia (1983), and Canada (1991). C-Linkers are essentially floating-rate notes for which the principal is fixed and the variable coupon rate is linked to the ΔCPI. They tend to be issued by commercial banks and life insurance companies.

While inflation-adjusted linkers might seem to be straightforward securities, they are quite complex in theory and in practice. That's because inflation is arbitrarily measured and reported. There are many conceptual and political issues: Whose "consumption bundle" is measured for month-to-month price changes? When and how should that bundle be reweighted as new products are introduced and consumer spending patterns change?

Should the bundle be adjusted when consumers substitute one good for another because of relative price changes? How should quality improvements be handled, that is, buying a better widget that costs more and not just the same old widget at an inflated price? How is the cost of residential housing (a major household budget item) measured and included in the CPI? Does it matter that the government collects the data and calculates the official inflation rate that directly impacts the cost of its own debt? To focus on the bond math aspects of linkers, we'll neglect these issues and just assume that inflation is measured and reported accurately.

First, consider a highly stylized 2.50%, annual payment, 10-year P-Linker that adjusts the principal yearly based on the percentage change in the CPI. In practice, TIPS make semiannual interest payments and adjust the principal for the 2-month lagged ΔCPI—that lag makes it difficult to model intra-period valuation. Table 7.1 shows the nominal and real cash flows for the P-Linker assuming a low-inflation scenario. The CPI starts at 100 on date 0 and rises for arbitrarily chosen values to 118.752 on date 10 for an average annual inflation rate of 1.734%, including a couple of years of deflation. Inflation is calculated as the percentage change in the CPI from one year to the next. For instance, the inflation rate of 2.863% for the tenth year is 118.752/115.447 – 1.

TABLE 7.1 2.50%, 10-Year, Annual Payment P-Linker, Low-Inflation Scenario

Date	CPI	Inflation Rate	Accrued Principal	Nominal Cash Flow	Real Value
0	100.000		1,000.00	–1,000.00	–1,000.00
1	102.700	2.700%	1,027.00	25.68	25.00
2	105.233	2.466%	1,052.33	26.31	25.00
3	108.221	2.839%	1,082.21	27.06	25.00
4	107.988	–0.215%	1,079.88	27.00	25.00
5	107.820	–0.156%	1,078.20	26.96	25.00
6	108.223	0.374%	1,082.23	27.06	25.00
7	110.112	1.745%	1,101.12	27.53	25.00
8	112.338	2.022%	1,123.38	28.08	25.00
9	115.447	2.768%	1,154.47	28.86	25.00
10	118.752	2.863%	1,187.52	1,217.21	1,025.00
	Average Inflation Rate	1.734%	Internal Rate of Return	4.272%	2.500%

The accrued principal on a P-Linker is reported in Table 7.1 per $1,000 in par value. The key point is that the nominal interest payment each year is the fixed 2.50% coupon rate times the accrued principal. The $1,217.21 final payment at maturity is the accrued principal as of that date, $1,187.52, plus the interest payment, $29.69 (= 0.02 50 * $1,187.52). The real value deflates the nominal cash flow for the cumulative increase in the CPI since the base year. For the final payment, $1,217.21 is divided by 118.752/100 to get a real value of $1,025.00. The internal rates of return (IRR) are calculated for the nominal and real values assuming purchase at par value for $1,000—the cash flow on date 0 is negative to indicate an outflow to the investor. I use the IRR financial function in Excel to get those results.

Table 7.2 repeats the exercise assuming a high-inflation scenario, where the CPI rises from 100 to 240.805, resulting in an average inflation rate of 9.186%. Obviously, the nominal IRR is much higher. The salient point is that the real values of the cash flows for each date and the real IRR, overall, are the same in each scenario. That is the essence of inflation protection—to provide a predictable rate of return in real (i.e., after inflation) terms (assuming no default, of course). Note that the real yield of 2.50% is not really "locked in" because there still is coupon reinvestment risk

TABLE 7.2   2.50%, 10-Year, Annual Payment P-Linker, High-Inflation Scenario

Date	CPI	Inflation Rate	Accrued Principal	Nominal Cash Flow	Real Value
0	100.000		1,000.00	−1,000.00	−1,000.00
1	104.566	4.566%	1,045.66	26.14	25.00
2	110.823	5.984%	1,108.23	27.71	25.00
3	118.398	6.835%	1,183.98	29.60	25.00
4	128.005	8.114%	1,280.05	32.00	25.00
5	139.556	9.024%	1,395.56	34.89	25.00
6	161.363	15.626%	1,613.63	40.34	25.00
7	188.857	17.039%	1,888.57	47.21	25.00
8	211.312	11.890%	2,113.12	52.83	25.00
9	228.523	8.145%	2,285.23	57.13	25.00
10	240.805	5.375%	2,408.05	2,468.25	1,025.00
	Average Inflation Rate	9.186%	Internal Rate of Return	11.814%	2.500%

with respect to changes in future real rates of interest. Also, TIPS provide deflation protection as well because at maturity, the investor receives the accrued principal or par value, whichever is higher.

Second, consider a stylized annual payment C-Linker paying 2.50% plus the percentage change in the CPI (i.e., the inflation rate) for the year. C-Linkers in practice often make monthly interest payments. Tables 7.3 and 7.4 show the nominal and real cash flows for the annual payment C-Linker purchased at par value for the same low- and high-inflation scenarios. On date 3 in Table 7.3, the inflation rate for the third year is determined to be 2.839%, making the coupon rate 5.339% (= 2.50% + 2.839%). The nominal interest payment is $53.39, the coupon rate times the constant principal amount of $1,000. The following year experiences deflation—in particular, an inflation rate of –0.215%. The coupon rate is 2.285% (= 2.50% – 0.215%). C-Linkers offer protection in that the coupon rate will go no lower than zero if the deflation rate is more than 2.50%.

Notice that the cash flows are more front-loaded on the C-Linker than on the P-Linker. That is because the compensation for inflation on the C-Linker is paid as it is realized, whereas it is mostly deferred until maturity on the P-Linker. Three implications of this difference in the timing of cash

TABLE 7.3   2.50%, 10-Year, Annual Payment C-Linker Low-Inflation Scenario

Date	CPI	Inflation Rate	Coupon Rate	Nominal Cash Flow	Real Value
0	100.000			–1,000.00	–1,000.00
1	102.700	2.700%	5.200%	52.00	50.63
2	105.233	2.466%	4.966%	49.66	47.19
3	108.221	2.839%	5.339%	53.39	49.34
4	107.988	–0.215%	2.285%	22.85	21.16
5	107.820	–0.156%	2.344%	23.44	21.74
6	108.223	0.374%	2.874%	28.74	26.55
7	110.112	1.745%	4.245%	42.45	38.56
8	112.338	2.022%	4.522%	45.22	40.25
9	115.447	2.768%	5.268%	52.68	45.63
10	118.752	2.863%	5.363%	1,053.63	887.25
	Average Inflation Rate	1.734%	Internal Rate of Return	4.234%	2.458%

TABLE 7.4 2.50%, 10-Year, Annual Payment C-Linker High-Inflation Scenario

Date	CPI	Inflation Rate	Coupon Rate	Nominal Cash Flow	Real Value
0	100.000			−1,000.00	−1,000.00
1	104.566	4.566%	7.066%	70.66	67.57
2	110.823	5.984%	8.484%	84.84	76.55
3	118.398	6.835%	9.335%	93.35	78.85
4	128.005	8.114%	10.614%	106.14	82.95
5	139.556	9.024%	11.524%	115.24	82.58
6	161.363	15.626%	18.126%	181.26	112.33
7	188.857	17.039%	19.539%	195.39	103.46
8	211.312	11.890%	14.390%	143.90	68.10
9	228.523	8.145%	10.645%	106.45	46.58
10	240.805	5.375%	7.875%	1,078.75	447.97
	Average Inflation Rate	9.186%	Internal Rate of Return	11.227%	2.301%

flows are: (1) more coupon reinvestment risk with C-Linkers (more cash flow received sooner subject to fluctuation in real rates); (2) higher real rate durations with P-Linkers (longer times to the receipt of cash flow); and (3) less potential credit risk on C-Linkers, depending on the issuer (credit risk typically is an increasing function of time to the receipt of cash flow). These differences, along with taxation, are important when an investor has a choice between P-Linkers and C-Linkers.

Before turning to linker taxation, notice that the real IRR on the 2.50% C-Linker is lower than on the 2.50% P-Linker, even though both are purchased at par value. Given low inflation averaging 1.734%, the C-Linker underperforms by 4.2 basis points. For high inflation averaging 9.186%, the difference is 19.9 basis points. The reason for this is that the typical C-Linker does not provide complete inflation protection—the interest payment formula leaves out the cross-product between the inflation rate and the real rate in setting the nominal rate. Recall from Chapter 3 the relationship among the three rates: (1 + nominal rate) = (1 + real rate) * (1 + inflation rate). Multiplying the terms, this becomes: nominal rate = real rate + inflation rate + (real rate * inflation rate). The typical C-Linker only includes the first two terms.

Hopefully, investors are aware of the interest payment formula on typical C-Linkers and that deficiency is reflected in the market price, especially if high inflation rates are expected. In reality, some C-Linkers do include the cross-product. The U.S. Treasury issues retail-oriented Series I Savings Bonds (called *I-Bonds*). These nonmarketable, 30-year C-Linkers can be purchased at par value in small denominations of $25. The coupon interest rate is reset semiannually based on the ΔCPI, including the cross-product. Interest accrues over the lifetime of the I-Bond and is paid at redemption. These, like P-Linkers, have the same real IRR for all subsequent paths for inflation. But that is before taxes.

LINKER TAXATION

This discussion of the taxation of inflation-indexed bonds is going to be simplistic, especially after the detail of Chapter 4. The stylized P-Linker and C-Linker are assumed to be purchased at par value and held to maturity. There are no capital gains or losses and no *de minimis* OID, just ordinary income tax. My objective is to demonstrate that these two designs offering inflation protection generate very different after-tax cash flows. Moreover, when the inflation rate is high, the after-tax real rates of return become negative. That explains why linkers usually are held in tax-deferred, retirement portfolios like defined-benefit and defined-contribution pension funds.

Table 7.5 shows the after-tax cash flows on the 2.50%, annual payment, 10-year P-Linker assuming a 30% tax rate on ordinary income and the high-inflation scenario. On date 6, the inflation rate for the year reaches double digits, 15.626%, raising the accrued principal up to $1,613.63 from $1,395.56. The interest payment is $40.34 (= 0.0250 * $1,613.63). The tax obligation on the interest income is $12.10 (= 0.30 * $40.34). But P-Linker taxation does not stop there—the increase in the accrued principal is taxed as ordinary income in the current year even though that compensation for inflation is not received until maturity. This is another example of phantom income. The tax liability on the increase in the accrued principal is $65.42 [= 0.30 * ($1,613.63 – $1,395.56)]. The total tax obligation is $77.52 (= $12.10 + $65.42), resulting in an after-tax cash flow of –$37.18 (= $40.34 – $77.52).

Negative after-tax cash flows for the P-Linker start in the third year and last until maturity in this high-inflation scenario. A useful calculation for the investor is the *threshold inflation rate*, shown in equation 7.11, which indicates the point at which negative after-tax cash flows arise. It's derived in the Technical Appendix.

TABLE 7.5 After-Tax Cash Flows on the 2.50%, 10-Year, Annual Payment P-Linker, High-Inflation Scenario, 30% Tax Rate

Date	CPI	Inflation Rate	Accrued Principal	Before-Tax Cash Flow	Taxes Due	After-Tax Cash Flow	After-Tax Real Value
0	100.000		1,000.00	−1,000.00		−1,000.00	−1,000.00
1	104.566	4.566%	1,045.66	26.14	21.54	4.60	4.40
2	110.823	5.984%	1,108.23	27.71	27.08	0.62	0.56
3	118.398	6.835%	1,183.98	29.60	31.60	−2.01	−1.69
4	128.005	8.114%	1,280.05	32.00	38.42	−6.42	−5.02
5	139.556	9.024%	1,395.56	34.89	45.12	−10.23	−7.33
6	161.363	15.626%	1,613.63	40.34	77.52	−37.18	−23.04
7	188.857	17.039%	1,888.57	47.21	96.65	−49.43	−26.17
8	211.312	11.890%	2,113.12	52.83	83.21	−30.39	−14.38
9	228.523	8.14%5	2,285.23	57.13	68.77	−11.64	−5.09
10	240.805	5.375%	2,408.05	2,468.25	54.91	2,413.34	1,002.20
			IRR	11.814%		8.362%	−0.763%

$$Threshold\ Inflation\ Rate = \frac{Fixed\ Rate * (1 - Tax\ Rate)}{Tax\ Rate - Fixed\ Rate * (1 - Tax\ Rate)} \quad (7.11)$$

Fixed Rate is the coupon rate on the P-Linker, here 2.50%, and *Tax Rate* is the applicable rate on ordinary income, here 30%. Substituting those into equation 7.11 gives a threshold rate of 6.195%.

$$Threshold\ Inflation\ Rate = \frac{0.0250 * (1 - 0.30)}{0.30 - .0250 * (1 - 0.30)} = 0.06195$$

In general, the lower the fixed coupon rate and the higher the tax rate, the lower is the threshold inflation rate that results in negative after-tax cash flow.

The after-tax cash flows for the 2.50%, annual payment, 10-year C-Linker are shown in Table 7.6 for the same high-inflation scenario. For the sixth year when the inflation rate is 15.626%, the coupon rate is set at 18.126% (= 2.50% + 15.626%) and the interest payment is $181.26 per $1,000 in par value. The tax obligation is $54.38 (= 0.30 * $181.26), leaving

TABLE 7.6 After-Tax Cash Flows on the 2.50%, 10-Year, Annual Payment C-Linker, High-Inflation Scenario, 30% Tax Rate

Date	CPI	Inflation Rate	Coupon Rate	Before-Tax Cash Flow	Taxes Due	After-Tax Cash Flow	After-Tax Real Value
0	100.000			−1,000.00		−1,000.00	−1,000.00
1	104.566	4.566%	7.066%	70.66	21.20	49.46	47.30
2	110.823	5.984%	8.484%	84.84	24.45	59.39	53.59
3	118.398	6.835%	9.335%	93.35	28.01	65.35	55.19
4	128.005	8.114%	10.614%	106.14	31.84	74.30	58.04
5	139.556	9.024%	11.524%	115.24	34.57	80.67	57.80
6	161.363	15.626%	18.126%	181.26	54.38	126.88	78.63
7	188.857	17.039%	19.539%	195.39	58.62	136.77	72.42
8	211.312	11.890%	14.390%	143.90	43.17	100.73	47.67
9	228.523	8.145%	10.645%	106.45	31.93	74.51	32.61
10	240.805	5.375%	7.875%	1,078.75	23.62	1,055.12	438.16
			IRR	11.227%		7.975%	−0.819%

an after-tax cash flow of $126.88 (= $181.26 − $54.38). This is much more straightforward than the P-Linker—there is no taxable phantom income or negative after-tax cash flow.

The sad news is that both of these linkers are projected to deliver negative after-tax real IRRs. To be sure, the realized real rates of return will depend on actual real rates when the coupons are reinvested. These results ultimately depend on the particular price and rate assumptions. It's easy to put these stylized linkers onto a spreadsheet to see the impact of lowering the purchase price, raising the fixed coupon rate, lowering the tax rate, and lowering the average inflation rate. Those changes raise the after-tax real IRR and can make it a positive outcome. For instance, other things being equal, if the tax rate is less than 23.04% on this 2.50%, 10-year P-Linker, and less than 22.21% on the C-Linker, the after-tax IRRs are above zero. An individual investor can manage the tax problem by holding the linker in a tax-deferred, retirement savings account like a 401(k) or 403(b). Doing so won't make the tax obligation go away, but will allow the investment to compound at the before-tax real yield.

LINKER DURATION

Yield duration in Chapter 6 is defined as the sensitivity of the fixed-income bond price to a change in the nominal yield to maturity. Inflation-indexed bonds require that we focus on *why* the nominal rate changes and distinguish between a change in the real rate and a change in the inflation rate. Let's start by formalizing the stylized linkers, keeping close to the notation of Chapter 3. Let the nominal rate be y, the real rate r, and the inflation rate i. Also, let the number of periods to maturity be N, the fixed coupon rate c, the par (or face) value of the linker FV, and the current price PV. For these stylized linkers, we are on a coupon payment date so there is no accrued interest to sully the equations.

P-Linker valuation is based on the assumed path for the accrued principal. Given a constant inflation rate, this path will be $(1 + i) * FV, (1 + i)^2 * FV, \ldots,$ $(1 + i)^N * FV$. Then the price of the P-Linker, denoted PV_{PLINK}, is the present value of the cash flows, discounted at the nominal rate.

$$
PV_{PLINK} = \left[\frac{c * (1+i) * FV}{(1+y)^1} + \frac{c * (1+i)^2 * FV}{(1+y)^2} + \cdots + \frac{c * (1+i)^N * FV}{(1+y)^N} \right]
$$
$$
+ \frac{(1+i)^N * FV}{(1+y)^N} \tag{7.12}
$$

This equation is simplified using the standard relationship among the nominal, real, and inflation rates: $(1 + y) = (1 + r) * (1 + i)$.

$$PV_{PLINK} = \left[\frac{c*FV}{(1+r)^1} + \frac{c*FV}{(1+r)^2} + \cdots + \frac{c*FV}{(1+r)^N} \right] + \frac{FV}{(1+r)^N} \qquad (7.13)$$

This can be written more compactly as shown in equation 7.14.

$$PV_{PLINK} = \frac{c*FV}{r} * \left(1 - \frac{1}{(1+r)^N} \right) + \frac{FV}{(1+r)^N} \qquad (7.14)$$

The inflation rate drops out in equations 7.13 and 7.14, so the inflation duration for the stylized P-Linker is zero. That's because the first derivative of the pricing equation with respect to a change in the inflation rate is zero. In practice, the time between measuring the ΔCPI and changing the accrued principal (i.e., the indexation lag) matters, and the inflation duration for TIPS is close to but not exactly zero.

In equation 7.14, only changes in the real rate impact the market value of the P-Linker. Its Macaulay duration, derived in the Technical Appendix and denoted *RealMacDurPLINK* in equation 7.15, is going to look familiar to you.

$$RealMacDurPLINK = \frac{1+r}{r} - \frac{1+r+\left[N*(c-r)\right]}{c*\left[(1+r)^N - 1\right] + r} \qquad (7.15)$$

This is the same as equation 6.15 for the Macaulay duration of a standard fixed-rate bond on a coupon date (when $t/T = 0$). Real rate durations on TIPS are relatively high compared to Treasury notes and bonds for the same maturity because their fixed coupon rates and the real yields are relatively low. In general, the Macaulay yield duration statistic is inversely related to both the coupon rate and yield to maturity.

The present value of the C-Linker, PV_{CLINK}, assuming a constant inflation rate, is shown in equation 7.16.

$$PV_{CLINK} = \left[\frac{(i+c)*FV}{(1+y)^1} + \frac{(i+c)*FV}{(1+y)^2} + \cdots + \frac{(i+c)*FV}{(1+y)^N} \right] + \frac{FV}{(1+y)^N} \qquad (7.16)$$

The principal is fixed and the inflation rate simply is added to the fixed coupon rate without the cross-product term. The projected cash flows again are discounted using the nominal rate. In closed-form, this reduces to equation 7.17.

$$PV_{CLINK} = \frac{(i+c)*FV}{y} * \left(1 - \frac{1}{(1+y)^N}\right) + \frac{FV}{(1+y)^N} \qquad (7.17)$$

The real rate Macaulay duration for the C-Linker (*RealMacDurCLINK*) is derived in the Technical Appendix. It entails taking the first derivative of equation 7.17 with respect to changes in r, which is contained in y, and doing some algebraic manipulation.

$$RealMacDurCLINK = \frac{1+y}{y} - \frac{1+y+\left[N*(c-r*(1+i))\right]}{(c+i)*\left((1+y)^N - 1\right)+y} \qquad (7.18)$$

This equation has a similar structure to equation 7.15 for the P-Linker (and to equation 6.15 for the traditional fixed-rate bond). The key point is that, unlike the P-Linker, the real rate duration of the C-Linker is a function of the inflation rate, which enters the equation directly as i and indirectly in y. This will matter in Chapter 10 when we get to strategies, in particular, an immunization strategy that rests on matching the duration of the bond portfolio to some target. It will be much easier to implement such a strategy using P-Linkers than with C-Linkers.

The inflation Macaulay duration for the C-Linker (*InflationMacDurCLINK*) will turn out to be low but not equal to zero, even for these stylized securities. Equation 7.19 is derived in the Technical Appendix.

$$InflationMacDurCLINK = \frac{1+y}{y} - \frac{1+y+\left[N*(c-r*(1+i))\right]}{(c+i)*\left((1+y)^N - 1\right)+y} \qquad (7.19)$$

$$- \frac{(1+i)*\left((1+y)^N - 1\right)}{(c+i)*\left((1+y)^N - 1\right)+y}$$

Notice that the first two terms are the same as *RealMacDurCLINK*. The third term reduces *InflationMacDurCLINK*—sometimes all the way into negative territory. Some numerical examples will establish the circumstances when negative inflation duration occurs. It's not obvious from looking at equation 7.19.

Suppose that someday an inspired government offers a full array of long-term P-Linkers and C-Linkers. Perhaps this is to allow individuals to build low-risk retirement portfolios protected from inflation and deflation and hold them as either tax-deferred or currently taxable investments. Or perhaps the government seeks to assure holders of its traditional fixed-income debt that it has no intention of "inflating" its way out of its obligations. Assume that at present there are 20-year, annual payment P-Linkers and C-Linkers having coupon rates of 1.00%, 2.50%, and 4.00%. Investors require a real rate of 2.50%, so the 1.00% linkers trade at substantial discounts and the 4.00% linkers at substantial premiums. Assume that they originally were issued as 25-year or 30-year securities at par value and since then the real rates have been volatile. The 2.50%, 20-year linkers are the newly issued on-the-run offerings.

Table 7.7 shows the prices and Macaulay durations for these 20-year linkers given two inflation rates, 1.00% and 4.00%. For the real rate of 2.50%, the nominal rates are 3.525% (= 1.0250 * 1.01 – 1) and 6.60% (= 1.0250 * 1.04 – 1). The prices and durations are calculated by substituting $N = 20$, $FV = 100$, $r = 0.0250$, $i = 0.01$ or 0.04, $y = 0.03525$ or 0.0660, and $c = 0.01$, 0.0250, or 0.04 into equations 7.12, 7.13, 7.15, 7.16, and 7.17 (using a spreadsheet). There is a lot going on these numerical examples, so it is worthwhile to examine them closely.

First, notice that the prices and durations for the P-Linker are the same for both inflation rates. The Macaulay real rate durations are high, given the 20-year time to maturity, and are inversely related to the fixed coupon rate (as is a traditional fixed-rate bond). The modified real rate durations are easily calculated. For instance, the modified duration for the 1%, 20-year P-Linker is 17.464 (= 17.901/1.025). The inflation durations are all zero.

You might be questioning these prices for the P-Linker, thinking that if expected future inflation were to jump suddenly from 1.00% to 4.00%, the prices of P-Linkers such as TIPS surely would react. The demand for inflation-protected securities would go up, driving their prices up and the real rate down. So, if a change in inflation impacts the price of the P-Linker, how could its inflation duration be zero? Good point. Table 7.7 implicitly assumes that the real rate remains the same whereas your analysis has the real rate changing. However, how much so is estimated by the real rate duration statistic, not the inflation duration. Suppose you figure that the heightened demand for linkers will reduce the real rate by 10 basis points from 2.50% to 2.40%. The price of the 4%, 20-year P-Linker would go up from 123.384 by approximately 1.780, estimated by the modified real rate duration times the price times the change in the real rate.

The key point is that these real rate and inflation duration statistics are what we call *comparative static* properties of the security—we assume other variables are held constant when we change one in particular. In reality, when the nominal interest rate goes up or down, both inflation and

TABLE 7.7   Prices and Real Rate and Duration Macaulay Duration Statistics on 20-Year P-Linkers and C-Linkers

Inflation 1.00%, Real Rate 2.50%, Nominal Rate 3.525%			
Fixed Coupon Rate	**1.00%**	**2.50%**	**4.00%**
P-Linker			
Price (% of Par Value)	76.616	100.000	123.384
Real Rate Duration	17.901	15.979	14.786
Inflation Duration	0	0	0
C-Linker			
Price (% of Par Value)	78.375	99.645	120.916
Real Rate Duration	16.149	14.699	13.759
Inflation Duration	–2.125	0.326	1.915

Inflation 4.00%, Real Rate 2.50%, Nominal Rate 6.60%			
Fixed Coupon Rate	**1.00%**	**2.50%**	**4.00%**
P-Linker			
Price (% of Par Value)	76.616	100.000	123.384
Real Rate Duration	17.901	15.979	14.786
Inflation Duration	0	0	0
C-Linker			
Price (% of Par Value)	82.510	98.907	115.304
Real Rate Duration	12.336	11.689	11.225
Inflation Duration	–1.443	0.194	1.365

real rates change as well, but not necessarily by the same amount or in the same direction or in any consistent manner. One way of dealing with this is to calculate the duration of the linker with respect to the nominal rate and just *assume* some breakdown between the two component rates. That breakdown sometimes is called the "yield beta." For example, if you assume a yield beta of 0.50, you would get a nominal Macaulay duration for the 4% P-Linker of 7.393 (= 14.786/2). That means you assume that a 1.00%

change in the nominal rate is half due to inflation and that the other half is attributable to the real rate. In my opinion, this is a rather ad hoc approach. I think it is more insightful to work with the underlying real rate and inflation duration statistics.

Notice that the prices on the 2.50% C-Linker are less than par value even though the real rate is also 2.50%. That's because of the absence of the cross-product term. This effect is heightened when the inflation rate is higher. The real rate durations for the C-Linkers are high but still are lower than the corresponding P-Linker because, by design, the compensation for inflation is more front-loaded. That reduces the weighted-average time to the receipt of cash flow. Importantly, we now see that negative inflation duration occurs when the C-Linker is trading at a price sufficiently below par value.

The reason why discount C-Linkers have negative inflation duration and why premium C-Linkers have positive inflation duration is that they fundamentally are floating-rate notes. Their real rate durations are like the credit duration on a traditional floater; their inflation durations are like rate duration. The key difference is the location of the real rate. With a floater, it's in the nominal money market reference rate. With a C-Linker, it's in the fixed coupon rate along with compensation for credit and liquidity risk.

When the real rate goes up, the C-Linker trades at a discount. The amount of the discount is the present value of the annuity representing the deficiency in the fixed coupon. If there is no further change in the real rate, a drop in the inflation rate lowers the nominal rate used to get that present value. A lower discount rate increases the present value of the annuity, increasing the amount of the discount and lowering the price of the C-Linker. In sum, a lower inflation rate reduces the price—that's negative inflation duration.

Not understanding the inflation duration of C-Linkers could lead to real surprises for aggressive traders positioning a portfolio based on an expected level of inflation. Suppose that the trader's view is that inflation will go up by more than is generally expected by other market participants. Normally the trader is not particularly concerned whether bonds are trading at a discount or a premium. With C-Linkers, however, it definitely does matter—the trader would want to hold low-coupon C-Linkers trading at a discount and having negative inflation duration. If the view is toward lower-than-expected inflation, the trader prefers high-coupon, premium C-Linkers having positive inflation duration. The trader in each case also has to factor in the likely impact on real rates and use the real rate duration to assess the additional price change.

CONCLUSION

Floating-rate notes and inflation-indexed bonds demonstrate how we can employ a toolkit of bond math techniques to go beyond basic fixed-rate and zero-coupon securities. We have to extend our duration analysis to assess *why* the required rate of return changes and *how* that impacts market value. For floaters, changes in credit spreads and benchmark yields impact market value differently. For linkers, changes in the real rate and inflation have different impacts. Best of all, we can understand why and when floaters and linkers have negative duration. Now we can use the toolkit to delve into derivatives and the most commonly used product to manage fixed-income portfolios of assets or liabilities—interest rate swaps.

CHAPTER 8

Interest Rate Swaps

The unprecedented interest rate volatility in the United States in the 1970s and 1980s created demand for risk management products and strategies. Swaps emerged from that time period and since then have become the primary derivative contract used in practice to hedge interest rate risk. There are some actively traded fixed-income and interest rate futures contracts, in particular, on Treasury notes and bonds and on 3-month LIBOR, but swaps have come to dominate because of their flexibility and operational ease for many *end users*. End users are those entities (including financial institutions, investment funds, companies, universities, and state and local governments) that either want or need an interest rate derivative. It's surely a vast simplification, but I like to think that those who *want* derivatives essentially are *speculating* on rates and those who *need* them are *hedging* risk exposures. In reality, decisions regarding risk management often are a play between those two motivations, sometimes called *strategic hedging*.

Interest rate swaps are also a great product to illustrate bond math techniques. We focus on swap valuation in this chapter. The traditional method is called LIBOR discounting. Later in the chapter we see how the financial crisis of 2007 to 2009 has led to some significant changes in derivatives valuation and what is called OIS discounting. To start, I use basic bond math to show that a standard (or *plain vanilla*) fixed-for-floating swap can be priced initially and valued later using the implied spot and forward curves corresponding to the reference rate, that is, LIBOR. "Pricing" here means determining the fixed rate at issuance. Typically, it is set so that the initial value of the swap is zero to each of the two counterparties to the contract. Subsequently, as time passes and swap market rates change, the swap will take on positive value to one of the parties and an equal but negative value to the other. Swaps are what we call a zero-sum game—gains to one side are offset by the losses to the counterparty.

The primary risk statistics (i.e., duration in its various forms) for an interest rate swap are calculated by interpreting the derivative as a "long-short" combination of a fixed-rate and a floating-rate bond. To the party paying the fixed rate and receiving the floating rate, the swap has *negative duration*. The idea is that the swap has the same net cash flows as owning a (low-duration) floater financed by issuing a (higher-duration) fixed-rate bond. Because swaps are a zero-sum game, the counterparty receiving the fixed rate and paying the floating rate has a swap having positive duration. It's like owning a fixed-rate bond financed by issuing the floater.

We calculate the duration of the implicit fixed-rate bond in the interest rate swap using the equations developed in Chapter 6. Unfortunately, the general formula in Chapter 7 for the duration of a floater that might be trading at a premium or discount is not used with interest rate swaps. Market practice traditionally has been to assume that the floater always is priced at par value on payment dates—that dramatically simplifies its duration calculations.

PRICING AN INTEREST RATE SWAP

Figure 8.1 portrays an interest rate swap in the customary box-and-arrow format. Party A and Party B agree to exchange an interest rate that varies from period to period, specifically 3-month LIBOR (hence, it's the "floating" rate), for a fixed rate of 3.40% on a quarterly basis for two years. Net settlement payments are in arrears, meaning 3-month LIBOR is determined at the beginning of the period and then a payment for the rate difference, times the *notional principal*, times the fraction of the year, is made at the end of the period. Importantly, there is no exchange of principal at initiation or at maturity. That's why the principal is merely "notional"—it's the scale factor for the transaction.

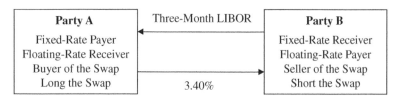

FIGURE 8.1 Two-Year, Quarterly Net Settlement, Interest Rate Swap 3.40% Fixed versus 3-Month LIBOR

Party A, the fixed-rate payer and floating-rate receiver, sometimes is said to be the "buyer" of the swap, or is "long" the swap. Party B, the fixed-rate receiver and floating-rate payer, then is the "seller" and is "short" the swap. In this context, the reference rate (here 3-month LIBOR) is the presumptive commodity, and the fixed rate is the price paid or received for it. In practice, Party A is often just called the *payer* and Party B is the *receiver*, referring to the fixed-rate leg of the transaction.

Settlement payments are easily calculated on interest rate swaps. They depend on the specific day-count convention, payment frequency, and the amount of notional principal. For simplicity, I assume quarterly settlements on a 30/360 basis for both rates, although actual/360 is common with actual transactions. Suppose the notional principal is $60 million and 3-month LIBOR is 2.25%. Party A owes its counterparty $172,500 at the end of the quarter.

$$(3.40\% - 2.25\%) * (90/360) * \$60,000,000 = \$172,500$$

If 3-month LIBOR is 3.90%, Party B owes $75,000.

$$(3.90\% - 3.40\%) * (90/360) * \$60,000,000 = \$75,000$$

Where does the fixed rate of 3.40% on this 2-year interest rate swap come from? The answer is that it is the "average" of the first two years of the forward curve, specifically the sequence of forward rates on 3-month LIBOR. Where those come from is the real challenging question that I get to later. For now, let's take as given the rates in Table 8.1. The notation is

TABLE 8.1 Initial 3-Month LIBOR Forward Curve and Calculated Implied Spot Rates and Discount Factors

Time Period	Forward Rates	Time Period	Implied Spot Rates	Discount Factors
0 × 3	0.5000%	0 × 3	0.5000%	0.998752
3 × 6	1.5821%	0 × 6	1.0407%	0.994817
6 × 9	2.6694%	0 × 9	1.5829%	0.988222
9 × 12	3.7647%	0 × 12	2.1272%	0.979008
12 × 15	3.7468%	0 × 15	2.4506%	0.969922
15 × 18	4.4047%	0 × 18	2.7756%	0.959358
18 × 21	5.0696%	0 × 21	3.1025%	0.947352
21 × 24	5.7427%	0 × 24	3.4316%	0.933943

the same as in Chapter 5 for implied forwards. The 3 × 6 forward rate of 1.5821% means the 3-month rate on a transaction between months 3 and 6—the first number is the starting month and the second the ending month. The 21 × 24 forward rate of 5.7427% means the 3-month rate between months 21 and 24. (Alternate notation for these forward rates is 3m3m and 21m3m, where the first number is the forward time period and the second is the tenor of the rate.) The rates are annualized as usual, all for a periodicity of 4 because of the assumed 30/360 day-count. This forward curve is quite steep. A true believer in the expectations theory is expecting a dramatic jump in rates over the next year. Also, notice the quirky 12 × 15 rate—the forward curve is not always smooth or monotonically increasing or decreasing.

These forward rates can be used to bootstrap the sequence of implied spot rates, which also are shown in Table 8.1. They are annual rates for quarterly compounding, same as the LIBOR forwards. Technically, they are computed as the *geometric average* of the forward rates. A few examples illustrate the process.

$$\left(1+\frac{0.005000}{4}\right) * \left(1+\frac{0.015821}{4}\right) = \left(1+\frac{Spot_{0\times6}}{4}\right)^2, \quad Spot_{0\times6} = 0.010407$$

$$\left(1+\frac{0.010407}{4}\right)^2 * \left(1+\frac{0.026694}{4}\right) = \left(1+\frac{Spot_{0\times9}}{4}\right)^3, \quad Spot_{0\times9} = 0.015829$$

$$\left(1+\frac{0.015829}{4}\right)^3 * \left(1+\frac{0.037647}{4}\right) = \left(1+\frac{Spot_{0\times12}}{4}\right)^4, \quad Spot_{0\times12} = 0.021272$$

Notice the bootstrapping—the result for one time frame is used as an input in the next as we move out along the term structure of spot rates.

The "average" of the 3-month LIBOR forward curve is the solution for *SFR* (swap fixed rate) in the lengthy expression to follow. The idea is that each forward rate is "monetized" by multiplying by the notional principal (assumed to be 100) and by the fraction of the year (0.25). That amount is discounted using the corresponding implied spot rate. *SFR*, which is the same for every period, is "monetized" as well using the same notional principal, the same day-count factors, and the same spot rates.

$$\frac{0.5000\% * 100 * 0.25}{\left(1 + \dfrac{0.005000}{4}\right)^{1}} + \frac{1.5821\% * 100 * 0.25}{\left(1 + \dfrac{0.010407}{4}\right)^{2}} + \frac{2.6694\% * 100 * 0.25}{\left(1 + \dfrac{0.015829}{4}\right)^{3}}$$

$$+ \frac{3.7647\% * 100 * 0.25}{\left(1 + \dfrac{0.021272}{4}\right)^{4}} + \frac{3.7468\% * 100 * 0.25}{\left(1 + \dfrac{0.024506}{4}\right)^{5}} + \frac{4.4047\% * 100 * 0.25}{\left(1 + \dfrac{0.027756}{4}\right)^{6}}$$

$$+ \frac{5.0696\% * 100 * 0.25}{\left(1 + \dfrac{0.031025}{4}\right)^{7}} + \frac{5.7427\% * 100 * 0.25}{\left(1 + \dfrac{0.034316}{4}\right)^{8}}$$

$$= \frac{SFR * 100 * 0.25}{\left(1 + \dfrac{0.005000}{4}\right)^{1}} + \frac{SFR * 100 * 0.25}{\left(1 + \dfrac{0.010407}{4}\right)^{2}} + \frac{SFR * 100 * 0.25}{\left(1 + \dfrac{0.015829}{4}\right)^{3}} + \frac{SFR * 100 * 0.25}{\left(1 + \dfrac{0.021272}{4}\right)^{4}}$$

$$+ \frac{SFR * 100 * 0.25}{\left(1 + \dfrac{0.024506}{4}\right)^{5}} + \frac{SFR * 100 * 0.25}{\left(1 + \dfrac{0.027756}{4}\right)^{6}} + \frac{SFR * 100 * 0.25}{\left(1 + \dfrac{0.031025}{4}\right)^{7}} + \frac{SFR * 100 * 0.25}{\left(1 + \dfrac{0.034316}{4}\right)^{8}}$$

For the 2-year swap on 3-month LIBOR, *SFR* = 3.40%.

The key idea in this swap pricing equation is that the forward curve indicates the sequence of "hedge-able" future 3-month spot rates. The no-arbitrage condition is that the present values of each leg of the swap are equal. Therefore, the initial value of the interest rate swap is zero to both counterparties. Notice that if we included the costs and risks of hedging the future spot rates, our forward *curve* would become a forward *cone* or *cylinder*. Then we would not get a precise answer; instead we would have a range for the swap fixed rate. Another way of expressing this is that 3.40% is the *mid-market rate* around which a swap market maker will build the bid-ask spread to reflect the costs and risks of hedging.

This approach portrays a general model of swap pricing that clearly begs for spreadsheet analysis using the discount factors instead of the spot rates. Recall from Chapter 5 that spot rates and discount factors contain the same information. Spot rates are more visual in that it is easier to see the discounting process at work, whereas discount factors lend themselves to the precision produced on a spreadsheet. Using the discount factors in

Table 8.1, which are calculated using equation 5.9, the same swap fixed rate is obtained: SFR = 3.40%.

$$(0.5000\% * 100 * 0.25 * 0.998752) + (1.5821\% * 100 * 0.25 * 0.994817)$$
$$+ (2.6694\% * 100 * 0.25 * 0.988222) + (3.7647\% * 100 * 0.25 * 0.979008)$$
$$+ (3.7468\% * 100 * 0.25 * 0.969922) + (4.4047\% * 100 * 0.25 * 0.959358)$$
$$+ (5.0696\% * 100 * 0.25 * 0.947352) + (5.7427\% * 100 * 0.25 * 0.933943)$$

$$=$$

$$(SFR * 100 * 0.25 * 0.998752) + (SFR * 100 * 0.25 * 0.994817)$$
$$+ (SFR * 100 * 0.25 * 0.988222) + (SFR * 100 * 0.25 * 0.979008)$$
$$+ (SFR * 100 * 0.25 * 0.969922) + (SFR * 100 * 0.25 * 0.959358)$$
$$+ (SFR * 100 * 0.25 * 0.947352) + (SFR * 100 * 0.25 * 0.933943)$$

This is a 2-year *plain vanilla swap* in that the notional principal is constant and the transaction starts immediately. We could have the notional principal vary from period to period or even be zero for the first few periods. The same pricing model can be used to calculate the fixed rate for such "flavored" varieties as a *varying notional principal swap* or a *forward-starting swap*. The principle is that the swap fixed rate is the "average" of the relevant segment of the LIBOR forward curve, appropriately weighted. Notice that I'm neglecting transactions costs and counterparty credit risk in these calculations.

Where does the forward curve for the reference rate come from? It could be the sequence of implied forward rates, as calculated in Chapter 5, given a series of cash market bonds issued by banks. However, there is a Eurodollar futures contract on 3-month LIBOR, and the observed rates from that futures market serve as a foundation for the forward curve. In general, market makers set the bid-and-ask rates on over-the-counter (OTC) derivatives such as forwards and swaps based on the cost and risk of the most efficient way of hedging risk. When available, actively traded futures contracts offer the best hedge. When a commercial bank is the OTC market maker, it is in effect a financial risk intermediary between an end user and the futures exchange.

INTEREST RATE FORWARDS AND FUTURES

There is a very important difference between interest rate forwards and futures that matters for bond math. This has to do with the timing of the gains and losses on the contracts. Suppose that in June 2014 a hedge fund asks a commercial bank for pricing on a 60 × 63 OTC forward contract on 3-month LIBOR—these exist and are called *forward rate agreements* (FRAs). That FRA is essentially a bet on the level of 3-month LIBOR in June 2019. The bank in turn observes that June 2019 Eurodollar futures are trading at price index of 94.00, implying a futures rate of 6.00%. (In this market, the price index is 100 minus the rate.) If the bank sets the cost and risk of hedging the OTC forward over the five years at 4 basis points, would the bank show the hedge fund a bid FRA rate of 5.98% and an ask rate of 6.02%? That means the bank would be willing to "buy" LIBOR in the future, paying 5.98%, or to "sell" LIBOR, receiving 6.02%.

The answer is no, those forward rates are too high. An *adjustment factor* first must be subtracted from the futures rate. The amount of that adjustment is a subject of advanced bond math theory and goes well beyond this book. To do justice to this problem, we really would need to study theoretical term structure models that often are named after their developers (e.g., the Ho-Lee model, the Heath-Jarrow-Morton model, the Hull-White model, the Black-Derman-Toy model). A problem is that each model gives a somewhat different adjustment factor.

Equation 8.1 is an example of the relationship between the forward and futures rates based on the Ho-Lee model.

$$Forward\ Rate = Futures\ Rate - (1/2 * Variance * Time1 * Time2) \quad (8.1)$$

The rates are stated for continuous compounding. *Variance* is the square of the standard deviation of daily changes in the reference rate (3-month LIBOR), and *Time1* and *Time2* are the years to the forward dates (for a 60 × 63 forward, 5.00 and 5.25 years). Suppose the standard deviation is 0.012 and the observed futures rate is 6.00% (annualized for a periodicity of 4). Equation 2.3 from Chapter 2 converts that rate to 5.9554% for continuous compounding.

$$APR_\infty = 4 * LN\left(1 + \frac{0.0600}{4}\right) = 0.059554$$

The Ho-Lee adjusted forward rate is 5.7664%.

$$Forward\ Rate = 0.059554 - [1/2 * (0.012)^2 * 5.00 * 5.25] = 0.057664$$

Equation 2.4 converts that rate back to a conventional quote for 3-month LIBOR of 5.8082%.

$$APR_4 = 4 * EXP\left(\frac{0.057664}{4}\right) - 1 = 0.058082$$

Therefore, given these assumptions, the adjustment factor is 19.2 basis points for the 5-year forward (0.06000 − 0.05808 = 0.00192). For the same standard deviation, the adjustment is only 3.3 basis points for a 2-year forward but 74.8 basis points for a 10-year forward. The longer the time frame, the more significant is the adjustment factor.

Why is the forward interest rate lower than the otherwise comparable futures rate? The key idea is that the gains and losses on an OTC forward contract are realized in a lump sum at the future delivery date. In contrast, the gains and losses on an exchange-traded futures contract are realized day by day over the lifetime of the transaction. The salient feature of the futures market is daily mark-to-market valuation and settlement into a margin account. That allows for the potential to invest gains and perhaps the need to finance losses. Usually there is no persistent pattern of correlation between market interest rates and the payoffs on a commodity, stock index, or foreign exchange futures contract. However, one-to-one correlation between gains and losses and changes in market rates is the essence of an interest rate futures contract, such as the one on 3-month LIBOR.

Suppose the commercial bank market maker is pricing the bid side of the 60 × 63 FRA. That is, the bank commits to "buy" LIBOR on a forward basis, paying a preset "price." The risk is that LIBOR turns out to be less than that fixed rate, so the hedge is to go long June 2019 Eurodollars futures. The problem is that gains occur on days when the futures price rises and the rate goes down; losses occur on days when the price falls and the rate rises. Systematically, the bank hedging its risk on the OTC forward gets to invest when rates are lower and might have to finance losses when rates are higher. The opposite scenario plays out when the bank is pricing the ask side of the FRA. The futures hedge is to go short; thereby the bank is able to invest gains when rates rise (and the futures price falls) and to finance losses when rates fall (and the futures price rises).

Both circumstances of hedging the OTC contract with exchange-traded futures have the effect of dragging the forward rate down. On the bid side, the hedge is "bad," so the pay-fixed rate on the FRA is lowered relative to the futures rate as compensation. On the ask side, the hedge is "good" and the received-fixed rate is lowered due to market competition. How much lower depends on the anticipated volatility of rates and the time frame. That is evident in the Ho-Lee adjustment factor shown in equation 8.1. A more developed model also could include a term for the correlation between the short-term rate driving the gains and losses on the futures contract (e.g., 3-month LIBOR) and the long-term rate representing the time to the delivery date on the forward contract.

INFERRING THE FORWARD CURVE

Suppose that you do not have access to a term structure model or the requisite adjustment to the futures rates. You still can infer the LIBOR forward curve if you observe the fixed rates on plain vanilla interest rate swaps. For example, suppose that you know the current level of 3-month LIBOR is 0.50% and that the fixed rates on 1-year and 2-year swaps are 2.12% and 3.40%. These swaps are for quarterly settlements and 30/360 day-counts. Suppose further that you observe the full range for the intermediate-maturity swaps: The 0.50-year fixed rate is 1.04%, the 0.75-year is 1.58%, the 1.25-year is 2.44%, the 1.50-year is 2.76%, and the 1.75-year is 3.08%.

Okay, it is incredibly unrealistic that you could observe all these swap fixed rates. In practice, commercial banks making markets in swaps quote fixed rates for standard time frames, such as for the 1-year and 2-year contracts. Typically, you will need to *interpolate* to get the other rates. Suppose you use simple straight-line interpolation, adding 54 basis points to the observed level of 3-month LIBOR to get 1.04% and 1.58% and then 32 basis points for each quarter in the second year to go from 2.12% to 3.40%. This is clearly arbitrary and adds *model risk* to the analysis.

Given these observed or interpolated swap fixed rates, we can dip into our bond math toolkit to infer the LIBOR forward curve. The trick is to transform these swaps into bonds by adding 100 in par value to date 0 and to the maturity date and then use the bootstrapping technique from Chapter 5 to get the implied spot rates. Here are the equations to solve for the series of spot ($Spot$) rates, quoted in terms of months. $Spot_{0\times6}$ is the 6-month rate as of today (day 0); $Spot_{0\times9}$ is the 9-month rate, and so forth.

$$100 = \frac{1.04/4}{\left(1+\dfrac{0.0050}{4}\right)} + \frac{1.04/4+100}{\left(1+\dfrac{Spot_{0\times6}}{4}\right)^2}, \quad Spot_{0\times6} = 0.010407$$

$$100 = \frac{1.58/4}{\left(1+\dfrac{0.0050}{4}\right)} + \frac{1.58/4}{\left(1+\dfrac{0.010407}{4}\right)^2} + \frac{1.58/4+100}{\left(1+\dfrac{Spot_{0\times9}}{4}\right)^3}, \quad Spot_{0\times9} = 0.015829$$

$$100 = \frac{2.12/4}{\left(1+\dfrac{0.0050}{4}\right)} + \frac{2.12/4}{\left(1+\dfrac{0.010407}{4}\right)^2} + \frac{2.12/4}{\left(1+\dfrac{0.015829}{4}\right)^3} + \frac{2.12/4+100}{\left(1+\dfrac{Spot_{0\times12}}{4}\right)^4},$$

$$Spot_{0\times12} = 0.021272$$

$$100 = \frac{2.44/4}{\left(1+\dfrac{0.0050}{4}\right)} + \frac{2.44/4}{\left(1+\dfrac{0.010407}{4}\right)^2} + \frac{2.44/4}{\left(1+\dfrac{0.015829}{4}\right)^3}$$

$$+ \frac{2.44/4}{\left(1+\dfrac{0.021272}{4}\right)^4} + \frac{2.44/4+100}{\left(1+\dfrac{Spot_{0\times15}}{4}\right)^5}, \quad Spot_{0\times15} = 0.024506$$

$$100 = \frac{2.76/4}{\left(1+\dfrac{0.0050}{4}\right)} + \frac{2.76/4}{\left(1+\dfrac{0.010407}{4}\right)^2} + \frac{2.76/4}{\left(1+\dfrac{0.015829}{4}\right)^3} + \frac{2.76/4}{\left(1+\dfrac{0.021272}{4}\right)^4}$$

$$+ \frac{2.76/4}{\left(1+\dfrac{0.024506}{4}\right)^5} + \frac{2.76/4+100}{\left(1+\dfrac{Spot_{0\times18}}{4}\right)^6},$$

$$Spot_{0\times18} = 0.027756$$

$$100 = \frac{3.08/4}{\left(1+\dfrac{0.0050}{4}\right)} + \frac{3.08/4}{\left(1+\dfrac{0.010407}{4}\right)^2} + \frac{3.08/4}{\left(1+\dfrac{0.015829}{4}\right)^3} + \frac{3.08/4}{\left(1+\dfrac{0.021272}{4}\right)^4}$$

$$+ \frac{3.08/4}{\left(1+\dfrac{0.024506}{4}\right)^5} + \frac{3.08/4}{\left(1+\dfrac{0.027756}{4}\right)^6} + \frac{3.08/4+100}{\left(1+\dfrac{Spot_{0\times21}}{4}\right)^7},$$

$$Spot_{0\times21} = 0.031025$$

$$100 = \frac{3.40/4}{\left(1+\dfrac{0.0050}{4}\right)} + \frac{3.40/4}{\left(1+\dfrac{0.010407}{4}\right)^2} + \frac{3.40/4}{\left(1+\dfrac{0.015829}{4}\right)^3} + \frac{3.40/4}{\left(1+\dfrac{0.021272}{4}\right)^4}$$

$$+ \frac{3.40/4}{\left(1+\dfrac{0.024506}{4}\right)^5} + \frac{3.40/4}{\left(1+\dfrac{0.027756}{4}\right)^6} + \frac{3.40/4}{\left(1+\dfrac{0.031025}{4}\right)^7} + \frac{3.40/4+100}{\left(1+\dfrac{Spot_{0\times24}}{4}\right)^8},$$

$$Spot_{0\times24} = 0.034316$$

Can you imagine doing these types of repetitive calculations in the olden days before spreadsheets and being able to do the bootstrapping with discount factors? Anyway, now we have the implied spots, all annualized for the same periodicity. We can use equation 5.4 from Chapter 5 to get the sequence of implied forward rates.

$$Rate_{3\times6} = \left(\frac{\left(1+\dfrac{0.010407}{4}\right)^2}{\left(1+\dfrac{0.005000}{4}\right)^1} - 1 \right) * 4 = 0.015821$$

$$Rate_{6\times9} = \left(\frac{\left(1+\dfrac{0.015829}{4}\right)^3}{\left(1+\dfrac{0.010407}{4}\right)^2} - 1 \right) * 4 = 0.026694$$

$$Rate_{9\times12} = \left(\frac{\left(1+\dfrac{0.021272}{4}\right)^4}{\left(1+\dfrac{0.015829}{4}\right)^3} - 1 \right) * 4 = 0.037647$$

$$Rate_{12\times15} = \left(\frac{\left(1+\dfrac{0.024506}{4}\right)^5}{\left(1+\dfrac{0.021272}{4}\right)^4} - 1 \right) * 4 = 0.037468$$

$$Rate_{15\times18} = \left(\frac{\left(1+\dfrac{0.027756}{4}\right)^6}{\left(1+\dfrac{0.024506}{4}\right)^5} - 1 \right) * 4 = 0.044047$$

$$Rate_{18\times21} = \left(\frac{\left(1+\dfrac{0.031025}{4}\right)^7}{\left(1+\dfrac{0.027756}{4}\right)^6} - 1 \right) * 4 = 0.050696$$

$$Rate_{21\times24} = \left(\frac{\left(1+\dfrac{0.034316}{4}\right)^8}{\left(1+\dfrac{0.031025}{4}\right)^7} - 1 \right) * 4 = 0.057427$$

You'll notice that this forward curve on 3-month LIBOR turns out to be the same as in Table 8.1—this is how I put together the example on my spreadsheet. There are two points to this exercise. First, implied spot rates can be bootstrapped by working either *down* from the forward curve or *up* from the cash market for fixed-coupon securities (I'm envisioning upwardly sloped curves). Second, and more important, this demonstrates how we can infer the forward curve that is consistent with observed (and, likely, interpolated) swap fixed rates. That provides the inputs needed to price nonvanilla swaps.

Suppose a corporation plans to issue at par value a 1-year, fixed-rate bond in three months to refinance some maturing debt. This is a classic *pre-issuance* interest rate risk management problem. The risk is that market rates jump up unexpectedly prior to issuance, raising the coupon rate on the new debt. "Unexpectedly" here is important; nothing can be done about widely anticipated rate changes because they already are priced into the derivatives that might be used to hedge the risk. The corporation could sell some interest rate futures contracts but a commonly used strategy is to enter a 3 × 15 *forward-starting swap* as the fixed-rate payer. This is a 1-year swap that starts in three months. In practice, this might be referred to as the *3m1y* forward swap.

A concern for the corporate treasurer is that this is not a plain vanilla swap having a widely quoted fixed rate. Suppose a commercial bank offers to "sell" the swap to the corporation for a fixed rate of 2.98%. Is that reasonable pricing? You only know for sure that 3-month LIBOR is 0.50% and that 1-year and 2-year vanilla swaps are at 2.12% and 3.40% but you assume it is reasonable to use straight-line interpolation between those observed rates. Given your now fully loaded bond math toolkit, you can set up and solve this equation.

$$\frac{1.5821\% * 100 * 0.25}{\left(1 + \dfrac{0.010407}{4}\right)^2} + \frac{2.6694\% * 100 * 0.25}{\left(1 + \dfrac{0.015829}{4}\right)^3}$$

$$+ \frac{3.7647\% * 100 * 0.25}{\left(1 + \dfrac{0.021272}{4}\right)^4} + \frac{3.7468\% * 100 * 0.25}{\left(1 + \dfrac{0.024506}{4}\right)^5}$$

$$= \frac{SFR * 100 * 0.25}{\left(1 + \dfrac{0.010407}{4}\right)^2} + \frac{SFR * 100 * 0.25}{\left(1 + \dfrac{0.015829}{4}\right)^3}$$

$$+ \frac{SFR * 100 * 0.25}{\left(1 + \dfrac{0.021272}{4}\right)^4} + \frac{SFR * 100 * 0.25}{\left(1 + \dfrac{0.024506}{4}\right)^5}$$

This solves for the "average" of the relevant 3 × 15 segment of the LIBOR forward curve. The answer is *SFR* = 2.93%. This neglects credit risk and transactions costs. Once again, you can think of it as the mid-market rate around which the swap market maker builds the bid-ask spread as compensation for the costs and risks of entering the derivative. The corporation now has a basis to negotiate, perhaps arguing that 2.98% is too high a fixed rate.

VALUING AN INTEREST RATE SWAP

Pricing a swap is the determination of the fixed rate at origination; *valuing* the swap is determining its fair value thereafter. A plain vanilla swap starts with an initial value of zero because by construction the present values of the fixed-rate leg and the floating-rate leg are equal. As time passes and as interest rates change, the swap takes on positive or negative value. That's important because accounting rules for derivatives require that the fair value of the swap be recognized on the balance sheet as an asset or liability. Moreover, depending on the applicability of hedge accounting treatment, the change in fair value from period to period might have to flow through the income statement. That can impact the closely watched earnings per share numbers.

Let's go back to the 2-year, 3.40% fixed versus 3-month LIBOR, quarterly settlement in arrears, $60 million notional principal, plain vanilla interest rate swap between Party A and B depicted in Figure 8.1. Suppose that three months go by. Party A, the fixed-rate payer, makes a net settlement payment of $435,000 to its counterparty because the initial observation for 3-month LIBOR is 0.50% in Table 8.1.

$$(3.40\% - 0.50\%) * (90/360) * \$60,000,000 = \$435,000$$

The fair value of the swap now depends on the current market and, in particular, on the relevant segment of the new LIBOR forward curve. This

TABLE 8.2 3-Month LIBOR Forward Curve and Implied Spot Rates and Discount Factors Three Months Later

Time Period	Forward Rates	Time Period	Implied Spot Rates	Discount Factors
0 × 3	0.7500%	0 × 3	0.7500%	0.998129
3 × 6	1.6210%	0 × 6	1.1853%	0.994100
6 × 9	2.6780%	0 × 9	1.6822%	0.987489
9 × 12	3.5460%	0 × 12	2.1474%	0.978812
12 × 15	3.5980%	0 × 15	2.4371%	0.970086
15 × 18	4.2520%	0 × 18	2.7390%	0.959882
18 × 21	4.7090%	0 × 21	3.0198%	0.948713

forward curve and the implied spot rates are shown in Table 8.2. Notice that the forward curve has twisted and flattened—the near-term rates have gone up a bit and the longer-term rates have come down.

Now we can solve for the fixed rate on a 1.75-year swap using the forward rates and the discount factors in Table 8.2.

$$(0.7500\% * 100 * 0.25 * 0.998129) + (1.6210\% * 100 * 0.25 * 0.994100)$$
$$+ (2.6780\% * 100 * 0.25 * 0.987489) + (3.5460\% * 100 * 0.25 * 0.978812)$$
$$+ (3.5980\% * 100 * 0.25 * 0.970086) + (4.2520\% * 100 * 0.25 * 0.959882)$$
$$+ (4.7090\% * 100 * 0.25 * 0.948713)$$

$$=$$

$$(SFR * 100 * 0.25 * 0.998129) + (SFR * 100 * 0.25 * 0.994100)$$
$$+ (SFR * 100 * 0.25 * 0.987489) + (SFR * 100 * 0.25 * 0.978812)$$
$$+ (SFR * 100 * 0.25 * 0.970086) + (SFR * 100 * 0.25 * 0.959882)$$
$$+ (SFR * 100 * 0.25 * 0.948713)$$

The result is that SFR = 3.00%.

Therefore, after three months, the swap has become a liability to Party A because it has an obligation to pay 3.40% fixed for the next seven quarterly periods when the going market rate is only 3.00%. Likewise, the swap has become an asset to Party B. Notice that these changes in market value since origination have occurred with 3-month LIBOR going up from 0.50% to 0.75%. A common mistake based on looking at Figure 8.1 is to conclude that Party A gains when LIBOR goes up and Party B gains when LIBOR goes down. The current observation on LIBOR is important—it determines who pays whom on the next settlement date. In this case, Party A now owes Party B $397,500 at the end of the period.

$$(3.40\% - 0.75\%) * (90/360) * \$60,000,000 = \$397,500$$

However, it is the entire forward curve that determines the market value of the swap. Current 3-month LIBOR is merely the first observation on that forward curve.

The fair value of the swap is the present value of the annuity representing the difference between the contractual fixed rate of 3.40% and the mark-to-market rate of 3.00%. The amount of the annuity is $60,000 per period for the remaining seven quarterly periods, given the $60 million notional principal and the 30/360 day-count.

$$(3.40\% - 3.00\%) * (90/360) * \$60,000,000 = \$60,000$$

This is the unambiguous part of swap valuation. The idea is that the two counterparties could enter a "mirror swap" at 3.00% to offset 3-month LIBOR for the remaining 1.75 years. In principle, Party A owes B a total of $420,000 to be paid in seven installments of $60,000.

The ambiguous part of swap valuation is in calculating the present value of the $60,000 per period annuity. Suppose this is a voluntary unwind of the derivative contact. Party A or B for some reason wants to exit the deal and asks for a settlement payment. If this is an unsecured swap, Party A might argue that the appropriate discount rate is its 1.75-year cost of funds on fully amortizing debt because it is extinguishing its liability. However, if this swap is collateralized in some manner, Party B might argue for a lower discount rate (and higher settlement payment from Party A to close out the contract). For routine accounting valuations, the traditional method has been to get the discount rate (or rates) from the current swap market.

What do you suggest—discount the $60,000 annuity at the current swap fixed rate of 3.00% or the sequence of implied spot rates (or discount factors)? Are you anticipating the same result, differing perhaps only by rounding? It's an interesting bond math problem. First use 3.00% to get $407,678 for the value of the swap. Here's the full equation, but it's easily obtained on a calculator.

$$\frac{\$60,000}{\left(1+\frac{0.0300}{4}\right)^1} + \frac{\$60,000}{\left(1+\frac{0.0300}{4}\right)^2} + \frac{\$60,000}{\left(1+\frac{0.0300}{4}\right)^3} + \frac{\$60,000}{\left(1+\frac{0.0300}{4}\right)^4}$$

$$+ \frac{\$60,000}{\left(1+\frac{0.0300}{4}\right)^5} + \frac{\$60,000}{\left(1+\frac{0.0300}{4}\right)^6} + \frac{\$60,000}{\left(1+\frac{0.0300}{4}\right)^7} = \$407,678$$

Now use the implied spot rates to get $410,233. The discount factors would obtain the same value with any difference due only to rounding.

$$\frac{\$60,000}{\left(1+\frac{0.007500}{4}\right)^1} + \frac{\$60,000}{\left(1+\frac{0.011853}{4}\right)^2} + \frac{\$60,000}{\left(1+\frac{0.016822}{4}\right)^3} + \frac{\$60,000}{\left(1+\frac{0.021474}{4}\right)^4}$$

$$+ \frac{\$60,000}{\left(1+\frac{0.024371}{4}\right)^5} + \frac{\$60,000}{\left(1+\frac{0.027390}{4}\right)^6} + \frac{\$60,000}{\left(1+\frac{0.030198}{4}\right)^7} = \$410,233$$

Party A should recognize the interest rate swap on its balance sheet as a liability, as Party B books an asset, but for how much: $407,678 or $410,233? There is not a big difference between the two values given the $60 million notional principal; the issue is theoretical correctness. Here's a hint: The new swap fixed rate of 3.00%, as an "average" of the forward curve, is also the 1.75-year *par yield* as described in Chapter 5. It's the solution for *PMT* in the next expression.

$$100 = \frac{PMT/4}{\left(1+\dfrac{0.007500}{4}\right)^1} + \frac{PMT/4}{\left(1+\dfrac{0.011853}{4}\right)^2} + \frac{PMT/4}{\left(1+\dfrac{0.016822}{4}\right)^3} + \frac{PMT/4}{\left(1+\dfrac{0.021474}{4}\right)^4}$$

$$+ \frac{PMT/4}{\left(1+\dfrac{0.024371}{4}\right)^5} + \frac{PMT/4}{\left(1+\dfrac{0.027390}{4}\right)^6} + \frac{PMT/4+100}{\left(1+\dfrac{0.030198}{4}\right)^7}, \quad PMT = 3.00$$

Given this implied spot curve, a 3.00%, quarterly payment, 1.75-year bond is priced at par value. Its yield to maturity of 3.00% is the weighted average of the spot rates, with most of the weight on the last rate that has largest cash flow. But our swap valuation problem entails the present value of an annuity, not a fixed-rate bond that redeems principal at maturity. The theoretically correct value is $410,233, obtained using the sequence of implied spot rates (or discount factors).

The key point here is that the fixed rate on a swap is the initial "average" of the relevant segment of the forward curve for the money market reference rate. Later, the value of the swap depends on the new "average" of the remaining segment of the new forward curve. In our example, the 3.40% swap is marked to market using a 3.00% fixed rate. But notice that any number of shifts and twists to the forward curve after three months could have resulted in a new "average" of 3.00%. The annuity component of value is still $60,000 per period. However, the present value of the annuity depends on the particular shift and twist—they determine the new implied spot curve and the fair value for the swap.

INTEREST RATE SWAP DURATION

We know from the numerical example above that when the swap fixed rate falls, the fixed-rate payer loses market value and the fixed-rate receiver gains. Therefore, the swap has negative duration to the payer (i.e., the long position or the "buyer" of the swap) and positive duration to the receiver (the short position or the "seller"). We see in Chapter 10 that adding a pay-fixed swap to a fixed-income investment portfolio reduces average portfolio duration while adding a receive-fixed swap increases average duration. How much of an increase or decrease depends on the duration of the swap and the amount of notional principal.

The duration of a plain vanilla interest rate swap is derived by recognizing that the net settlement cash flows on the derivative are the same (assuming no default) as on a pair of bonds, one a fixed-rate bond and the other a floater. The swap to Party A in Figure 8.1 is as if it has purchased a 2-year floater paying 3-month LIBOR flat and has issued a 2-year, 3.40% quarterly payment, fixed-rate bond. Both bonds are priced at par value because the initial value of the swap is zero. In the same manner, the swap to Party B provides the same net cash flows as if it buys a 3.40% fixed-rate bond financed by issuing the LIBOR flat floater.

Equation 6.13 from Chapter 6 provides a closed-form formula for the Macaulay duration (*MacDur*) of a standard fixed-rate bond. It is repeated here as equation 8.2.

$$MacDur = \left[\frac{1+y}{y} - \frac{1+y+[N*(c-y)]}{c*[(1+y)^N - 1]+y} \right] - t/T \tag{8.2}$$

The current date is t days into the T-day period. The yield per period prevailing on date t is y; the fixed coupon rate per period is c; the number of periods to maturity as of the beginning of the period is N.

Equation 7.10 in Chapter 7 shows the general formula for the Macaulay duration of a floater that might be trading at a premium or discount on a payment date. Following market practice, I assume that the floating-rate note component of the swap always is priced at par value on a payment date, so that $PV_{ANN} = 0$. That dramatically simplifies the equation for floater duration.

$$MacDur = 1 - t/T \tag{8.3}$$

As shown in equations 8.4 and 8.5, the Macaulay duration of an interest rate swap (*MacDurSWAP*) subtracts one formula from the other because one bond is an implicit asset and the other a liability.

$$\text{Pay-Fixed Swap: } MacDurSWAP = 1 - \left[\frac{1+y}{y} - \frac{1+y+[N*(c-y)]}{c*[(1+y)^N - 1]+y} \right] \tag{8.4}$$

$$\text{Receive-Fixed Swap: } MacDurSWAP = \left[\frac{1+y}{y} - \frac{1+y+[N*(c-y)]}{c*[(1+y)^N - 1]+y} \right] - 1 \tag{8.5}$$

It's interesting that the t/T term drops out of the two expressions. Fixed-rate bonds and floaters have a "saw-tooth" pattern for the duration statistic during the period. The duration of each declines smoothly (assuming no change in market interest rates) and then jumps up on the payment date. Because a swap can be interpreted as a "long-short" combination of two bonds, the "saw-teeth" are smoothed out. That's not to say that the duration is constant—it still is inversely related to the yield (i.e., the fixed rate on the mark-to-market swap). Remember that y is the yield on the implicit fixed-rate bond that prevails on date t and likely will change during the period. The other terms in the equation, c and N, are constants.

Equations 8.4 and 8.5 are formulas for rate duration, not for credit duration. That is, they can be used to estimate the change in the market value of the swap arising from a change in benchmark interest rates, in particular, the forward curve for the money market reference rate. Counterparty credit risk is not an issue. This justifies the simplifying assumption for the duration of the floater. The pair-of-bonds interpretation of the swap is fine for assessing the impact of market rates but is inappropriate for default risk. A swap is an exchange of interest cash flows, not of principal. For example, if Party A defaults, the loss to Party B is limited to the fixed-rate cash flows no longer received less the floating-rate cash flows that no longer need to be paid.

Let's use these duration statistics to see how well they estimate the actual change in the value of the swap once three months go by and the LIBOR forward curve has shifted and twisted from Table 8.1 to Table 8.2. We know that leads to a loss of $410,233 to Party A, the fixed-rate payer, and an equivalent gain to Party B, the fixed-rate receiver. Let the contractual fixed rate on the swap $c = 0.0085$ ($= 0.0340/4$), the number of periods to maturity as of the beginning of the period $N = 8$, and the fixed rate on the mark-to-market swap $y = 0.0075$ ($= 0.0300/4$).

Pay-Fixed Swap:

$$MacDurSWAP = 1 - \left[\frac{1.0075}{0.0075} - \frac{1.0075 + [8 * (0.0085 - 0.0075)]}{0.0085 * \left[(1.0075)^8 - 1\right] + 0.0075} \right]$$

$$= 1 - 7.769 = -6.769$$

Receive-Fixed Swap:

$$MacDurSWAP = \left[\frac{1.0075}{0.0075} - \frac{1.0075 + [8 * (0.0085 - 0.0075)]}{0.0085 * \left[(1.0075)^8 - 1\right] + 0.0075} \right] - 1$$

$$= 7.769 - 1 = 6.769$$

It's no surprise that the pay-fixed swap has negative duration and the receive-fixed swap positive duration. Annualized, the Macaulay durations are −1.69225 and +1.69225 after dividing by four periods in the year. The annual modified durations are −1.67965 and +1.67965, the Macaulay durations divided by 1.0075.

For a notional principal of $60 million and a 40-basis-point decrease in the swap rate, duration estimates the change in market value (ΔMV) to be a gain of $403,116 to Party B, the fixed-rate receiver, and a loss to Party A, the fixed-rate payer, for the same amount.

Fixed-Rate Payer: $\quad \Delta MV \approx -(-1.67965 * \$60,000,000 * -0.0040)$

$\quad\quad\quad\quad\quad\quad\quad\quad = -\$403,116$

Fixed-Rate Receiver: $\quad \Delta MV \approx -(1.67965 * \$60,000,000 * -0.0040)$

$\quad\quad\quad\quad\quad\quad\quad\quad = \$403,116$

Another version of this calculation is to use the basis-point-value (BPV) for the swap, which is its modified duration times the notional principal, times one basis point (0.0001). For the fixed-rate payer, the BPV is −$10,077.90 (= −1.67965 * $60,000,000 * 0.0001) whereas for the fixed-rate receiver it is +$10,077.90. Then, for a 40 basis point change in the swap fixed rate, the estimated change in value to the payer is −$10,077.90 * 40 = −$403,116. The BPV, as a measure of money duration, relates directly to a change in value in currency units. Modified duration relates to a percentage change in value—that can be awkward for a newly initiated swap that has a value of zero. Therefore, some derivatives analysts prefer to work with the BPV (or the DV01 or PV01, which are very similar statistics) rather that modified duration. In any case, the modified duration and the BPV of the swap contain the same information and produce the same estimated change in value.

When the swap fixed rate goes down from 3.40% to 3.00%, the estimated change in value of $403,116 is not a bad approximation for the actual change, which we determined above to be $410,233. The reason for the difference between the estimated and actual results concerns the change in the swap rate, 40 basis points in this example. (Also, the convexity of the swap has been neglected. It, too, can be inferred from the convexities of the implied fixed-rate and floating-rate bonds.) The new swap fixed rate of 3.00% could have resulted from many twists and shifts to the LIBOR forward curve. Each one of those twists and shifts would produce a different implied spot curve and a different present value of the annuity. However, the only input into our estimation is the 40 basis point change in the swap fixed rate. Although we do not have to assume a parallel shift to the forward curve to use duration, we do have to keep in mind that we are estimating outcomes with error.

COLLATERALIZED SWAPS

An important development in the interest rate swap market in recent years has been widespread use of collateralization to mitigate counterparty credit risk. When the market started in the 1980s, most swap contracts were unsecured and any imbalance in the credit standings between the two counterparties was "priced into" the fixed rate or managed by having the weaker party get some type of credit enhancement. In the 1990s, after the introduction of the CSA (Credit Support Annex) to the standard ISDA (International Swap and Derivatives Association) master agreement, posting cash collateral when the market value of the swap is negative became more common and nowadays is the industry norm.

The main implication of collateralization is that the credit risk on the swap transaction becomes minimal, similar to exchange-traded futures contracts. To be sure, futures require initial margin accounts by both counterparties to provide an additional buffer to potential default loss. Bilateral CSAs usually entail a zero threshold, meaning only the counterparty having the negative market value for the swap posts collateral, so there still is some "tail" risk of default. In any case, minimal credit risk on the swap implies that the discount factors to get the present value of the annuity for the difference between the contractual and current swap market fixed rates, which remains unambiguous, should be based on risk-free interest rates or, at least, nearly risk-free from the perspective of the rating agencies.

Why then is it not market practice to use actively traded U.S. Treasury notes and bonds, for which there are ample price data, to get the discount factors to value collateralized swaps denominated in U.S. dollars? The problem is that U.S. Treasury yields are in general too low for this purpose. Treasuries are by far the most liquid debt security in the fixed-income market and are in high demand as collateral for the repo transactions. Exemption from state and local income taxes lowers their yields even more. Also, Treasury yields typically are more volatile than swap rates because they are the first asset class to absorb fluctuations in demand and supply arising from international capital flows, especially during flights to quality.

The ideal discount factors to value collateralized derivatives contracts would come from traded securities having the same liquidity, tax status, and volatility as interest rate swaps but credit risk approaching zero. Pre-2007, fixed rates on LIBOR swaps were viewed to be a reasonable and workable proxy for the risk-free yield curve. However, in the post-2007 world the presence of a persistent and sizable spreads between LIBOR and overnight indexed swap (OIS) rates exposes the "credit risk approaching zero" presumption.

An overnight indexed swap is a derivative contract on the total return of a reference rate that is compounded daily over a set time period. In the U.S. dollar market, the reference rate is the effective federal funds rate. It is calculated and reported by the Federal Reserve each day in its H.15 Report and is the weighted average of brokered trades between banks for overnight ownership of deposits at the Fed (i.e., bank reserves). The *effective* fed funds rate is not necessarily equal to the *target* rate set by the Federal Open Market Committee (FOMC) and announced at regularly scheduled FOMC meetings. The Fed merely aims to keep the effective rate close to its target via open market operations of buying and selling securities. [In the Euro-zone, the OIS reference rate is EONIA (Euro Overnight Index Average), which essentially is the 1-day interbank rate. In the U.K., the reference rate is SONIA (Sterling Overnight Index Average).]

Until August 2007, the LIBOR-OIS spread was consistently narrow, typically just 8 to 10 basis points. That justified the use of rates on LIBOR swaps as proxies for risk-free transactions. Some commentators date the onset of the financial crisis at August 9, 2007, which was the day when the LIBOR-OIS spread first spiked upward. It remained high, oscillating between 50 and 100 basis points, and then jumped again in the fall of 2008, reaching its pinnacle at about 350 basis points after the announcement of the Lehman bankruptcy on September 15, 2008. It then returned to more normal levels in 2009 only to go up again in 2011 reflecting concerns over the Euro-zone sovereign debt crisis. The LIBOR-OIS spread has become a widely used indicator for bank credit and liquidity risk.

The OIS curve is now preferred by swap dealers because it removes the bank credit and liquidity risk that is being priced into LIBOR. Moreover, central clearing of standardized swaps and collateralization of uncleared transactions are mandated for dealers by the Dodd-Frank Act of 2010. In response, central clearers such as CME and LCH specifically use the OIS curve to value swaps and to establish collateral requirements.

TRADITIONAL LIBOR DISCOUNTING

To see the impact of OIS discounting, let's first do another example of swap valuation under traditional LIBOR discounting. Suppose that a 3.85% fixed-rate, $50 million notional principal, quarterly settlement interest rate swap on 3-month LIBOR has 12 months remaining. This swap might originally have had a tenor of five years and four years have gone by. Its current market value is based on a comparison to the 2.12% fixed rate on the 12-month swap. The annuity is the difference between the contractual and the current market fixed rates, times the notional principal and the day-count factor.

$$(3.85\% - 2.12\%) * \$50,000,000 * 0.25 = \$216,250$$

The present value of this annuity can be calculated using the sequence of bootstrapped implied spot rates shown in Table 8.1. The value of the swap is $856,523.

$$\frac{\$216,250}{\left(1+\dfrac{0.005000}{4}\right)^1} + \frac{\$216,250}{\left(1+\dfrac{0.010407}{4}\right)^2} + \frac{\$216,250}{\left(1+\dfrac{0.015829}{4}\right)^3}$$

$$+ \frac{\$216,250}{\left(1+\dfrac{0.021272}{4}\right)^4} = \$856,523$$

The bootstrapped discount factors give the same result.

$$(\$216,250 * 0.998752) + (\$216,250 * 0.994817) + (\$216,250 * 0.988222)$$
$$+ (\$216,250 * 0.979008) = \$856,523$$

This interest rate swap is an asset worth $856,523 to the fixed-rate receiver and a liability for the same amount to the fixed-rate payer because market rates are lower than when the swap was originated.

Another approach to swap valuation is to use the interpretation of the contract as a long/short combination of floating-rate and fixed-rate bonds. The implicit $50 million, floating-rate bond pays interest quarterly based on 3-month LIBOR. In principle, the unknown levels for future LIBOR can be hedged using FRAs or Eurodollar futures to lock in the sequence of forward rates. Therefore, the value of the floater is the present value of the projected cash flows. Using the LIBOR discount factors, this present value is $50 million.

$$(\$50,000,000 * 0.5000\% * 0.25 * 0.998752)$$
$$+ (\$50,000,000 * 1.5821\% * 0.25 * 0.994817)$$
$$+ (\$50,000,000 * 2.6694\% * 0.25 * 0.988222)$$
$$+ (\$50,000,000 * 3.7647\% * 0.25 * 0.979008)$$
$$+ (\$50,000,000 * 0.979008) = \$50,000,000$$

The implicit, $50 million, 3.85% fixed-rate bond pays interest in the amount of $481,250 each quarter (= $50,000,000 * 0.0385/4). The value of this bond, also using the LIBOR discount factors, is $50,856,523. (All of the calculations are done on a spreadsheet using unrounded discount factors.)

$$(\$481,250 * 0.998752) + (\$481,250 * 0.994817) + (\$481,250 * 0.988222)$$
$$+ (\$50,481,250 * 0.979008) = \$50,856,523$$

The value of the swap is just the difference in the bond prices, $856,523.

$$\$50,856,523 - \$50,000,000 = \$856,523$$

The reason for illustrating the two methods to value an interest rate swap is that with traditional LIBOR discounting, the same result is obtained. That will not be true in a world of OIS discounting. That's an important theme in the remainder of this chapter.

The two key assumptions to this calculation of market value are: (1) The swap is not collateralized (or, if it is, the collateral is not considered in the valuation methodology), and (2) the fixed-rate payer is a "LIBOR-flat" borrower. The second assumption means that the owing counterparty, here the fixed-rate payer, has credit quality consistent with the banks that are used to establish the LIBOR index. In other words, this counterparty can borrow funds for 12 months at LIBOR flat (meaning a margin of zero above the reference rate) on a quarterly payment floating-rate basis or at 2.12% fixed. In sum, the LIBOR-based implied spot rates and discount factors are appropriate to get the present value of its future obligations. Usually, this corresponds to an investment-grade borrower having a quality rating of A+ to AA– on its debt.

Suppose instead that the fixed-rate payer is a financially distressed company that has had its debt liabilities downgraded to noninvestment grade. If the fixed-rate receiver requested early termination of the swap, the payer would offer to settle the obligation for something less than $856,523. That counterparty to the contract would argue that the present value of the (unambiguous) $216,250 annuity should be calculated with discount factors that reflect its higher-than-LIBOR-flat or higher-than-2.12%-fixed 12-month cost of borrowed funds. In sum, the fair value of the swap would be overstated at $856,523.

While using default-risk-adjusted discount factors is appropriate in principle for an early termination, it would be unwieldy for routine valuations carried out daily by swap dealers having a multitude of open contracts. The advantage to using the LIBOR swap curve is that there are good publically available data for a full range of maturities. Importantly, the bootstrapped numbers are "internal" to the valuation problem. In this traditional approach, one can start with either the LIBOR forward curve or fixed rates on at-market swaps and easily infer the implied spot rates and discount factors needed to value the swap book.

OIS DISCOUNTING

Let's now assume that this 12-month, 3.85% fixed-rate, $50 million notional principal, quarterly settlement interest rate swap is collateralized. Cash that is posted to meet the collateral obligation earns the OIS rate. To get the OIS discount factors, we need to assume some things about that market. Suppose the 3-month fixed rate is 0.10% on an OIS for a notional principal of $50 million. At settlement, the payoff will be based on the difference between the fixed and floating legs on the swap. Assuming 90 days for the three months (i.e., for simplicity, the 30/360 day-count convention), the fixed leg is:

$$\$50,000,000 * \frac{90}{360} * 0.0010 = \$12,500$$

The floating leg depends on the sequence of realized daily reference rates.

$$\$50,000,000 * \left[\left(1 + \frac{EFF_1}{360}\right) * \left(1 + \frac{EFF_2}{360}\right) * \cdots * \left(1 + \frac{EFF_{90}}{360}\right) - 1\right]$$

EFF_1, EFF_2, . . . , EFF_{90} are the reported daily observations for the effective fed funds rate. (Note that this neglects the odd manner in which the Friday fed funds rates is used for Saturday and Sunday—rather than being compounded for three days, simple interest is used.) Net settlement on the OIS is the difference between the two legs. The 3-month OIS fixed rate determines the 0x3 discount factor.

$$DF_{0\times3} = \frac{1}{\left(1 + \frac{0.00100}{360/90}\right)} = 0.999750$$

Suppose that the fixed rate on a 6-month OIS is 0.62%. Given 180 days for the time period and $50 million in notional principal, the fixed and floating legs are:

$$\$50,000,000 * \frac{180}{360} * 0.0062 = \$155,000$$

$$\$50,000,000 * \left[\left(1 + \frac{EFF_1}{360}\right) * \left(1 + \frac{EFF_2}{360}\right) * \cdots * \left(1 + \frac{EFF_{180}}{360}\right) - 1\right]$$

The 6-month discount factor for the OIS curve is:

$$DF_{0\times6} = \frac{1}{\left(1 + \dfrac{0.0062}{360/180}\right)} = 0.996910$$

In general, the divisor is "Year/Days," where Year is 360 or 365 days, and Days is the actual or assumed number of days in the time period.

OIS fixed rates for other maturities out to one year typically are quoted in the same manner, that is, on a simple interest basis common for money market instruments. Suppose that the fixed rates for 9 and 12 months are 1.10% and 1.64% and that these apply to 270 and 360 days given the simplifying assumption of the 30/360 day-count. The 0×9 and 0×12 OIS discount factors are:

$$DF_{0\times9} = \frac{1}{\left(1 + \dfrac{0.0110}{360/270}\right)} = 0.991818$$

$$DF_{0\times12} = \frac{1}{\left(1 + \dfrac{0.0164}{360/360}\right)} = 0.983865$$

OIS contracts maturing in more than one year usually are designed to have periodic settlements against the fixed rate, as is standard for LIBOR swaps. To stay with the simplistic design of these numerical examples, assume that the annual OIS fixed rates for quarterly settlement are: 1.98% for 15 months, 2.32% for 18 months, 2.63% for 21 months, and 2.90% for 24 months. For these, the discount factors are obtained using a bootstrapping technique equivalent to that shown in Chapter 5. The difference in presentation here is that the discount factors are used directly rather than the implied spot rates.

$$100 = (1.98/4 * 0.999750) + (1.98/4 * 0.996910) + (1.98/4 * 0.991818)$$
$$+ (1.98/4 * 0.983865) + (1.98/4 + 100) * DF_{0\times15}, \quad DF_{0\times15} = 0.975508$$

$$100 = (2.32/4 * 0.999750) + (2.32/4 * 0.996910) + (2.32/4 * 0.991818)$$
$$+ (2.32/4 * 0.983865) + (2.32/4 * 0.975508) + (2.32/4 + 100) * DF_{0\times18},$$
$$DF_{0\times18} = 0.965701$$

$$100 = (2.63/4 * 0.999750) + (2.63/4 * 0.996910) + (2.63/4 * 0.991818)$$
$$+ (2.63/4 * 0.983865) + (2.63/4 * 0.975508) + (2.63/4 * 0.965701)$$
$$+ (2.63/4 + 100) * DF_{0 \times 21}, \quad DF_{0 \times 21} = 0.954840$$

$$100 = (2.90/4 * 0.999750) + (2.90/4 * 0.996910) + (2.90/4 * 0.991818)$$
$$+ (2.90/4 * 0.983865) + (2.90/4 * 0.975508) + (2.90/4 * 0.965701)$$
$$+ (2.90/4 * 0.954840) + (2.90/4 + 100) * DF_{0 \times 24}, \quad DF_{0 \times 24} = 0.943365$$

Consider again the valuation of the seasoned LIBOR swap from the previous section. It has a fixed rate of 3.85%, a notional principal of $50 million, and 12 months remaining until maturity. Using the LIBOR swap discount factors, the market value is shown above to be $856,523. Now, using the slightly higher OIS discount factors, the market value of the swap goes up to $859,019.

$$(\$216,250 * 0.999750) + (\$216,250 * 0.996910) + (\$216,250 * 0.991818)$$
$$+ (\$216,250 * 0.983865) = \$859,019$$

Clearly, the difference is not large but that is due to the low level of interest rates and the relatively short time frame in the example. The impact of using OIS rather than LIBOR discount factors is greater for longer-term swaps and when the difference between the contractual rate and the current market swap rate is larger. What matters is that this market value better captures the minimal credit risk on a collateralized interest rate swap. It's better bond math.

THE LIBOR FORWARD CURVE FOR OIS DISCOUNTING

A useful application for the OIS discount factors is to calculate the implied LIBOR forward curve that is consistent with the observed rates on collateralized interest rate swaps. To see the difference between LIBOR and OIS discounting, assume that the fixed rates on the sequence of collateralized swaps are the same as before. That is, the fixed rates are 1.04%, 1.58%, 2.12%, 2.44%, 2.76%, 3.08%, and 3.40% for quarterly settlement swaps against 3-month LIBOR for maturities ranging from 6 to 24 months.

Given that 3-month LIBOR is assumed to be 0.50%, the 3×6 implied LIBOR forward is calculated using the 0×3 and 0×6 OIS discount factors and the 6-month swap fixed rate.

$$(0.50\% * 100 * 0.25 * 0.999750) + (Rate_{3\times6} * 100 * 0.25 * 0.996910)$$
$$= (1.04\% * 100 * 0.25 * 0.999750) + (1.04\% * 100 * 0.25 * 0.996910),$$
$$Rate_{3\times6} = 1.5815\%$$

This equation follows the principle of swap pricing—the fixed rate, here 1.04% for the 6-month maturity, is the "average" of the forward curve in that the present values are the same after the rates are monetized by multiplying by the notional principal (100) and the day-count factor (0.25). Previously, we used the relevant segment of the forward curve to get the swap fixed rate. Now, we use the known swap fixed rate to solve for the incremental forward rate.

The 6 × 9 implied forward rate further illustrates the property that OIS discounting lowers the implied LIBOR forward curve when the LIBOR-OIS spread is positive and the forward curve is upwardly sloped.

$$(0.50\% * 100 * 0.25 * 0.999750) + (1.5815\% * 100 * 0.25 * 0.996910)$$
$$+ (Rate_{6\times9} * 100 * 0.25 * 0.991818) = (1.58\% * 100 * 0.25 * 0.999750)$$
$$+ (1.58\% * 100 * 0.25 * 0.996910) + (1.58\% * 100 * 0.25 * 0.991818),$$
$$Rate_{6\times9} = 2.6671\%$$

In Table 8.1, the 6 × 9 implied forward rate for 3-month LIBOR is shown to be 2.6694%. That rate is consistent with LIBOR discount factors. Here it is 2.6671% for OIS discounting.

The difference in the implied forward rates becomes a bit larger moving out along the curve. These are the remaining implied rates for LIBOR using the OIS discount factors. Notice that in each equation, the incremental forward rate is the unknown variable. The known inputs are the forward rates up to that time period and the swap fixed rate. You probably can envision the spreadsheet that would do these calculations for you.

$$(0.50\% * 100 * 0.25 * 0.999750) + (1.5815\% * 100 * 0.25 * 0.996910)$$
$$+ (2.6671\% * 100 * 0.25 * 0.991818) + (Rate_{9\times12} * 100 * 0.25 * 0.983865)$$
$$= (2.12\% * 100 * 0.25 * 0.999750) + (2.12\% * 100 * 0.25 * 0.996910)$$
$$+ (2.12\% * 100 * 0.25 * 0.991818) + (2.12\% * 100 * 0.25 * 0.983865),$$
$$Rate_{9\times12} = 3.7602\%$$

$(0.50\% * 100 * 0.25 * 0.999750) + (1.5815\% * 100 * 0.25 * 0.996910)$

$+ (2.6671\% * 100 * 0.25 * 0.991818) + (3.7602\% * 100 * 0.25 * 0.983865)$

$+ (Rate_{12x15} * 100 * 0.25 * 0.975508) = (2.44\% * 100 * 0.25 * 0.999750)$

$+ (2.44\% * 100 * 0.25 * 0.996910) + (2.44\% * 100 * 0.25 * 0.991818)$

$+ (2.44\% * 100 * 0.25 * 0.983865) + (2.44\% * 100 * 0.25 * 0.975508),$

$Rate_{12x15} = 3.7431\%$

$(0.50\% * 100 * 0.25 * 0.999750) + (1.5815\% * 100 * 0.25 * 0.996910)$

$+ (2.6671\% * 100 * 0.25 * 0.991818) + (3.7602\% * 100 * 0.25 * 0.983865)$

$+ (3.7431\% * 100 * 0.25 * 0.975508) + (Rate_{15x18} * 100 * 0.25 * 0.965701)$

$= (2.76\% * 100 * 0.25 * 0.999750) + (2.76\% * 100 * 0.25 * 0.996910)$

$+ (2.76\% * 100 * 0.25 * 0.991818) + (2.76\% * 100 * 0.25 * 0.983865)$

$+ (2.76\% * 100 * 0.25 * 0.975508) + (2.76\% * 100 * 0.25 * 0.965701),$

$Rate_{15x18} = 4.3995\%$

$(0.50\% * 100 * 0.25 * 0.999750) + (1.5815\% * 100 * 0.25 * 0.996910)$

$+ (2.6671\% * 100 * 0.25 * 0.991818) + (3.7602\% * 100 * 0.25 * 0.983865)$

$+ (3.7431\% * 100 * 0.25 * 0.975508) + (4.399\% * 100 * 0.25 * 0.965701)$

$+ (Rate_{18x21} * 100 * 0.25 * 0.954840) = (3.08\% * 100 * 0.25 * 0.999750)$

$+ (3.08\% * 100 * 0.25 * 0.996910) + (3.08\% * 100 * 0.25 * 0.991818)$

$+ (3.08\% * 100 * 0.25 * 0.983865) + (3.08\% * 100 * 0.25 * 0.975508)$

$+ (3.08\% * 100 * 0.25 * 0.965701) + (3.08\% * 100 * 0.25 * 0.954840),$

$Rate_{18x21} = 5.0618\%$

$(0.50\% * 100 * 0.25 * 0.999750) + (1.5815\% * 100 * 0.25 * 0.996910)$

$+ (2.6671\% * 100 * 0.25 * 0.991818) + (3.7602\% * 100 * 0.25 * 0.983865)$

$+ (3.7431\% * 100 * 0.25 * 0.975508) + (4.3995\% * 100 * 0.25 * 0.965701)$

$+ (5.0618\% * 100 * 0.25 * 0.954840) + (Rate_{21x24} * 100 * 0.25 * 0.943365)$

$= (3.40\% * 100 * 0.25 * 0.999750) + (3.40\% * 100 * 0.25 * 0.996910)$

$+ (3.40\% * 100 * 0.25 * 0.991818) + (3.40\% * 100 * 0.25 * 0.983865)$

$+ (3.40\% * 100 * 0.25 * 0.975508) + (3.40\% * 100 * 0.25 * 0.965701)$

$+ (3.40\% * 100 * 0.25 * 0.954840) + (3.40\% * 100 * 0.25 * 0.943365),$

$Rate_{21x24} = 5.7298\%$

In this example, the use of OIS rather than LIBOR discount factors does not make for a large difference in the implied LIBOR forward curve. It is only 1.29 basis points, 5.7427% compared to 5.7298%, for the 21 × 24 time period. Nevertheless, these are the correct forward (or projected) rates to use on collateralized swaps when determining the fixed rate on a nonvanilla design, for instance, a varying notional principal, forward-starting swap, or when pricing options on swaps (i.e., "swaptions").

These implied forward rates are also important when valuing a swap using the combination-of-bonds approach. Consider again the 3.85%, $50 million notional principal, 12-month quarterly settlement swap shown earlier to have a market value of $859,019 when collateralized and marked against a 2.12% at-market contract. That amount is the annuity of $216,250 for the difference in the fixed swap rates discounted using the OIS curve. The equation is repeated here.

$$(\$216,250 * 0.999750) + (\$216,250 * 0.996910) + (\$216,250 * 0.991818)$$
$$+ (\$216,250 * 0.983865) = \$859,019$$

The implicit 3.85% fixed-rate bond pays a quarterly coupon of $481,250. It can be valued using the OIS discount factors as if the bond has been upgraded to risk-free status.

$$(\$481,250 * 0.999750) + (\$481,250 * 0.996910) + (\$481,250 * 0.991818)$$
$$+ (\$50,481,250 * 0.983865) = \$51,104,920$$

This is greater than the bond price of $50,856,523 found earlier, where it is calculated using the (lower) LIBOR discount factors.

The key point is that it would be incorrect to assume that the implicit floating-rate bond continues to be priced at par value. That would value the swap wrongly at $1,104,920 (= $51,104,920 – $50,000,000). This "floater" should be treated as a risk-free security having a price greater than $50,000,000 because it is collateralized. To get that price, assume that the implied forward rates based on the OIS discount factors are the fixed rates on collateralized FRAs. That means the cash flows on the LIBOR floating-rate bond can be fixed via hedging. The value of the implicit floater is $50,245,902.

$$(\$50,000,000 * 0.5000\% * 0.25 * 0.999750) + (\$50,000,000 * 1.5815\%$$
$$* 0.25 * 0.996910) + (\$50,000,000 * 2.6671\% * 0.25 * 0.991818)$$
$$+ (\$50,000,000 * 3.7602\% * 0.25 * 0.983865)$$
$$+ (\$50,000,000 * 0.983865) = \$50,245,902$$

The difference in the (unrounded) values for the two implicit bonds is $859,019, which is the same as found directly by discounting the $216,250 annuity with the OIS discount factors.

$$\$51,104,920 - \$50,245,902 = \$859,019$$

This valuation exercise assumes the same series of swap fixed rates whether the contracts are uncollateralized or collateralized. But that is not likely to happen in reality. Other things being equal, the fixed rate on the collateralized swap should be higher than when it is uncollateralized. The reasoning is similar to the adjustment between interest rates on exchange-traded futures and over-the-counter forwards. The idea is that posting cash collateral is costly to the counterparty for which the swap is underwater, meaning it has a negative market value. Either the funds need to be borrowed or are diverted from other uses, thereby imposing a financial or, at least, an opportunity cost to the entity. Moreover, the rate earned on cash collateral nowadays is the OIS rate whereas the bank's cost of funds is LIBOR (or above).

The reason for the higher fixed rate on a collateralized swap is that the impact of having to post costly collateral is not symmetric between the two counterparties—the fixed-rate receiver suffers from interest rate volatility while the payer benefits. Suppose the contract is underwater to the fixed-rate receiver because swap rates have risen since entrance. If rates rise further, more collateral is needed; if rates fall, less is required. In contrast, suppose the swap is underwater to the fixed-rate payer because rates have fallen. If rates then rise somewhat, less collateral is needed; and if rates fall further, more is required. Systematically, the fixed-rate receiver posts more costly collateral when rates go up and the fixed-rate payer posts more when rates go down. This asymmetry, other things being equal, leads to a higher fixed rate on the collateralized swap.

CONCLUSION

Interest rate swaps demonstrate how once again we can employ a toolkit of bond math techniques to go beyond basic fixed-rate and zero-coupon securities. Interest rate swaps combine aspects of fixed-rate and floating-rate bonds. They can be interpreted as holding a long position in one and a short position in the other. That allows us to get reasonable estimates of the modified duration and basis-point-value for a swap. Most important, pricing swaps at initiation and valuing them thereafter are direct applications of spot and forward curve analysis. Getting the "source" forward curve from futures markets is a difficult technical matter, and one that requires an adjustment factor drawn from a mathematical model of the term structure of interest rates. Alternatively, we can work with observed fixed rates on standard swaps and interpolate rates for the intermediate maturities. Then we can bootstrap the implied spot and forward rates. Once we have a forward curve, our swap pricing and valuation analysis is merely a spreadsheet away. We can do this in the traditional world of LIBOR discounting or in the brave new world of OIS discounting.

CHAPTER 9

Bond Portfolios

Finally, we get to bond portfolios. In reality, investors do not hold, and borrowers do not issue, bonds in isolation; they are clustered in asset and liability portfolios. The question for analysis is how well the statistics about an individual bond—its yield to maturity, its duration and convexity—translate to a portfolio. That is, how do we calculate the yield, duration, and convexity of the overall portfolio? It's not as obvious as it might seem because it is not just a matter of calculating the market-value-weighted averages of the individual statistics. Sometimes that produces a reasonable number; other times it is very misleading. Sometimes when we work with portfolio summary statistics we even venture into the realm of theoretical incorrectness and make assumptions that allow for arbitrage opportunities.

Once we understand the risk and return profile of a bond portfolio in theory and in practice, we can turn our attention to strategy. That comes in the next chapter.

BOND PORTFOLIO STATISTICS IN THEORY

We can think of a portfolio of fixed-income bonds as just one big bond representing many promised payments on scheduled future dates. In doing this we focus on cash flow, not on how the payments are accounted for as interest income or redemption of principal. This big-bundle-of-cash-flow approach makes sense only if the bonds are fairly homogeneous with respect to credit risk and taxation. It would be hard to interpret the summary statistics on a bond portfolio made up of half low-yield, high-quality, federal tax-exempt municipals and half high-yield, non–investment-grade corporate bonds.

Suppose that our portfolio is composed of a homogeneous class of traditional fixed-income securities, for instance, semiannual payment U.S. Treasury notes and bonds. There are no floaters or linkers, and for now not even callables. In general, the current market value of the portfolio is MV, which includes both the flat price and the accrued interest of the constituent securities. However, to simplify, I assume in this chapter that all the bonds have either just been issued or have made a coupon payment so that the accrued interest is zero. In any case, all the results here extend to between-coupon dates and for any other periodicity (e.g., payments made monthly, quarterly, or annually).

The future cash flows are designated CF_1, CF_2, . . . , CF_N. The longest-maturity bond redeems its principal in N semiannual periods, where N is an integer. The cash flow for each period consists of coupon interest on all remaining securities and principal on any maturing bonds. Some of the cash flows can even be zero, for instance, if the longest-maturity bond in the portfolio is a zero-coupon Treasury STRIPS.

The *portfolio yield* is the internal rate of return on the cash flows: MV, CF_1, CF_2, . . . , CF_N. It's the solution for $YieldPORT$ in equation 9.1.

$$MV = \frac{CF_1}{(1 + YieldPORT)^1} + \frac{CF_2}{(1 + YieldPORT)^2} + \cdots + \frac{CF_N}{(1 + YieldPORT)^N}$$

$$(9.1)$$

This is the same as solving for the yield to maturity on an ordinary fixed-income bond, as in Chapter 3, where CF_1 to CF_{N-1} are the coupon payments (PMT) and CF_N is the final payment including the principal ($PMT + FV$). Moreover, I can make a similar statement about the portfolio yield as I made about a yield to maturity—it does need to assume a flat yield curve. That is, the underlying Treasury yield curve corresponding to the many bonds in the portfolio can be upwardly sloped, downwardly sloped, or perfectly flat. $YieldPORT$, which also is called the *cash flow yield*, is in a sense an "average" of the various yields to maturity, which are in turn "averages" of the implied spot rates.

Given the portfolio yield and the schedule of cash flows, we calculate the Macaulay duration of the portfolio as the weighted-average time to the receipt of cash flow, as in equation 6.14 in Chapter 6. This statistic is denoted $MacDurPORT$.

$$MacDurPORT = \frac{\left(1 * \dfrac{CF_1}{(1 + YieldPORT)^1} \right) + \left(2 * \dfrac{CF_2}{(1 + YieldPORT)^2} \right) + \cdots + \left(N * \dfrac{CF_N}{(1 + YieldPORT)^N} \right)}{\dfrac{CF_1}{(1 + YieldPORT)^1} + \dfrac{CF_2}{(1 + YieldPORT)^2} + \cdots + \dfrac{CF_N}{(1 + YieldPORT)^N}}$$

$$(9.2)$$

The denominator in equation 9.2 is the market value of the portfolio, MV. In the numerator, the times to the receipt of cash flow (i.e., 1 out to N periods) are each multiplied by the share of the portfolio market value corresponding to that period.

The equation for portfolio Macaulay duration can be written more compactly using the summation sign.

$$MacDurPORT = \sum_{n=1}^{N} n * \left(\frac{\dfrac{CF_n}{(1 + YieldPORT)^n}}{MV} \right) \qquad (9.3)$$

Here we see that Macaulay duration is a weighted average of the times to receipt of cash flow. Another statistic for the portfolio, one that we have not seen yet, is the *dispersion* of the cash flow. It is denoted *DispPORT* and is calculated in equation 9.4:

$$DispPORT = \sum_{n=1}^{N} (n - MacDurPORT)^2 * \left(\frac{\dfrac{CF_n}{(1 + YieldPORT)^n}}{MV} \right) \qquad (9.4)$$

Portfolio dispersion is the *variance* of the times to the receipt of cash flow; like Macaulay duration, it uses the shares of market value for each period as the weights. The same formula can be used to calculate the cash flow dispersion for an individual bond.

A change in the market value of the portfolio (dMV) resulting from a change in the portfolio yield ($dYieldPORT$) is estimated in the same manner as in Chapter 6 for individual bonds.

$$dMV \approx -\left(\frac{MacDurPORT}{1 + YieldPORT} \right) * MV * dYieldPORT \qquad (9.5)$$

The term in parenthesis is the modified duration of the portfolio (*ModDurPORT*). It is important to note once again that using equation 9.5 does not inherently assume a parallel shift in the yield curve. Just as many shapes to the underlying yield curve can produce the same portfolio yield, many shifts and twists to the yield curve can produce that same change in the portfolio yield. It's just an estimation that happens to be better if the underlying curve is flat and its shift is parallel. Moreover, the estimation can be improved by adding the convexity adjustment.

The convexity statistic for the portfolio ($ConvPORT$) is derived in the Technical Appendix.

$$ConvPORT = \frac{1}{(1+YieldPORT)^2} * \sum_{n=1}^{N} * (n+1) * \left(\frac{\frac{CF_n}{(1+YieldPORT)^n}}{MV} \right)$$

$$(9.6)$$

This convexity statistic also can be expressed as a function of the portfolio cash flow yield, Macaulay duration, and dispersion.

$$ConvPORT = \frac{(MacDurPORT)^2 + MacDurPORT + DispPORT}{(1+YieldPORT)^2} \qquad (9.7)$$

This formula is also derived in the Technical Appendix. It is a general relation, and it holds between coupon payment dates and regardless of the shape of the underlying yield curve. It's a very neat result that might surprise you if you've never seen it before. We see in equation 9.7 that for a given Macaulay duration of the portfolio (or individual bond), convexity is directly linked to the dispersion of cash flow—the greater the dispersion, the higher the convexity. The more concentrated are the cash flows, the lower the dispersion and the convexity.

A fixed-income money manager might think of a "laddered" portfolio as a way of addressing liquidity needs. Hence, the maturities of the bonds are spread out along the yield curve (the rungs of the ladder), so that a portion is always soon to mature and provide cash. Laddering also increases convexity by spreading out the cash flows. Greater convexity, other things being equal, generally is a good thing for the portfolio, increasing gains when yields go down and reducing losses when yields go up.

In the extreme, a "barbell" portfolio maximizes convexity by putting all the weight in the "wings" (i.e., in the shortest-term and longest-term maturities). In contrast, a "bullet" portfolio in which the maturities are tightly clustered has less dispersion and lower convexity. After this dose of street lingo, we are ready to tackle the portfolio statistics in practice.

BOND PORTFOLIO STATISTICS IN PRACTICE

The equations earlier suggest that calculating the summary statistics for a fixed-income portfolio is a straightforward matter. But it is not easy to do so, starting with *YieldPORT*, which is an input in the other equations. I assumed for convenience a nice, evenly spaced, semiannual pattern to the timing of cash flows. In reality, a typical portfolio of hundreds of bonds has coupon and principal payments occurring on many business days throughout the year, so N has to be measured in days, not semiannual periods. In reality, it's a really big internal rate of return calculation.

Imagine solving for *YieldPORT* back in the olden days before computers. Picture a back-office analyst working all day to get the solution by slow trial-and-error search, only to be told that the trading desk just sold some bonds and bought some others. The analyst has to start all over again the next day—it's the bond math version of the Myth of Sisyphus!

In practice, summary statistics for a fixed-income portfolio typically are calculated as weighted averages of those for the individual bonds. As we've seen, these statistics are reported on various Bloomberg pages and become the inputs to the averaging process. Suppose that the portfolio is composed of *J* bonds, each having a market value (including accrued interest) denoted MV_j and interest rate sensitivities denoted $MacDur_j$, $ModDur_j$, and $Convexity_j$. The market-value-weighted averages for Macaulay duration, modified duration, and convexity are shown in equations 9.8 to 9.10.

$$AvgMacDur = \sum_{j=1}^{J} MacDur_j * \left(\frac{MV_j}{MV} \right) \qquad (9.8)$$

$$AvgModDur = \sum_{j=1}^{J} ModDur_j * \left(\frac{MV_j}{MV} \right) \qquad (9.9)$$

$$AvgConvexity = \sum_{j=1}^{J} Convexity_j * \left(\frac{MV_j}{MV} \right) \qquad (9.10)$$

How well do these *estimate* the "true" portfolio statistics, *MacDurPORT*, *ModDurPORT*, and *ConvPORT*? The answer depends on the shape of the yield curve. If ever the curve is perfectly flat, the estimations are perfect. Usually the weighted averages are lower because of the normal, upward slope to the yield curve: *AvgMacDur* < *MacDurPORT*, *AvgModDur* < *ModDurPORT*, and *AvgConvexity* < *ConvPORT*. The discrepancy is smaller when rates overall are lower, the yield curve is flatter, and when more of the market-value weights are farther out the curve where intra-portfolio yield differences usually are smaller. In the occasional circumstance of an inverted yield curve, the weighted averages are higher than the "theoretically correct" portfolio statistics.

Notice that I did not include a market-value-weighted average for the portfolio dispersion statistic, *DispPORT*. That's because it is not commonly calculated. One reason is that dispersion is not a statistic reported on Bloomberg. The Bloomberg Yield and Spread Analysis pages have lots of data but not cash flow dispersion, even though its inputs are the same as Macaulay duration. A second, and more important, reason is that the weighted average of individual dispersion statistics can be very misleading, even if the yield curve is flat. Suppose a portfolio is composed entirely of zero-coupon Treasury STRIPS having a range of maturities. Each individual zero has a dispersion of zero—and, obviously, a weighted average of zeros is zero. However, the portfolio overall clearly has positive dispersion; its *DispPORT* > 0.

The main reason for estimating portfolio statistics via a weighted average is that fixed-income bonds other than Treasuries often contain embedded call options and sometimes even put options. Then there is no way to project with confidence the future cash flows needed to get *YieldPORT*, *MacDurPORT*, and so on. Fortunately, the relevant statistics can be calculated (and are available on Bloomberg) for individual bonds, but it is important to factor in the correct numbers.

We saw in Chapter 6 that for callable bonds, you need to be careful in selecting the duration and convexity statistics off Bloomberg pages. Those calculated using the yield to first call, the yield to worst, or the yield to maturity are just data. More useful numbers are the curve duration and convexity (also called *OAS* and *effective duration and convexity*). Floating-rate notes also might be present in the portfolio. Once again you need to be careful about which statistics to use. Recall from Chapter 7 that Bloomberg reports modified duration and convexity to the next coupon payment date as well as OAS duration and convexity for floaters. The former essentially is the price sensitivity with respect to benchmark interest rates and the latter to credit risk. If there are C-Linkers or P-Linkers in the portfolio, you should think about summarizing real rate versus inflation durations.

Suppose you have a portfolio of investment-grade corporate bonds, including both callable and noncallable securities, and want statistics for average modified duration and convexity. Clearly, you use the *curve* durations and convexities on the callable bonds. But what do you use for the noncallable bonds? The Bloomberg Yield and Spread Analysis page reports both the yield and curve durations and convexities. To be consistent, you should use their curve durations and convexities as well. Then you would be averaging apples with apples, not apples with oranges.

There is another reason to aggregate the curve durations and convexities even on a portfolio of all (noncallable) Treasury notes and bonds. That is theoretical correctness. Often the risk management problem is framed as the gain or loss on the portfolio given a *parallel shift* in the yield curve, sometimes described as a *shape-preserving shift* because all yields are assumed to change by the same amount. For instance, the concern is how much the portfolio declines in market value if all yields go up by 25 basis points. You could solve that what-if scenario directly by summing the new prices after increasing each yield. Or you can estimate the result using average duration and convexity.

The problem is that the benign-sounding assumption of a parallel shift to the yield curve is inconsistent with the principle of no arbitrage. That's because when all the yields go up by 25 basis points, the implied spot rates change as well but not by the same amount—recall the example at the end of Chapter 6. For instance, zero-coupon bonds in the portfolio would be overpriced (relative to their no-arbitrage value) because their implied spot rates go up by more than 25 basis points (assuming the yield curve is upward sloping). So, it's theoretically impossible for all yields to shift by the same amount and still preserve the no-arbitrage assumption.

The key point is that the curve durations and convexities are calculated using a common assumption, namely a parallel shift in the benchmark Treasury curve, based on a model that itself keeps the no-arbitrage assumption intact. The model calibrates the change in the price of the bond, which depends on its coupon rate and maturity, and backs out the effective duration and convexity, as demonstrated in Chapter 6. Therefore, aggregating the curve durations and convexities by calculating the market-value-weighted average is theoretically correct. On the other hand, yield durations and convexities are well-defined statistics for a fixed-income bond that you can verify for yourself. Curve durations and convexities come from a "black box" and you need to trust the numbers (unless you build or have access to the underlying term structure model).

Calculating the average yield for the portfolio is another interesting problem. An obvious choice for the summary statistic is the market-value-weighted average of the individual yields. Denote these $Yield_j$ for each of the J bonds and the portfolio average $AvgYieldMV$.

$$AvgYieldMV = \sum_{j=1}^{J} Yield_j * \left(\frac{MV_j}{MV} \right) \qquad (9.11)$$

For callable bonds, the *option-adjusted yield* can be used. This is the yield to maturity after increasing the price for the value of the embedded call option. That depends on the assumed volatility of interest rates and requires an option-pricing model.

As with average duration and convexity, this market-value-weighted average yield is an accurate estimator of the portfolio internal rate of return only when the yield curve is flat. Typically, it is an underestimate, that is, $AvgYieldMV < YieldPORT$, the more so the steeper the curve. Nevertheless, $AvgYieldMV$ does offer information—it indicates the annual return on the portfolio over the next year assuming a static yield curve.

You might be wondering why I put the "MV" in $AvgYieldMV$. It's because there is another way of averaging the individual yields to maturity. Instead of using market-value weights, we can use risk-based weights, in particular, the basis point value. Define the basis point value for each security (BPV_j) to be the modified duration times the market value, times one basis point: $BPV_j = ModDur_j * MV_j * 0.0001$. The portfolio basis point value (BPV) is the sum of the BPV_j over the J securities in the portfolio. The BPV-weighted-average yield, $AvgYieldBPV$, is shown in equation 9.12.

$$AvgYieldBPV = \sum_{j=1}^{J} Yield_j * \left(\frac{BPV_j}{BPV} \right) \qquad (9.12)$$

Sometimes this is expressed as the weighted average of money durations (or, as commonly said, dollar durations). Recall from Chapter 6 that money duration is modified duration times market value. The weights are the same, just scaled differently.

Here's the good news: $AvgYieldBPV$ is a really good approximation for $YieldPORT$. You'll see this in the numerical example in the next section. This—and not the market-value-weighted average yield—is a reasonable measure of the rate of return for the portfolio on a hold-to-maturity basis. The usual caveats apply—no default and reinvestment of cash flow at the same rate. The advantage of $AvgYieldBPV$ is that it typically is easier to calculate than $YieldPORT$ because it uses readily available inputs (i.e., on Bloomberg) from the individual bonds that compose the portfolio, including callables.

There is an interesting application here to the liability side of the balance sheet—usually we think about bond portfolios as assets using the perspective of the investor. Try to remember what you learned in school about calculating the weighted average cost of capital (the WACC) used to get the net present value of an investment project expanding the current line of business. To get the after-tax cost of debt, you probably were taught to use the yields (not the coupon rates) on existing debt liabilities and market values (not the par values). Essentially, you calculate an after-tax version of $AvgYieldMV$—a market-value-weighted average of yields.

Suppose that you do the capital budgeting exercise. Assume that debt is the primary component in the cost of capital—it's a very highly leveraged firm. The problem is that if the yield curve is upward sloping (so that $AvgYieldMV <$ $YieldPORT$) and you invest MV to earn $AvgYieldMV$ each period, you do not earn enough to pay off your liabilities—you need to earn $YieldPORT$ on the project. A better cost of debt to get your "hurdle rate" is to use an after-tax version of $AvgYieldBPV$ because it's a much better approximation for $Yield$-$PORT$ and can be easily calculated with our bond math tools.

We can combine the various weighted averages to estimate the change in market value resulting from some instantaneous yield "event," described summarily by a change in the average yield ($dAvgYield$) for the portfolio.

$$dMV \approx -\left(AvgModDur * MV * dAvgYield\right)$$
$$+\left[1/2 * AvgConvexity * MV * (dAvgYield)^2\right] \qquad (9.13)$$

However, we know that there is more than one way to formulate this expression. We can use the *yield* durations and convexities or the *curve* durations and convexities for $AvgModDur$ and $AvgConvexity$. We can use the change in the MV-weighted or the BPV-weighted average yield for $dAvgYield$.

It's time for a numerical example to elucidate these portfolio statistics in theory and practice.

A REAL BOND PORTFOLIO

This portfolio is composed of four U.S. Treasury securities, including short-term and intermediate-term T-notes, a long-term T-bond, and, just to make things interesting, a position in long-term P-STRIPS. Figures 9.1 to 9.4 show

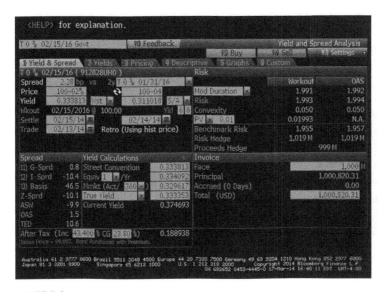

FIGURE 9.1 Bloomberg Yield and Spread Analysis Page, 0.375% Treasury Note Due 2/15/2016
Used with permission of Bloomberg.com © 2014. All rights reserved.

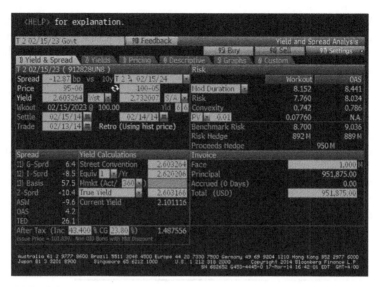

FIGURE 9.2 Bloomberg Yield and Spread Analysis Page, 2% Treasury Note Due 2/15/2023
Used with permission of Bloomberg.com © 2014. All rights reserved.

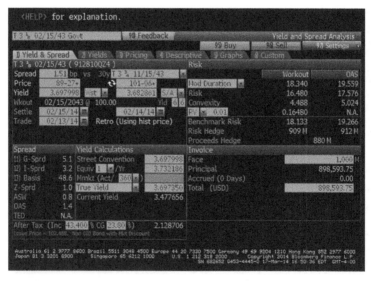

FIGURE 9.3 Bloomberg Yield and Spread Analysis Page, 3.125% Treasury Bond Due 2/15/2043
Used with permission of Bloomberg.com © 2014. All rights reserved.

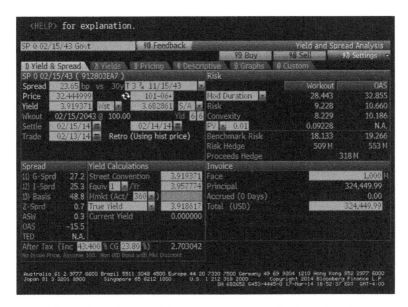

FIGURE 9.4 Bloomberg Yield and Spread Analysis Page, 0% Treasury P-STRIPS Due 2/15/2043

the Bloomberg Yield and Spread Analysis pages for each security backdated for settlement on February 15, 2014, using the historical prices—this is a nice feature to Bloomberg. Conveniently (and intentionally) each Treasury matures on February 15, so the accrued interest is zero and all future cash flows are scheduled for February 15 and August 15 of each year. That makes it easy to build a spreadsheet to illustrate the portfolio statistics.

Table 9.1 summarizes the risk and return characteristics on the individual Treasuries using the Bloomberg data. These numbers are easily verified on Excel, other than curve duration and convexity, which emerge from the "black box" behind the OAS1 pages. Notice that I report the convexity statistics in their more natural and mathematical form, multiplying Bloomberg convexity by 100. Notice also the significant differences between the modified durations and the curve durations, especially on the long-term bonds. The difference between the yield and curve convexities is even larger. This is because of the steepness in the Treasury yield curve at that time. It's no surprise that the yield on the P-STRIPS is considerably higher than the T-bond maturing on the same date, 3.919371% compared to 3.697998%.

Before turning to the portfolio, let's focus a bit on the individual yield and curve durations and convexities. Consider the price sensitivity of a

TABLE 9.1 Individual Treasury Statistics for Settlement on 2/15/14

	T-Note	T-Note	T-Bond	P-STRIPS
Coupon Rate	0.375%	2.00%	3.125%	0%
Maturity	2/15/16	2/15/23	2/15/43	2/15/43
Price	100.08203125	95.1875	89.859375	32.444999
Yield to Maturity	0.333813%	2.603264%	3.697998%	3.919371%
Macaulay Duration	1.994	8.258	18.679	29.000
Modified Duration	1.991	8.152	18.340	28.443
Curve Duration	1.992	8.441	19.559	32.855
Yield Convexity	5.0	74.2	448.8	822.9
Curve Convexity	5.0	78.6	502.4	1,018.6
PV01	0.01993	0.07760	0.16480	0.09228
Par Value	$120,000,000	$100,000,000	$100,000,000	$125,000,000

$100 million (par value) position in the 3.125% long-term Treasury bond in isolation, for instance, resulting from a 25-basis-point jump in its yield to maturity. The modified yield duration and convexity are the correct inputs to the estimation. The estimated loss is $3.994 million.

$$dMV \approx -(18.340 * \$89,859,375 * 0.0025)$$
$$+[1/2 * 448.8 * \$89,859,375 * (0.0025)^2] = -\$3,994,025$$

Now consider a $100 million (par value) P-STRIPS holding. If its yield goes up by 25 basis points, the estimated loss is $2.224 million.

$$dMV \approx -(28.443 * \$32,444,999 * 0.0025)$$
$$+[1/2 * 822.9 * \$32,444,999 * (0.0025)^2] = -\$2,223,648$$

On a percentage basis, the loss on the P-STRIPS is much higher than on the coupon bond because of its much lower price as a percentage of par value.

Let's turn this into a hedging problem. Suppose you own the $100 million par value position in the P-STRIPS and fear an imminent rise in Treasury yields. You decide to hedge fully your position by short-selling the more actively traded comparable maturity T-bond. Your problem is to calculate the *hedge ratio*, which is the amount of T-bonds you need to short sell. A common way to get this amount is to use the ratio of the PV01s (or BPVs). A formula for the hedge ratio between two bonds is written in equation 9.14.

$$\text{Hedge Ratio} = \frac{\text{PV01 of the Exposed Position}}{\text{PV01 of the Hedge}} \qquad (9.14)$$
$$* \text{ Par Value of the Exposed Position}$$

From Table 9.1, the PV01 for the P-STRIPS is 0.09228 and 0.16480 for the T-Bond. Entering those in 9.14 for a par value of $100 million gives the result that you would need to short sell about $56 million in par value of the T-bond to hedge the exposure on the P-STRIPS.

$$\text{Hedge Ratio} = \frac{0.09228}{0.16480} * \$100,000,000 = \$55,995,146$$

The same hedge ratio would be obtained with a ratio of DV01s, which are just the PV01s scaled up to a given par value, for instance, $1 million.

Do you see the error—or at least the violation of the principle of no arbitrage? It is in the implicit assumption that both bond yields change by the same amount. That would be fine if the Treasury yield curve is flat—but it's not; it's steeply and upwardly sloped. If the yield on the 3.125%, 29-year T-bond goes up by 25 basis points, the yield on the 29-year P-STRIPS will go up by more than that and its market value will fall by more than is estimated. You need a bigger hedge; a $56 million short position in the coupon-bearing T-bond is simply not enough.

A better hedge ratio uses "revised PV01s." First notice that the given PV01s are essentially equivalent to the modified duration times the full price of the bond, times one basis point.

$$28.443 * 32.444999 * 0.0001 = 0.09228$$
$$18.340 * 89.859375 * 0.0001 = 0.16480$$

The revised PV01s use the *curve* durations instead of the *yield* durations.

$$32.855 * 32.444999 * 0.0001 = 0.10660$$
$$19.559 * 89.859375 * 0.0001 = 0.17576$$

The new-and-improved hedge is to short sell about $60.65 million in the T-bond.

$$\text{Hedge Ratio} = \frac{0.10660}{0.17576} * \$100,000,000 = \$60,650,888$$

The key point is that the curve durations (and the revised PV01s) are based on a parallel shift in the entire Treasury yield curve and are calibrated so that there are no arbitrage opportunities.

The no-arbitrage assumption is particularly important in the U.S. Treasury market because of the presence of zero-coupon C-STRIPS and P-STRIPS. When their yields to maturity veer away from the implied spot curve by enough to compensate for transactions costs, arbitrageurs can and will exploit opportunities for coupon-stripping and bond reconstitution. If these were corporate bonds, it would be a different story. Our bond math techniques allow us to say, "If a zero-coupon corporate bond exists, its no-arbitrage yield would equal the implied spot rate." But without a series of actual zero-coupon corporate securities to carry out the trades to eliminate any mispricing, it's a weak argument. The zero-coupon corporate bond yield could differ from the theoretical implied spot rate by a lot and for quite a while.

Let's now build a portfolio of the four Treasury securities using the par values indicated in Table 9.1. The market value for settlement on February 15, 2014, is $345,701,561, which easily is calculated when there is no accrued interest to deal with. As usual, the prices are quoted as percentages of par value in Table 9.1.

$$\$120,000,000 * (100.08203125/100) + \$100,000,000 * (95.1875/100)$$
$$+ \$100,000,000 * (89.859375/100) + \$125,000,000 * (32.444999/100)$$
$$= \$345,701,561$$

Table 9.2 shows an abridged version of the spreadsheet I use to calculate the portfolio statistics. The date-0 cash flow for the purchase price of the portfolio is $345,701,561—this amount needs to be made negative for internal rate of return calculations. There are 58 future cash flows, occurring on February 15 and August 15 of each year until February 15, 2043. The first three semiannual payments are coupon interest totaling $2,787,500.

$$(\$120,000,000 * 0.00375 * 1/2) + (\$100,000,000 * 0.0200 * 1/2)$$
$$+ (\$100,000,000 * 0.03125 * 1/2) = \$2,787,500$$

TABLE 9.2 Portfolio Cash Flows and Calculations

Date	Date	Cash Flow	PV of Cash Flow	Weight	Date * Weight	Dispersion	Convexity
0	02/15/14	−345,701,561					
1	08/15/14	2,787,500	2,741,389	0.007930	0.007930	4.217	0.016
2	02/15/15	2,787,500	2,696,041	0.007799	0.015598	3.795	0.047
3	08/15/15	2,787,500	2,651,443	0.007670	0.023009	3.401	0.092
4	02/15/16	122,787,500	114,862,257	0.332258	1.329034	133.690	6.645
5	08/15/16	2,562,500	2,357,452	0.006819	0.034097	2.477	0.205
6	02/15/17	2,562,500	2,318,455	0.006707	0.040239	2.187	0.282
17	08/15/22	2,562,500	1,929,801	0.005582	0.094899	0.278	1.708
18	02/15/23	102,562,500	75,961,396	0.219731	3.955160	8.067	75.148
19	08/15/23	1,562,500	1,138,099	0.003292	0.062551	0.084	1.251
20	02/15/24	1,562,500	1,119,273	0.003238	0.064754	0.053	1.360
56	02/15/42	1,562,500	613,966	0.001776	0.099456	1.812	5.669
57	08/15/42	1,562,500	603,810	0.001747	0.099557	1.895	5.774
58	02/15/43	226,562,500	86,104,181	0.249071	14.446109	286.926	852.320
			345,701,561	1.000000	24.059117	480.571	1,083.471

On February 15, 2016, the first T-note having a par value of $120 million matures and the total payment is $122,787,500. Between August 15, 2016, and August 15, 2022, the coupon interest is $2,562,500.

$$(\$100,000,000 * 0.0200 * 1/2) + (\$100,000,000 * 0.03125 * 1/2)$$
$$= \$2,562,500$$

After the next T-note is retired on February 15, 2023, entailing a total payment of $102,562,500, the cash flows are just the coupon interest on the remaining T-bond.

$$\$100,000,000 * 0.03125 * 1/2 = \$1,562,500$$

On February 15, 2043, the T-bond and the P-STRIPS mature and the final payment is $226,562,500.

This sequence of evenly spaced, semiannual cash flow is the MV, CF_1, CF_2, . . ., CF_N in equation 9.1 needed to get the internal rate of return for the portfolio. I use the IRR function in Excel to get $YieldPORT = 1.682\%$, which is the yield per semiannual period. (Actually, given the full precision of the spreadsheet, $YieldPORT = 1.682028892\%$.) Annualized, the cash flow yield for this portfolio is 3.364% (s.a.).

The fourth column of Table 9.2 is the present value of the cash flow for each date, discounted using the (full precision) $YieldPORT$. The sum of those present values is $345,701,561, the market value of the portfolio, thereby verifying the internal rate of return calculation. Following equation 9.3, the fifth column divides each present value by the overall market value, giving the weights that sum to one. The sixth column multiplies the time to the receipt of the cash flow (measured in semiannual periods, column 1) times the weight. The sum of column 6 produces the Macaulay duration for the portfolio, $MacDurPORT = 24.059$. Annualized (by dividing by two), the portfolio Macaulay duration is 12.030. The annualized modified duration is 11.831, the Macaulay duration divided by one plus the cash flow yield per period.

$$ModDurPORT = \frac{12.030}{1.01682} = 11.831$$

The seventh column follows equation 9.4 to get the cash flow dispersion statistic for the portfolio. Whereas Macaulay duration is the *average* of the times to receipt of cash flow, dispersion is the *variance*. For each date, the difference between the time period (column 1) and the Macaulay duration (24.059) is squared and then multiplied by the present value of the cash flow (column 4). Summed over the 58 semiannual periods, *DispPORT* turns out to be 480.571. The eighth column gets the convexity of the portfolio using equation 9.6. For each date, the time period (column 1) is multiplied by one plus that time period, and then by the present value of the cash flow (column 4). The sum is 1,083.471. *ConvPORT* is found to be 1,047.9 by dividing the sum by one plus the portfolio yield (per period) squared.

$$ConvPORT = \frac{1,083.471}{(1.01682)^2} = 1,047.9$$

The portfolio yield, Macaulay duration, dispersion, and convexity statistics are linked by equation 9.7.

$$ConvPORT = \frac{(24.059)^2 + 24.059 + 480.571}{(1.01682)^2} = 1,047.9$$

Annualized, the portfolio dispersion is 120.1 and the convexity is 262.0, after dividing by four (the periodicity squared).

So, we have portfolio valued at $345,701,561. It has a cash flow yield of 3.364%, a Macaulay duration of 12.030, a modified duration of 11.831, a cash flow dispersion of 120.1, and a convexity of 262.0. Those annualized summary statistics use the big-bundle-of-cash-flow approach and represent the "true" risk and return profile for the portfolio. Now let's see how the statistics commonly used in practice compare.

The market value (MV) and basis point value (BPV) weights for the portfolio are shown in Table 9.3. The MV weights are straightforward (MV_j/MV); the BPV weights (BPV_j/BPV) entail multiplying the modified duration for each security by its market value, and then by one basis point. The differences between these weights are instructive—the P-STRIPS holding, while less than 12% of market value, represents a bit over 30% of interest

TABLE 9.3 Market Value and Basis Point Value Weights

Position	MV Weights	BPV Weights
0.375% T-note due 2/15/16	34.740%	6.265%
2.00% T-note due 2/15/23	27.535%	20.332%
3.125% T-bond due 2/15/43	25.993%	43.179%
0% P-STRIPS due 2/15/43	11.732%	30.224%
	100.000%	100.000%

rate risk. The short-term T-notes are almost one-third of market value but only about 6% of risk.

Due to the steepness of the yield curve, the market-value-weighted average yield is considerably less than the internal rate of return on the portfolio. *AvgYieldMV* is only 2.254% whereas *YieldPORT* is 3.362%.

$$AvgYieldMV = (0.333813\% * 0.34740) + (2.603264\% * 0.27535)$$
$$+ (3.697998\% * 0.25993) + (3.919371\% * 0.11732)$$
$$= 2.254\%$$

Suppose that the U.S. Treasury actually did use capital budgeting techniques as taught in introductory finance courses, and it has a long-term (29-year) project in mind. If it issues these four bonds at these prices to fund the project, the government has $345.7 million to invest. The point here is that if the project earns only 2.254% annually, the revenues are not sufficient to pay off that debt, especially the large payment due on February 15, 2043. The project would have to earn at least 3.364% to have positive net present value. The *BPV*-weighted average, 3.332%, is a better indicator of the "hurdle rate" for the project than the *MV*-weighted average.

$$AvgYieldBPV = (0.333813\% * 0.06265) + (2.603264\% * 0.20332)$$
$$+ (3.697998\% * 0.43179) + (3.919371\% * 0.30224)$$
$$= 3.332\%$$

Average yield duration and convexity are also lower than the "true" portfolio statistics. These correspond to changes in the yields to maturity on the individual securities.

$$AvgMacDur(Yield) = (1.994 * 0.34740) + (8.258 * 0.27535)$$
$$+ (18.679 * 0.25993) + (29.000 * 0.11732)$$
$$= 11.224$$

$$AvgModDur(Yield) = (1.991 * 0.34740) + (8.152 * 0.27535)$$
$$+ (18.340 * 0.25993) + (28.443 * 0.11732)$$
$$= 11.040$$

$$AvgConvexity(Yield) = (5.0 * 0.34740) + (74.2 * 0.27535)$$
$$+ (448.8 * 0.25993) + (822.9 * 0.11732)$$
$$= 235.403$$

The strong upward slope to the yield curve is the reason why these weighted averages understate the big-bundle-of-cash flow portfolio statistics: 12.030 for Macaulay duration, 11.831 for modified duration, and 262.0 for convexity. Moreover, these are not trivial differences.

The other set of market-value-weighted averages uses the curve duration and convexity as inputs.

$$AvgModDur(Curve) = (1.992 * 0.34740) + (8.441 * 0.27535)$$
$$+ (19.559 * 0.25993) + (32.855 * 0.11732)$$
$$= 11.955$$

$$AvgConvexity(Yield) = (5.0 * 0.34740) + (78.6 * 0.27535)$$
$$+ (502.4 * 0.25993) + (1,018.6 * 0.11732)$$
$$= 273.468$$

Notice that these are considerably higher than the averages based on the yield duration and convexities. Once again that's due to the upward slope of the Treasury yield curve. Also, these results are even higher than the "true" portfolio modified duration and convexity.

What is right? What numbers should an analyst use to understand the risk and return profile of the bond portfolio? Which statistics best measure risk exposure? In sum, which statistics are just data and which ones provide information? These are excellent questions.

THOUGHTS ON BOND PORTFOLIO STATISTICS

To be frank, I have more expertise at *producing* and *thinking about* individual bond and bond portfolio statistics than *using* them in practice. I've never built or managed an actual fixed-income portfolio. I offer some thoughts, but keep in mind that they come from someone looking at the world from an ivory tower. I'm going to imagine that I've been asked to manage, or at least advise, a large portfolio of investment-grade corporate bonds, made up of both noncallables and callables.

Obviously, my first step is to look at a variety of *descriptive statistics* for the portfolio, including the various weighted averages for yield, duration, and convexity. I'd want to see breakdowns by credit rating and industry. If not included in the spreadsheets provided to me, I'd ask someone to calculate the implied probabilities of default for each bond for a range of assumptions about recovery, as in Chapter 3. If my performance is measured against the return on some broad index of corporate bonds, I would want to see the descriptive statistics for that portfolio as well to identify any significant differences.

The key point here is that the descriptive statistics have informational value as long as they are measured consistently, even if they are theoretically flawed. I'll be watching for *changes* in those statistics over time. For instance, if average yield to maturity calculated for either MV or BPV weights is increasing, I'll want to know why. Is it due to higher yield on benchmark Treasuries? If so, is it because of higher real rates or higher expected inflation? Is it due to higher credit spreads over Treasuries? If so, is it due to a change in the probability of default or to projected recovery rates? Is the higher average yield due to a change in taxation or a loss in liquidity?

I'm going to use the average *curve*, rather than *yield*, duration and convexity in estimating potential changes in market value due to volatile interest rates. There are several reasons for this. Being an academic, I like theoretical correctness when possible and prefer to aggregate apples with apples. But, more important, I think about interest rate risk in the context of the Treasury yield curve. To me, the more intuitive what-if question is about a 25-basis-point shift in the Treasury curve, not a 25-basis-point change in the portfolio yield as estimated by the BPV-weighted average. Even though this is a portfolio of corporate bonds, interest rate risk commonly is *framed* with respect to benchmark Treasuries. Average *yield* duration and convexity are better thought of as primarily descriptive statistics, possibly useful in formulating portfolio strategy, as we see in Chapter 10.

There is another benefit to aggregating curve duration and convexity for the portfolio: The statistics can be decomposed into *partial* durations and convexities. Recall that the curve statistics are estimated using effective duration and convexity, as in Chapter 6. The entire Treasury yield curve is raised and lowered by a certain amount. Importantly, that shift translates to a nonparallel shift in the implied spot curve. Those implied spots are then used to value the bond assuming no arbitrage—that is, getting $MV(up)$ and $MV(down)$, the inputs to the calculations.

Rather than shift the entire Treasury yield curve, the same model can shift only one particular point, for instance, the 5-year or 10-year. That produces the sensitivity of the bond price (or portfolio) to an isolated shift in that particular Treasury yield. These are the partial (sometimes called *key rate*) durations and convexities. The sums of those partial durations and convexities are just the overall curve statistics. The point is that now it is possible to estimate the impact of various twists and turns to the shape of the Treasury yield curve. That is likely to be more insightful that just summarizing those "events" by the change in the overall average yield.

CONCLUSION

It is surely an unfair comparison, but sometimes bonds to me are like middle-school-age children. On their own, as individuals, they are fine and usually well behaved. The same can be said for bonds. I understand them and their risk-return profile. I can measure their comparative static properties. The problem is when they run together in portfolios, like children in a shopping mall. It's hard to predict pack behavior using weighted averages of their individual statistics.

You need a really good strategy to build and manage a bond portfolio. That comes next.

CHAPTER 10

Bond Strategies

Bond investment strategies usually are described as being either passive or active. However, I prefer the dichotomy to be "passive" or "aggressive" to focus attention on managerial intent rather than frequency of trading. Some passive strategies—for instance, tracking the performance of some published bond index or targeting a preset rate of return over a known investment horizon—require active trading to rebalance the portfolio. Trades in a passively managed bond fund are about "needs" and not "wants."

In contrast, an aggressively managed bond portfolio seeks to maximize the rate of return, typically over a given time period. For example, a fixed-income mutual fund manager focuses on changes in net asset value, subject to constraints on overall credit quality and maturity. When credit risk is a factor, the portfolio manager might overweight (or underweight) companies and industries expected to outperform (or underperform) market expectations. This draws more on equity analysis tools and not so much on bond math. Therefore, I focus on aggressive strategies having to do with an anticipated shift in the shape and level of the benchmark yield curve. The question is whether average portfolio duration and convexity are useful summary statistics for the strategy.

Some bond investment strategies can be described as passive-aggressive, borrowing loosely the term from psychology. In fact, I suspect that many bond portfolio managers in practice tread this middle ground, sometimes content to follow the market passively and at other times intentionally staking out some position that is hoped to achieve superior performance. For example, fixed-income portfolios often are judged relative to a published index. The fund manager might just track the index, holding positions very similar to the bonds that compose the benchmark, and wait for opportunities to be aggressive.

Before starting, let's try one more quiz—no tricks this time; there is no wrong or right answer. Suppose that some government trying to deal with its enormous debt decides to run a national lottery to raise needed funds—Big Bond Lotto, it's called. The payoff each week is a fixed-rate, long-term government bond. This is a pari-mutuel lottery in that the grand prize depends on the number of winning tickets. You pick your numbers strategically and are lucky enough to be the sole winner of Big Bond Lotto, fortunately after several months have gone by without a winner, thereby building up a huge payout. Now that you're a very rich fixed-income investor, what is your hope for benchmark interest rates? Are you hoping that government bond yields go down, go up, or are you indifferent?

If you are like most people to whom I've posed this scenario, you hope that yields go down so that the bond price goes up. You have revealed your investment horizon—you plan to sell the government bond soon to diversify into other, more fun, assets. Not only are you rich, you want capital gains, too! Occasionally, someone hopes that yields go up so that coupons can be reinvested at the higher rates. This is a revealed hold-to-maturity investor whose total return is a function of coupon reinvestment risk. The hope is that the real rate goes up, not inflation.

Suppose that some clever person, after checking a financial function on Excel or Bloomberg, or maybe digging out a bond math formula and using a financial calculator, announces that he or she is indifferent to yields going up or down. Granted, that indifference is subject to how and when yields change but still this person claims, "I'm good, I'm immunized from interest rate risk because it just so happens that the Macaulay duration of this government bond matches my investment horizon." Okay, this has never happened, but in theory it could.

Immunization strategy is a great way to conclude a study of bond math. The key point is that the difference between the duration of the fixed-income portfolio and the investment horizon measures interest rate risk. When those are matched, risk is minimized and the investor is immunized to a large extent from rate volatility. An implication is that two investors holding the same bond portfolio can have diametrically opposed risk profiles. One investor gains if yields rise; the other gains if yields fall. One hedges risk by entering a receive-fixed interest swap; the other hedges by entering a pay-fixed swap.

In sum, fixed-income strategy ultimately depends on the time horizon for the investment portfolio. That raises the specter of what I call *horizon risk*, which is the risk that a strategy is set assuming a particular holding period, only to find that the bonds need to be liquidated prematurely or unexpectedly rolled over.

ACTING ON A RATE VIEW

Suppose that you are the strategist for an aggressively (and actively) managed "long-only" portfolio of Treasury notes and bonds, having maturities spread out along the yield curve. You have to stay fully invested in Treasuries, cannot use derivatives, cannot take on short positions, and cannot use borrowed funds for leverage. You are authorized to buy and sell securities opportunistically in light of your view on an impending change to the level and shape of the Treasury yield curve. Your objective is to maximize quarterly returns, that is, achieve gains (when Treasury yields go down) as well as to minimize losses (when yields go up). Currently, the market-value-weighted average modified duration of your portfolio is 7.10 and the average convexity is 110.5 (using the Bloomberg convexities times 100). These are *descriptive statistics* and are averages of the *yield* durations and convexities.

Some decisions are quite straightforward. Suppose your view is that the Treasury yield curve will shift either upward or downward in a parallel manner, as illustrated in Figure 10.1. Surely when you anticipate the upward shift, you sell some long-term T-bonds and buy short-term T-notes, thereby reducing average duration. When your view is a downward parallel shift, you sell short-term T-notes and buy long-term T-bonds in order to increase the overall modified duration of the portfolio. That sounds simple enough, but in deciding how much to buy and sell, you have to consider trading costs and the chance that your rate view turns out to be incorrect. True believers in the expectations theory of the term structure will be quick to remind you that market expectations about factors driving yields up or down are already priced into the bonds.

The key point is that average duration is a perfectly acceptable summary statistic for the aggressive strategy. That is, you could instruct your traders to bring the average duration down to 6.10 from 7.10 in the first scenario or to take it up to 8.10 in the second. The change in the duration statistic captures the *extent* of the aggressive restructuring. For this purpose,

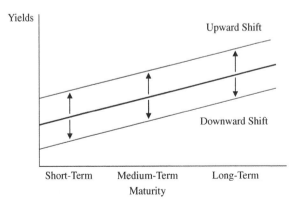

FIGURE 10.1 Parallel Upward and Downward Yield Curve Shifts

the standard market-value-weighted average of the yield duration statistics is fine. You are not estimating the change in market value—for that you would be better off using the weighted average of curve durations. Notice that your trades also change average convexity, but that is not the focus of your strategic move.

Although the assumption of a parallel shift to the yield curve is common (and might even allow for arbitrage opportunities), it is an abstraction from reality. In fact, most yield curve events entail upward or downward shifts combined with some steepening or flattening. Figure 10.2 illustrates these four shifts—bull and bear steepeners in the upper diagram and bull and bear "flatteners" in the lower diagram. A bull market means yields go down in general and bond prices rise; a bear market is when yields rise and prices fall.

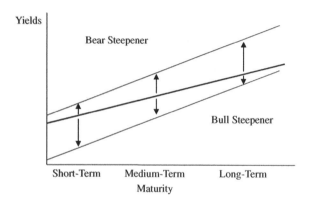

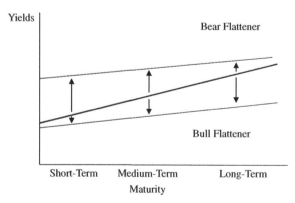

FIGURE 10.2   Steepening and Flattening Yield Curve Shifts

Our problem is that in two of the four scenarios, the change in average duration no longer serves as a reasonable descriptive statistic for aggressive strategy. In those circumstances, you cannot instruct your traders to execute buy-and-sell orders to change overall average duration by a certain amount. In fact, it's not always obvious what you should sell and what you should buy. Do you see the two scenarios when average duration "fails" as a summary statistic for strategy and the two in which it continues to work well, as in the case of a parallel shift? As you think about this, remember that the estimated change in the market value of a bond (or a cluster of bonds at a particular point on the yield curve) is the modified duration times the market value (that product being the money, or dollar, duration) times the change in the yield.

Look first at the bear steepener in Figure 10.2. Yields on long-term T-bonds are expected to rise more than yields on short-term T-notes. You know what to do: Sell the former and buy the latter, thereby reducing average duration. Our problem is the bull steepener because short-term T-note yields are expected to fall more than the yields on long-term T-bonds. Market values at each point on the yield curve go up—it's a rising-price bull market. However, the extent of the increase in market value depends critically on the extent of the change in yield. The short end of the curve has larger reductions in yields but lower durations; the long end has smaller changes in yields but higher durations. This is not to say that as a strategist you are stymied, just that you need to factor into your analysis the extent of the anticipated change in yield at the various points on the curve. Note that partial (or key rate) durations would come in handy here. In principle, you could end up increasing or decreasing average duration.

Now consider the bull flattener. It's clear that you want to sell some of your short-term positions to load up on the long end. Not only are the long-term T-bonds expected to experience the larger drop in their yields to maturity, they also have much higher modified durations. In this scenario you could tell your traders to increase average duration as well as convexity. The problem is with the bear flattener. Which positions will lose more value—the short-term T-notes that have the larger increases in yield but the lower durations, or the long-term T-bonds that have the smaller changes in yield but higher durations? Again, you need a more articulated rate view to provide instructions for your traders. Changing average duration by a certain amount is not enough.

Which of the four nonparallel shifts are most likely to occur? Recall from Chapter 5 the three stylized facts regarding the term structure of interest rates—the normal upward slope, usually (but not recently) greater rate volatility at the short-term end of curve, and positively correlated shifts up and down. When the curve is steep due to low short-term rates, the tendency is for rising rates and a flatter curve. When the curve is inverted because of high short-term rates, "regression to the mean" leads to lower rates and a steeper (more upwardly sloped) curve. These imply that the two most likely shifts are bull steepening and bear flattening—the two for which average duration does not provide a clear and simple guide to portfolio strategy. I realize that this is disappointing news to those of us who are inclined to think that Frederick Macaulay was a prophet and duration is imbued with mystical qualities.

Figure 10.3 shows two examples of changes in the *shape* of the yield curve. Sometimes we actually do see U-shaped curves in which medium-term maturities have the lowest yields and humped curves where they are highest. Consider first the "negative butterfly" twist to the yield curve portrayed in the upper diagram. Short-term and long-term yields are expected to fall while medium-term yields rise. Given this rate view, you want to sell the medium-term T-notes and buy both short-term T-notes and long-term T-bonds.

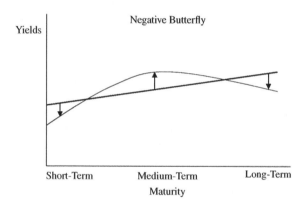

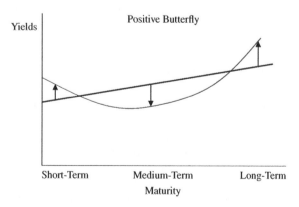

FIGURE 10.3   Shape-Changing Yield Curve Shifts

The key point is that once again you cannot use the change in average duration to describe the strategic rebalancing. Your negative butterfly trades could be duration neutral. However, transactions to "sell the belly and buy the wings" increase average convexity. You have increased cash flow dispersion by putting more weight at the ends of the yield curve. In this case, you could instruct your traders to keep average duration around 7.10 but raise average convexity from 110.5 to about 120. That signals how much restructuring you want for the portfolio.

I'm sure you now can deduce what to do with an anticipated "positive butterfly" shift in the lower diagram in Figure 10.3. You sell the wings, reducing your holdings of both short-term and long-term Treasuries, and add to the medium-term positions that you anticipate appreciating in value. Once again, the change in average duration is not obvious; however, you will be reducing average convexity and cash flow dispersion. You could charge your trading team to stay duration neutral but lower average convexity from 110.5 to about 100.

AN INTEREST RATE SWAP OVERLAY STRATEGY

Bond portfolios residing on either the asset or liability side of the balance sheet can be restructured internally or externally. I think of *internal risk management* as rebalancing via bond purchases and sales, for instance, as above, changing the average duration or convexity of the portfolio to conform to a particular rate view. The idea of "internal" is that the transactions are routine for the portfolio manager—buying and selling bonds. Often, *external risk management* accomplishes the same end. "External" here means using derivatives to transform some particular aspect of the asset or liability portfolio (i.e., its currency mix, credit exposure, or interest rate risk statistics). These are called *derivatives overlay strategies* in that the underlying portfolio is left intact while futures, options, or swaps modify its risk-return profile.

Now suppose that you are a passive-aggressive manager of an investment-grade corporate bond portfolio. You benchmark the quarterly returns on the portfolio against a widely used index that is produced and updated by an investment bank. You are essentially passive (i.e., a "closet indexer") in that the portfolio tracks the index. Therefore, it has a very similar distribution of bonds by credit quality and industry, and an average yield, duration, and convexity that are close to those of the benchmark. Note that it's important to know how those summary statistics are calculated for the index—probably they are market-value-weighted averages.

Your aggressive side comes out in overweighting and underweighting credit components that you expect to outperform and underperform recent trends and expectations from market commentators. Also, when you have a strong view on the Treasury yield curve, you extend or contract duration and convexity. Your problem is that it is costly to manage toward your particular rate view. Corporate bonds are not nearly as liquid as Treasuries, and there is a limited supply of certain maturities, especially long-term securities. You decide to manage the portfolio with a focus on getting the credit risk where you want it and then use interest rate swap overlays to reflect your view on the Treasury yield curve. Fortunately, interest rate swaps can be entered at low transactions costs and unwound expeditiously when your rate view happens to change.

Currently, your bond portfolio has a market value of $245 million and a market-value-weighted average modified yield duration of 6.50, matching the index used to benchmark your performance. The basis point value (BPV) of your portfolio is $159,250 (= $245,000,000 * 6.50 * 0.0001). Your rate view for the next several weeks is a bull flattener in which the long-term end of the yield curve drops more than the short-term end as inflationary fears dissipate. You decide to extend your modified duration out to about 7.50 using an interest rate swap. That restructuring corresponds to an increase in the BPV to about $183,750 (= $245,000,000 * 7.50 * 0.0001).

Thankfully, this is an anticipated yield curve shift for which average duration does serve as an indicator for the extent of the aggressive move. Suppose that 5-year and 10-year, quarterly settlement, fixed-versus-3-month-LIBOR, interest rate swaps are available to you from a swap dealer. Do you enter the swap as the fixed-rate payer or the fixed-rate receiver? Can you increase the average modified duration of the portfolio to 7.50 from 6.50 using a 5-year swap?

The answer to the first question is that you enter a *receive-fixed swap* that has positive duration. We saw in Chapter 8 that a receive-fixed/pay-LIBOR swap can be interpreted as a long position in a (high-duration) fixed-rate bond and a short position in a (very low-duration) floating-rate note paying LIBOR. The modified duration of the swap is the difference in the modified durations of the constituent bonds. In the same manner, the swap BPV is the difference in the BPVs of the implicit bonds. Suppose that the 5-year receive-fixed swap has a fixed rate of 1.75%, a modified duration of 4.56, and a BPV of 0.0456 per 100 of notional principal: 0.0456 = 100 * 4.56 * 0.0001. Also, a 10-year swap has a fixed rate of 3.00%, a modified duration of 8.36, and a BPV of 0.0836. Pay-fixed swaps have negative duration. Surely they do not reflect your bull flattener view.

The second question is harder and requires a deep understanding of swaps. It is tempting to conclude that entering a 5-year receive-fixed swap *lowers* the duration of the portfolio. After all, if the swap is like buying a 5-year fixed-rate bond financed by issuing a floater, then the duration of the portfolio that starts at 6.50 must go down if you add in lower duration assets. It would seem that only by entering a 10-year, receive-fixed swap can you lift the portfolio duration up to the 7.50 target.

This line of thinking, while compelling, misses a key idea—the interest rate swap does not change market value. Swaps simply modify, or transform, the duration of a segment of the portfolio. A receive-fixed swap, regardless of its time frame, adds duration to that segment. Equation 10.1 captures how to determine the notional principal (*NP*) needed to change the duration of a portfolio given its market value (*MV*) to the target duration.

$$
\begin{aligned}
&\left[\left(\frac{MV - NP}{MV}\right) * (Portfolio\ Duration)\right] \\
&+ \left[\left(\frac{NP}{MV}\right) * (Swap\ Duration + Portfolio\ Duration)\right] \\
&= Target\ Duration
\end{aligned}
\tag{10.1}
$$

This equation is based on two ideas. First, the duration of a segmented portfolio is estimated by a weighted average of the durations of the segments, using shares of total market value as the weights. Second, entering a plain vanilla interest rate swap transforms the duration of a segment of the portfolio but does not change the overall market value.

In equation 10.1, the segment of the original portfolio unaffected by the interest rate swap has a market-value weight of (*MV* – *NP*)/*MV*. The affected segment has the remaining weight, *NP*/*MV*, because the swap itself does not add nor subtract value at origination. It does, however, make the duration of the affected segment the sum of *Swap Duration* and the original *Portfolio Duration*. Therefore, a received-fixed swap increases, and a pay-fixed swap reduces, the duration of assets. In applying this formula, it is useful to isolate the *NP* term by algebraic rearrangement.

$$
NP = \frac{MV * [Target\ Duration - Portfolio\ Duration]}{Swap\ Duration}
\tag{10.2}
$$

Using the 10-year receive-fixed swap, you need a notional principal of about $29.3 million to increase the average duration of the portfolio from 6.50 to 7.50.

$$
NP = \frac{\$245\ million * [7.50 - 6.50]}{8.36} = \$29,306,220
$$

For the 5-year swap, you need more notional principal, about \$53.7 million, because the each unit of the derivative is less powerful.

$$NP = \frac{\$245 \text{ million} * [7.50 - 6.50]}{4.56} = \$53,728,070$$

In general, the higher the duration of the swap, less notional principal is required. It's like curing a headache—you can take a few low-dosage pills or just one gigantic pill providing a really big dose.

The hedge ratio for the swap, that is, the notional principal needed to achieve the new target risk measure, also can be calculated with the BPVs. The idea is to add the BPV of the swap to the original portfolio BPV to equal the target BPV. This is summarized in equation 10.3.

$$Portfolio\ BPV + \left(NP * \frac{Swap\ BPV}{100} \right) = Target\ BPV \qquad (10.3)$$

In this problem, the portfolio BPV is \$159,250 and the target BPV is \$183,750. Given the swap BPVs of 0.0456 and 0.0836 per 100 of notional principal for the 5-year and 10-year swaps, the same results are obtained.

$$\$159,250 + \left(NP * \frac{0.0456}{100} \right) = \$183,750, \quad NP = \$53,728,070$$

$$\$159,250 + \left(NP * \frac{0.0836}{100} \right) = \$183,750, \quad NP = \$29,306,220$$

This reminds us that modified duration and BPV contain the same information.

I've used the word "about" in setting the requisite notional principal judiciously because this is hardly an exact, tightly constructed calculation from a technical bond math perspective. The looseness arises in how average portfolio duration itself is calculated. I suggested in Chapter 9 that for corporate bond portfolios that inevitably contain callables, aggregating curve durations is more appropriate than yield durations to maintain apples with apples. But then what do you do if the benchmark index reports only the market-value-weighted average of yield durations?

How is the modified duration of those two swaps calculated? Is it yield duration or curve duration? Is your bond portfolio duration based on a periodicity of 2 (meaning the price sensitivity to changes in yields quoted on a semiannual bond basis) and your quarterly settlement swap on a periodicity of 4? If your rate view is based on Treasuries, how will the LIBOR swap curve shift if your bull flattener expectation prevails?

It's important not to fall for the *illusion of precision* just because your technology can deliver a very accurate-looking number. Sometimes you should round off your result to signal that it is measured with model error.

CLASSIC IMMUNIZATION THEORY

A great example of a passive fixed-income strategy is *immunization*. The objective is to try to lock in a target rate of return over a known investment horizon. This is accomplished by balancing the two opposing sources of interest rate risk over the holding period—cash flow reinvestment risk (on coupons and principal received prior to the horizon) and market price risk (on bonds that need to be liquidated at the horizon). If rates rise and remain risen, the future value of reinvested cash flow goes up but the sale price on the remaining bonds goes down. If, however, rates fall and remain fallen, the future value of reinvested cash flow goes down but the sale price on the remaining bonds goes up. As you no doubt are thinking, immunization requires assumptions about the timing and extent of interest rate volatility.

A numerical example here really helps. Assume that an investor has a firm 12-year investment horizon and buys on February 15, 2014, the Chapter 9 Treasury portfolio comprising some short-term notes, intermediate-term notes, and long-term bonds and zero-coupon STRIPS. For instance, this 12-year horizon could be the time until planned retirement or when payment is due for a child to attend a high-tuition (but very good) private university somewhere in Massachusetts. I'll lop off three digits of principal for each security to make the example more realistic. Note that all the summary statistics remain the same—bond math is invariant to scale.

So, we have a fixed-income bond portfolio valued at $345,701.56. The cash flow yield is 3.364%; the annual Macaulay and modified durations are 12.030 and 11.831; and the annual cash flow dispersion and convexity are 120.1 and 262.0. These are the "true" portfolio statistics based on the big-bundle-of-cash-flow approach and the cash flow yield, that is, the overall internal rate of return, and are not market-value-weighted averages.

The investor achieves a 12-year horizon yield of 3.364% if all coupon interest and principal cash flows received before February 15, 2026, are reinvested at 3.364% and if all bonds remaining in the portfolio at that time are sold at prices to yield 3.364%. This is the standard assumption about an internal rate of return that we first saw in Chapter 3. Essentially, if you stay on the constant-yield price trajectory, you can get off at any point and realize the original portfolio yield. Another way of saying this is that future transactions are made along the original implied forward curve. This assumes no default, of course. Also, this rate of return is in nominal terms. I'll get to immunization for real yields using linkers later.

Table 10.1 is an abridged version of the spreadsheet I use for this example. The third column is the cash flow for each semiannual period. The internal rate of return—that is, the solution for *YieldPORT* using equation 9.1 from Chapter 9—is 1.682% per semiannual period; annualized it is 3.364%.

TABLE 10.1   Total Returns for a 12-Year Horizon on February 15, 2026

Date	Date	Cash Flow	Total Return at 3.364%	Total Return at 2.364%	Total Return at 4.364%
0	02/15/14	−345,701.56			
1	08/15/14	2,787.50	4,090.99	3,652.50	4,579.58
2	02/15/15	2,787.50	4,023.32	3,609.83	4,481.79
3	08/15/15	2,787.50	3,956.77	3,567.66	4,386.09
4	02/15/16	122,787.50	171,409.84	155,317.13	189,078.49
5	08/15/16	2,562.50	3,518.05	3,203.51	3,861.69
16	02/15/22	2,562.50	2,928.31	2,815.07	3,045.50
17	08/15/22	2,562.50	2,879.87	2,782.19	2,980.47
18	02/15/23	102,562.50	113,358.24	110,054.59	116,744.11
19	08/15/23	1,562.50	1,698.40	1,657.05	1,740.57
20	02/15/24	1,562.50	1,670.31	1,637.70	1,703.40
21	08/15/24	1,562.50	1,642.68	1,618.56	1,667.03
22	02/15/25	1,562.50	1,615.50	1,599.66	1,631.43
23	08/15/25	1,562.50	1,588.78	1,580.97	1,596.59
24	02/15/26	1,562.50	1,562.50	1,562.50	1,562.50
25	08/15/26	1,562.50	1,536.65	1,544.25	1,529.13
26	02/15/27	1,562.50	1,511.23	1,526.21	1,496.48
55	08/15/41	1,562.50	931.65	1,085.47	800.23
56	02/15/42	1,562.50	916.24	1,072.79	783.14
57	08/15/42	1,562.50	901.08	1,060.26	766.42
58	02/15/43	226,562.50	128,495.91	151,941.78	108,757.31
			515,896.08	519,138.65	518,660.65

The fourth column is the value of each cash flow as of period 24, the horizon date on February 15, 2026. For example, the period-1 cash flow of $2,787.50 on August 15, 2014, grows to $4,090.99 over the 23 semiannual periods at the rate of 1.682%.

$$\$2,787.50 * (1.01682)^{23} = \$4,090.99$$

The period-58 cash flow of $226,562.50, which includes the redemption of principal on the two long-term bonds on February 15, 2043, has a discounted value of $128,495.91 over the 34 remaining semiannual periods between February 2026 and February 2043.

$$\frac{\$226,562.50}{(1.01682)^{34}} = \$128,495.91$$

The sum of the fourth column is $515,896.08. That's the total return on the horizon date under the strong assumption of reinvesting cash and selling bonds at the unchanged rate of 3.364%. It's no surprise that the realized holding-period rate (*HPR*) over the 12 years, as calculated in Chapter 3, is that same rate when annualized.

$$\$345,701.56 = \frac{\$515,896.08}{(1+HPR)^{24}}, \quad HPR = 0.01682, *2 = 0.03364$$

To see immunization at work, suppose that after purchasing the portfolio on February 15, 2014, the entire Treasury curve shifts upward or downward. In the first case, as shown in the fifth column, the new portfolio cash flow yield is 2.364%, a 100-basis-point decrease. Notice that I do not need to assume necessarily a parallel shift to the yield curve. That is, all I need for the exercise is a new, lower rate that applies when cash flows are reinvested and when bonds are sold at the horizon date. Alternatively, I can assume that future transactions are made at the new implied forward rates. To get the entries for each date, I subtract 50 basis points from the original yield per semiannual period and redo the time-value-of-money calculations.

$$\$2,787.50 * (1.01182)^{23} = \$3,652.50$$

$$\frac{\$226,562.50}{(1.01182)^{34}} = \$151,941.78$$

The total return on the horizon date is $519,138.65 and the horizon yield is 3.417%.

$$\$345,701.56 = \frac{\$519,138.65}{(1 + HPR)^{24}}, \quad HPR = 0.017086, * 2 = 0.03417$$

The sixth column shows the results from repeating the exercise for the increase in the rate up to 4.364% (s.a.). Again, a parallel shift is not required. We only need the assumption that cash flow reinvestment and bond sales can be made along the new, post-event implied forward curve that produces a portfolio yield of 4.364%. I add 50 basis points to the original yield per semiannual period and let the spreadsheet do the work. The total return as of February 15, 2026, is $518,660.65 and the horizon yield is 3.409% (s.a.).

$$\$345,701.56 = \frac{\$518,660.65}{(1 + HPR)^{24}}, \quad HPR = 0.017047, * 2 = 0.03409$$

If this is the first time you are seeing this demonstration of immunization, I hope that you are suitably impressed. Our investor essentially has locked in a total rate of return (in nominal terms) over the 12-year horizon. The holding-period rate of return remains close to the original cash flow yield of 3.364% (s.a.), in fact it is a little above, for a 100-basis-change in the interest rate. It's a bit higher because of convexity—this portfolio is more convex, that is, has a greater dispersion of cash flows, than a 12-year zero-coupon bond that would have provided "perfect" immunization. You can change the yield however you like—it works, as long as you keep that new rate constant going forward. Moreover, the yield curve event does not have to be instantaneous. The investor is immunized for the time until the first cash flow reinvestment date in six months.

How does immunization work? Why did I pick a 12-year investment horizon? It's because this portfolio happens to have an annual Macaulay duration of 12.030. The idea is that when the Macaulay duration of the portfolio matches (or, at least, is close to) the investment horizon, the cash flow reinvestment and market price risks offset. This is apparent in the last three columns of Table 10.1. When the yield goes up, the investor benefits from reinvesting the early (pre-horizon) cash flows but suffers from selling the late (post-horizon) coupon and principal payments. The opposite happens if yields go down.

Macaulay duration is quite remarkable. Not only does it provide a good first-order approximation for the change in market value following a sudden change in the yield, it also provides a measure of total return risk looking out into the future. When the investor's horizon is less than the duration, the risk is that yields go up because the market price effect dominates cash flow reinvestment. When the horizon is more than the duration, the risk is that yields fall because reinvestment dominates the market price risk. Remember this next time you win a big lottery.

Immunization is not without risk, however. Recall the underlying assumption that yields rise *and remain risen* or that yields fall *and remain fallen*. Surely, that's not likely. For example, suppose that the rate for reinvesting cash flows drops to 2.364% but then jumps up to 4.364% on the horizon date when the remaining bonds need to be sold. Summing the results for the first 24 periods from column 5 in Table 10.1 and then for the next 36 periods from column 6 give a total return of $469,947.62 and a realized rate of return of only 2.575%.

The amount of the interest rate risk in a duration-matching immunization strategy depends on the timing of the cash flows. This particular portfolio has significant cash flow dispersion. That short-term T-note maturing in 2016 is the major source of reinvestment risk. Where will 10-year notes be trading in two years? The long-term T-bond and STRIPS are a major source of market price risk. Where will 17-year Treasury prices be when those securities are scheduled to be sold in 12 years? The interest rate risk is mitigated by choosing bonds that match the Macaulay duration for the portfolio to the horizon and also *minimize* the dispersion statistic.

You probably are thinking that there is an obvious solution to this risk—just buy a zero-coupon bond that matures at the investment horizon. There is no cash flow subject to reinvestment risk, no market price risk (because the bond is redeemed at par value and not sold on the open market), and the dispersion is zero. In fact, it is productive to think of an immunization strategy using a portfolio of coupon bonds as "zero replication." This is illustrated in Figure 10.4. If the yield remains constant, the price of the

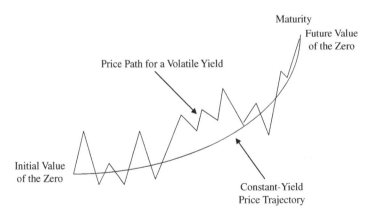

FIGURE 10.4 Immunization as Zero Replication

zero moves smoothly up the trajectory reaching its destination at maturity, which by design matches the horizon date. However, the actual price path getting there might be quite volatile as yields bounce around. That doesn't matter—the hold-to-maturity zero-coupon bond achieves its objective independent of the price path.

The idea of immunization is to *structure* and *manage* the portfolio of coupon bonds to reach the same destination as the maturity-matching zero. By "structure," I mean build the portfolio so that its Macaulay duration is close to the investment horizon. By "manage," I mean rebalance the portfolio regularly to stay on duration target. In sum, keep the relevant summary statistic close to that of the zero-coupon bond that provides for perfect immunization.

Suppose in Figure 10.4 that the first event is a lower yield on the zero; its price moves up. The bond portfolio should track that price movement closely assuming the change in the portfolio yield is the same as the change on the zero. If the next market movement is a higher yield, both should fall in market value by the same amount as long as their durations continue to match. But we need to rebalance regularly to deal with "duration drift." Remember from Chapter 6 that Macaulay duration on a coupon bond is inversely related to its yield to maturity. Also, as time passes duration declines in the saw-tooth pattern during the coupon period and then spikes upward on payment dates. The problem is that, as time passes and yields change, the durations of the portfolio of coupon bonds and the zero that provides perfect immunization do not change by the same amount.

The portfolio of coupon bonds needs to be managed actively to stay on duration target. How frequently the portfolio is rebalanced depends on transactions costs. Note that this can be done using derivative overlays such as interest rate swaps. Rebalancing means that the risk management problem starts over again each period. While the numerical examples assumed that rates rise and remain risen or that rates fall and remain fallen, immunization works in principle as long as the portfolio stays duration-matched—and as long as the yield curve is reasonably well behaved. That means generally parallel shifts to a generally flat curve. The real danger is a steepening twist, especially causing higher yields as the horizon nears and remaining bonds need to be sold.

IMMUNIZATION IMPLEMENTATION ISSUES

Immunization theory is based on the big-bundle-of-cash-flow portfolio statistics. In the example, we lock in the cash flow yield of 3.364% over the 12-year horizon because the portfolio Macaulay duration is 12.030. But that duration statistic is not commonly used in practice; instead it typically is estimated using the market-value-weighted average of the individual yield durations. In Chapter 9, we calculated $AvgMacDur(Yield)$ to be 11.224, considerably below the "true" portfolio duration because of the steep upward slope to the yield curve.

Bond strategies in practice inevitably have some degree of model risk arising from the statistics that we use to structure and manage the portfolio. Typically, we estimate those statistics using market-value-weighted averages. Sometimes they are accurate (e.g., when the yield curve is flat), but most of the time those averages introduce measurement error. For an immunization strategy, one way of mitigating the model risk as well as interest rate risk arising from not-so-well-behaved yield curves (i.e., nonparallel shifts, especially bear steepeners) is to build the portfolio to resemble that which works best—a zero-coupon bond maturing at or close to the horizon.

The standard textbook prescription to mitigate risk in an immunization strategy is to match the duration of a portfolio of coupon bonds to the horizon and to *minimize* cash flow dispersion. The intuition here is obvious—reducing dispersion by clustering the maturities of the bonds near the horizon makes the portfolio look more like the zero. In the extreme, *DispPORT*, the portfolio dispersion statistic introduced in Chapter 9, approaches zero. This not only reduces both cash flow reinvestment and market price risk, it also reduces model risk. In a tightly clustered, low-dispersion portfolio, the market-value-weighted averages are closer to the "true" portfolio statistics, even in a steep yield curve environment. For instance, $AvgMacDur(Yield)$ is closer to *MacDurPORT*, the lower is cash flow dispersion.

The problem with the prescription to duration match and minimize dispersion is not in theory; it is in implementation. In Chapter 9, I note that dispersion is not a statistic reported on Bloomberg (although it could be) and, more important, even if it were readily accessible, the market-value-weighted average of the statistics on individual bonds can be misleading. Fortunately, equation 9.7, repeated here as equation 10.4, offers a handy remedy.

$$ConvPORT = \frac{(MacDurPORT)^2 + MacDurPORT + DispPORT}{(1 + YieldPORT)^2} \quad (10.4)$$

For a given Macaulay duration for the portfolio, minimizing portfolio dispersion is equivalent to minimizing portfolio convexity. Note that this result is for the "true" statistics, not the weighted averages. However, given that it is common to calculate $AvgConvexity(Yield)$, the market-value-weighted average of the individual yield convexities, my suggestion is that an immunization strategy minimizes interest rate and model risk by duration matching and minimizing average convexity. On the other hand, a passive-aggressive approach to immunization is to match the duration to the investment horizon and, instead, *maximize* convexity. That will outperform the "extreme-zero-replication" approach to the extent that the yield curve is well behaved and does not twist in undesired ways.

There actually are practical applications for an immunization strategy to target a *nominal* rate of return. An example is *defeasance* whereby an issuer, often a corporation or municipality, has the cash to pay off debt liabilities and improve its leverage ratio and perhaps get an upgrade to its credit rating. However, unless the debt currently is callable, it can be difficult and expensive to buy back the bonds via a tender offer or an open market repurchase program. Seasoned corporate and municipal bonds are not very liquid and reside in hold-to-maturity portfolios. However, if the cash is invested in high-quality bonds, for instance, Treasury and agency notes, there are circumstances when for accounting purposes both the debt and the bond investments can be taken off the balance sheet. One way of building the defeasance portfolio is to match coupon and principal cash flows as closely as possible. Another is to match the durations and then actively rebalance to stay on duration target.

Many real-world investment problems are better described as attempts to target a *real*, i.e., after inflation, rate of return, for instance, on retirement savings. The same principle of immunization applies, only now it is to match the real rate duration to the horizon. Suppose that an individual plans to retire in 20 years. A 20-year P-Linker, such as TIPS, matches the horizon but still leaves coupon reinvestment risk on the table. Granted, the volatility in real rates is less than in nominal rates, but still a lower-risk strategy is to build a portfolio of TIPS that has an average real rate duration of 20 and then as time passes to stay on real rate duration target.

Recall from Chapter 7 that an advantage of P-Linkers is that the real rate duration statistic is high relative to traditional fixed-rate bonds and is not a function of the inflation rate. C-Linkers, however, are problematic for this strategy because their real rate durations are not only lower but, more importantly, depend on the projected inflation rate. It's much harder to build a real-rate immunizing portfolio using C-Linkers.

Another practical problem in implementing immunization strategy is *horizon risk*. This is the risk that once the portfolio is built, the investor's plans change, requiring early liquidation of the bonds or unexpected cash flow reinvestment. I think the biggest challenge that financial planners have is to get investors to reveal their financial objective, their true investment horizon, and their ability to stay committed to that time frame. Frankly, once the amount of desired total return and the time horizon are known, building a duration-matching bond portfolio is relatively easy.

LIABILITY-DRIVEN INVESTING

F. M. Redington, a British actuary, coined the term *immunization* in 1952. In an influential address to the Society of Actuaries, he proposed that life insurance companies manage interest rate risk by matching what he called the *mean term* of assets to liabilities. He described immunization to occur when the first derivative of the value of assets given a change in the interest rate equals the first derivative of the value of liabilities and the second derivative of the value of assets exceeds the second derivative of the value of liabilities. To me, Redington and Macaulay (along with Irving Fisher, who first decomposed nominal rates into the real rate and inflation) are the fathers of bond math.

We can translate Redington's criteria for immunization to be: (1) The modified duration of assets equals the modified duration of liabilities, and (2) the convexity of assets exceeds the convexity of liabilities. These rules are at the heart of what nowadays is called *liability-driven investing* (LDI). The idea is that an investment portfolio should not be structured and managed in isolation. Instead, one should look across the balance sheet to identify the sensitivity of liabilities to the main drivers of change in interest rates—that is, changes in the real rate, inflation, and credit risk. LDI is clearly applicable to pension funds, insurance companies, and university endowment funds.

Consider a defined-benefit pension plan. Its liabilities are the payments owed to employees in retirement. Typically, the obligations are tied to the employee's wage level and the number of years worked. Some plans index the retirement benefits to inflation; in others they are set in nominal terms. Obviously, measuring the plan's liabilities is a huge task requiring many assumptions, including future wage levels that depend on inflation and productivity growth, expected lifetime of the retirees, number of employees whose pensions become vested, and the interest rates used to discount the future payments back to the current date.

Suppose that the pension plan, or at least its actuarial consultant, has a big, complex model to measure its liabilities. It can raise and lower the baseline interest rate assumptions in the model to obtain estimates of $MV(initial)$, $MV(up)$, and $MV(down)$. From those, it can get the effective duration of liabilities and even effective convexity, although that might be pushing the analysis a bit too far. The key point is that the modified duration of pension fund assets also can be estimated. But this, too, is difficult because most defined benefit pension plans are heavily invested in equity. The interest rate sensitivity of common stock is not nearly as clean cut as it is with a fixed-rate bond because the change in value depends on *why* the nominal rate changes (i.e., due to the real rate or inflation), and that relationship might not be stable over time.

Despite these modeling problems—and the model risk that results—the pension plan still can measure the duration gap between the assets and liabilities. Usually asset duration is significantly lower than liability duration. The next step is to decide to maintain or to reduce that gap, for instance, using interest rate derivatives overlays, such as receive-fixed swaps, that have positive duration. Another possibility is to estimate the real rate and inflation durations of the liabilities and then to use linkers as part of the risk reduction strategy.

CLOSING THOUGHTS: TARGET-DURATION BOND FUNDS

I would like to close this book with a request to readers who might have some influence in the real world. There have been many innovations in the asset management industry over the years, including stock-index funds, industry-specific equity funds, exchange-traded funds, and, recently, target-date retirement funds. From my perspective as a conservative investor, I keep waiting for what seems to me to be the obvious next step—*target-duration bond funds*.

Fixed-income bond funds typically are identified by issuer type to signal credit risk—government, agency, (investment-grade) corporate, or high yield—and average maturity to signal interest rate risk—ultra-short, short-term, intermediate-term, or long-term. The bond portfolio often is managed to try to match or exceed the rate of return on some well-known benchmark index of bonds. The fund manager establishes and acts on an interest rate view, in general, regarding likely shifts in the shape and level of the relevant yield curve. I describe this as passive-aggressive.

The development I'd like to see is a family of passively managed bond funds, each targeting a designated average duration. These could be mutual funds or exchange-traded funds. The assets would be high-quality corporate, agency, or Treasury notes and bonds for which interest rate changes are the main drivers of performance. For example, suppose these target-duration bond funds are named D-0, D-1, D-3, D-5, D-8, and so on and are composed only of government securities. The D-0 fund holds overnight positions in very short-term money market instruments. The D-5 fund holds Treasury notes such that the market-value-weighted average modified duration for the portfolio is 5.0, but to be practical might range from day to day between, say, 4.9 and 5.1.

What is the difference between target-duration bond funds and the status quo? Most important, these funds would be passively managed, thereby minimizing operating expenses. The fund managers would not be buying and selling bonds based on a rate view. They would not be putting on flattener or steepener trades or looking for butterfly twists. If derivatives overlays are used, it is merely to keep the fund on its duration target as efficiently as possible. Each target-duration fund also would minimize average convexity.

There are two advantages of target-duration bond funds in my opinion, in addition to lower expenses. First, the investor is presented with a better articulated and more consistent interest rate risk profile than the typical fixed-income bond fund. There simply is more precise information in the names "D-5" and "D-7" than "intermediate-term." An active investor expecting long-term Treasury yields to fall would want to hold shares in the longest target-duration fund available, for instance, D-12. The investor then could expect that the net asset value of that particular fund will appreciate by about 12% if long-term Treasury yields fall by about 1%.

Second, the investor could use the family of target-duration bond funds to carry out "homemade" immunization. Suppose that an investor has a 7-year time horizon until retirement and would like to invest with minimal interest rate and credit risk. The investor initially would buy shares in the D-7 fund and then smoothly over time transfer the investment to other funds in the family. For example, assuming quarterly rebalancing, three months later one-fourth of the holdings would be transferred from D-7 to the D-6 fund. The average duration is then 6.75 years, matching the remaining time horizon. After another three months, the investment would be divided evenly between D-6 and D-7, and so forth. As the horizon date nears, the funds would end up entirely in D-0. The idea is that the total return over the 7 years tracks what could have been obtained from an initial investment in a 7-year zero-coupon bond, subject to the inevitable model and badly behaving yield curve risks.

Target-duration bond funds need not replace the current array of fixed-income fund offerings. Surely there are investors who are willing to pay the additional expenses to compensate managers who try to enhance returns vis-à-vis the benchmark index by raising and lowering average duration opportunistically. But surely there are others (like me) who would prefer lower expenses and to pursue via target-duration bond funds either a passive investment strategy, such as homemade immunization, or an aggressive strategy based on their own rate view.

Technical Appendix

CHAPTER 1 MONEY MARKET INTEREST RATES

Equation 1.8, which allows the conversion of a discount rate to an add-on rate when both are quoted for the same day-count convention, is derived by assuming that the cash flows, PV and FV, are the same for each rate quotation. To derive the equation, first rewrite equations 1.3 and 1.6.

$$\frac{FV}{PV} = \left[1 + \left(AOR * \frac{Days}{Year}\right)\right] \qquad \text{(A1.1)}$$

$$\frac{FV}{PV} = \frac{1}{\left[1 - \left(DR * \frac{Days}{Year}\right)\right]} \qquad \text{(A1.2)}$$

Equate these two expressions.

$$\left[1 + \left(AOR * \frac{Days}{Year}\right)\right] = \frac{1}{\left[1 - \left(DR * \frac{Days}{Year}\right)\right]} \qquad \text{(A1.3)}$$

Subtract 1 from each side.

$$\left(AOR * \frac{Days}{Year}\right) = \frac{1}{\left[1 - \left(DR * \frac{Days}{Year}\right)\right]} - 1 = \frac{1 - \left[1 - \left(DR * \frac{Days}{Year}\right)\right]}{\left[1 - \left(DR * \frac{Days}{Year}\right)\right]} \qquad \text{(A1.4)}$$

Simplify the numerator on the right side.

$$\left(AOR * \frac{Days}{Year} \right) = \frac{DR * \dfrac{Days}{Year}}{\left[1 - \left(DR * \dfrac{Days}{Year} \right) \right]} \tag{A1.5}$$

Multiply each side of the equation by *Year/Days*.

$$AOR = \frac{DR}{\left[1 - \left(DR * \dfrac{Days}{Year} \right) \right]} \tag{A1.6}$$

Multiply the numerator and denominator by *Year* to get equation 1.8.

$$AOR = \frac{Year * DR}{Year - (DR * Days)} \tag{A1.7}$$

Equation 1.11 is the official Investment Rate conversion formula for Treasury bill discount rates having six months or less to maturity. It converts the 360-day discount rate to a 365-day add-on basis. The equation can be derived by letting *IR* = *AOR* and *Year* = 365 in A1.1 and *Year* = 360 in A1.2.

$$\frac{FV}{PV} = \left[1 + \left(IR * \frac{Days}{365} \right) \right] \tag{A1.8}$$

$$\frac{FV}{PV} = \frac{1}{\left[1 - \left(DR * \dfrac{Days}{360} \right) \right]} \tag{A1.9}$$

Combine the equations.

$$\left[1 + \left(IR * \frac{Days}{365} \right) \right] = \frac{1}{\left[1 - \left(DR * \dfrac{Days}{360} \right) \right]} \tag{A1.10}$$

Proceed as above; subtract 1 from each side of the equation and simplify the numerator on the right side.

$$\left(IR * \frac{Days}{365}\right) = \frac{DR * \dfrac{Days}{360}}{\left[1 - \left(DR * \dfrac{Days}{360}\right)\right]} \tag{A1.11}$$

Multiply each side of the equation by *365/Days*.

$$IR = \frac{(365/360) * DR}{\left[1 - \left(DR * \dfrac{Days}{360}\right)\right]} \tag{A1.12}$$

Finally, multiply the numerator and denominator by 360 to get equation 1.11.

$$IR = \frac{365 * DR}{360 - (DR * Days)} \tag{A1.13}$$

Equation 1.12 is the official Investment Rate conversion formula for Treasury bill discount rates having more than six months to maturity. It is based on equation 1.13, repeated here.

$$100 = PV * \left(1 + \frac{182.5}{365} * IR\right) * \left(1 + \frac{Days - 182.5}{365} * IR\right) \tag{A1.14}$$

PV is the price of the T-bill, based on the discount rate pricing equation 1.6 assuming *FV* = 100, which is why 100 appears on the left-hand side. It implicitly converts to a 365-day basis. Rearrange A1.14 to display *IR* as an annual rate divided by 2 (periods in the year).

$$100 = PV * \left(1 + \frac{IR}{2}\right) * \left(1 + \frac{2 * (Days - 182.5)}{365} * \frac{IR}{2}\right) \tag{A1.15}$$

Simplify this expression by defining Z as follows:

$$Z \equiv \frac{2 * (Days - 182.5)}{365} = \frac{2 * Days}{365} - 1 \qquad \text{(A1.16)}$$

Substitute Z into A1.15 and divide both sides of the equation by PV.

$$\frac{100}{PV} = \left(1 + \frac{IR}{2}\right) * \left(1 + Z * \frac{IR}{2}\right) = 1 + \left(\frac{IR}{2}\right) + Z * \left(\frac{IR}{2}\right)^2 \qquad \text{(A1.17)}$$

Collect the $IR/2$ terms and rearrange further.

$$0 = Z * \left(\frac{IR}{2}\right)^2 + (1 + Z) * \left(\frac{IR}{2}\right) + \left(1 - \frac{100}{PV}\right) \qquad \text{(A1.18)}$$

This is now in the form of the general quadratic equation that has a well-known solution for x, here showing only the more positive root:

$$0 = a * x^2 + b * x + c \qquad \text{(A1.19)}$$

$$x = \frac{-b + \sqrt{b^2 - 4ac}}{2a} \qquad \text{(A1.20)}$$

Substitute $x = IR/2$, $a = Z$, $b = 1 + Z$, and $c = 1 - 100/PV$.

$$\frac{IR}{2} = \frac{-(1 + Z) + \sqrt{(1 + Z)^2 - 4 * Z * \left(1 - \frac{100}{PV}\right)}}{2 * Z} \qquad \text{(A1.21)}$$

Substitute the definition for Z from A1.16 back into the expression.

$$\frac{IR}{2} = \frac{-\left(\frac{2 * Days}{365}\right) + \sqrt{\left(\frac{2 * Days}{365}\right)^2 - 4 * \left(\frac{2 * Days}{365} - 1\right) * \left(1 - \frac{100}{PV}\right)}}{2 * \left(\frac{2 * Days}{365} - 1\right)}$$

$$\text{(A1.22)}$$

Finally, multiply both sides of the equation by 2 and simplify within the square root to get equation 1.12.

$$IR = \frac{-\dfrac{2 * Days}{365} + 2 * \sqrt{\left(\dfrac{Days}{365}\right)^2 - \left(\dfrac{2 * Days}{365} - 1\right) * \left(1 - \dfrac{100}{PV}\right)}}{\dfrac{2 * Days}{365} - 1}$$

(A1.23)

CHAPTER 3 PRICES AND YIELDS ON COUPON BONDS

Equation 3.4 is the standard relationship between the price of a fixed-income bond, PV, and its yield to maturity, y. The evenly spaced coupon payments of PMT each period and principal redemption of FV are discounted over the N periods to maturity. That equation is rewritten here.

$$PV = \left[\frac{PMT}{(1+y)^1} + \frac{PMT}{(1+y)^2} + \cdots + \frac{PMT}{(1+y)^N}\right] + \frac{FV}{(1+y)^N}$$

(A3.1)

The present value of the stream of coupon payments, in brackets, is the sum of a finite geometric series. Define that to be SUM.

$$SUM \equiv \left[\frac{PMT}{(1+y)^1} + \frac{PMT}{(1+y)^2} + \cdots + \frac{PMT}{(1+y)^N}\right]$$

(A3.2)

Divide both sides of this equation by $(1 + y)$.

$$\frac{SUM}{1+y} = \left[\frac{PMT}{(1+y)^2} + \frac{PMT}{(1+y)^3} + \cdots + \frac{PMT}{(1+y)^{N+1}}\right]$$

(A3.3)

Subtract A3.3 from A3.2. Notice that most of the terms in the brackets cancel.

$$SUM - \frac{SUM}{1+y} = \left[\frac{PMT}{(1+y)^1} - \frac{PMT}{(1+y)^{N+1}}\right]$$

(A3.4)

Multiply though by $(1 + y)$.

$$(1 + y) * SUM - SUM = \left[PMT - \frac{PMT}{(1 + y)^N} \right] \tag{A3.5}$$

Divide each side by y and pull the PMT term out of the brackets.

$$SUM = \frac{PMT}{y} * \left[1 - \frac{1}{(1 + y)^N} \right] \tag{A3.6}$$

Substitute A3.6 into A3.1 to get equation 3.5 in the text, repeated here.

$$PV = \frac{PMT}{y} * \left[1 - \frac{1}{(1 + y)^N} \right] + \frac{FV}{(1 + y)^N} \tag{A3.7}$$

CHAPTER 6 DURATION AND CONVEXITY

Equation 6.1 is the general bond pricing relationship between coupon payment dates. MV is the total price including accrued interest; PMT is the periodic coupon payment; FV is the principal redeemed in N periods as of the beginning of the current period, and t/T of the period has gone by and $1 - t/T$ remains.

$$MV = \frac{PMT}{(1 + y)^{1 - t/T}} + \frac{PMT}{(1 + y)^{2 - t/T}} + \cdots + \frac{PMT + FV}{(1 + y)^{N - t/T}} \tag{A6.1}$$

Multiply the numerator and denominator on the right side by $(1 + y)^{t/T}$.

$$MV = \left[\frac{PMT}{(1 + y)^1} + \frac{PMT}{(1 + y)^2} + \cdots + \frac{PMT + FV}{(1 + y)^N} \right] * (1 + y)^{t/T} \tag{A6.2}$$

Define the term in brackets to be PV, the price of the bond if the yield y prevailed at the beginning of the period when there were N full periods to maturity.

$$MV = PV * (1 + y)^{t/T} \tag{A6.3}$$

The first partial derivative of MV with respect to a change in the yield y is:

$$\frac{\partial MV}{\partial y} = \left(\frac{\partial PV}{\partial y} * (1+y)^{t/T} \right) + \left(t/T * PV * (1+y)^{t/T-1} \right) \qquad (A6.4)$$

Multiply this expression by $(1 + y)$ and divide by MV, using A6.3.

$$\frac{\partial MV}{\partial y} * \frac{1+y}{MV} = \left(\frac{\partial PV}{\partial y} * \frac{1+y}{PV} \right) + t/T \qquad (A6.5)$$

As defined in equation 6.3, the Macaulay duration of the bond is the negative of A6.5.

$$Macaulay\,Duration \equiv -\frac{\partial MV}{\partial y} * \frac{1+y}{MV} = -\left(\frac{\partial PV}{\partial y} * \frac{1+y}{PV} \right) - t/T$$

$$(A6.6)$$

Here we can use equations A3.7 for PV.

$$PV = \frac{PMT}{y} * \left[1 - \frac{1}{(1+y)^N} \right] + \frac{FV}{(1+y)^N} \qquad (A6.7)$$

Let the coupon rate per period be denoted c, such that $c = PMT/FV$. Equation A6.7 can now be written:

$$PV = \left(\frac{c}{y} * \left[1 - \frac{1}{(1+y)^N} \right] + \frac{1}{(1+y)^N} \right) * FV \qquad (A6.8)$$

The first partial derivative of this with respect to a change in the yield y is:

$$\frac{\partial PV}{\partial y} = \left\{ \left[\frac{c}{y} * \frac{N}{(1+y)^{N+1}} \right] - \left[\frac{c}{y^2} * \left(1 - \frac{1}{(1+y)^N} \right) \right] - \left[\frac{N}{(1+y)^{N+1}} \right] \right\} * FV$$

$$(A6.9)$$

Multiply this by $(1 + y)$ and divide by PV, as written in A6.8. Note the FV cancels.

$$\frac{\partial PV}{\partial y} * \frac{1+y}{PV} = \frac{\left[\frac{c}{y} * \frac{N}{(1+y)^N}\right] - \left[\frac{c*(1+y)}{y^2} * \left(1 - \frac{1}{(1+y)^N}\right)\right] - \left[\frac{N}{(1+y)^N}\right]}{\frac{c}{y} * \left[1 - \frac{1}{(1+y)^N}\right] + \frac{1}{(1+y)^N}}$$

$$(A6.10)$$

Next, multiply the numerator and denominator by $y * (1 + y)^N$.

$$\frac{\partial PV}{\partial y} * \frac{1+y}{PV} = \frac{(c*N) - \left[\frac{c*(1+y)}{y} * \left((1+y)^N - 1\right)\right] - [y*N]}{c * [(1+y)^N - 1] + y}$$

$$(A6.11)$$

Finally, add and subtract $(1 + y)$ in the numerator and rearrange terms.

$$\frac{\partial PV}{\partial y} * \frac{1+y}{PV} = -\frac{1+y}{y} + \frac{1+y+N*(c-y)}{c * [(1+y)^N - 1] + y}$$

$$(A6.12)$$

Substitute A6.12 into A6.6 to get the general formula for the Macaulay duration statistic, equation 6.13 in Chapter 6.

$$\textit{Macaulay Duration} = \left[\frac{1+y}{y} - \frac{1+y+N*(c-y)}{c * [(1+y)^N - 1] + y}\right] - t/T \quad (A6.13)$$

The weighted-average formula for Macaulay duration is obtained more directly. Take the first partial derivative of A6.2 with respect to the change in yield y.

$$\frac{\partial MV}{\partial y} = \left[-\frac{1*PMT}{(1+y)^2} - \frac{2*PMT}{(1+y)^3} - \cdots - \frac{N*(PMT+FV)}{(1+y)^{N+1}}\right] * (1+y)^{t/T}$$

$$+ \left[\frac{PMT}{(1+y)^1} + \frac{PMT}{(1+y)^2} + \cdots + \frac{PMT+FV}{(1+y)^N}\right] * t/T * (1+y)^{t/T-1}$$

$$(A6.14)$$

Multiply by $-(1 + y)$ and divide by MV, as defined in A6.2.

$$-\frac{\partial MV}{\partial y} * \frac{1+y}{MV} = \frac{\dfrac{1 * PMT}{(1+y)^1} + \dfrac{2 * PMT}{(1+y)^2} + \cdots + \dfrac{N * (PMT + FV)}{(1+y)^N}}{\dfrac{PMT}{(1+y)^1} + \dfrac{PMT}{(1+y)^2} + \cdots + \dfrac{PMT + FV}{(1+y)^N}} - t/T$$

$$(A6.15)$$

This is equation 6.14 in the text.

A6.4 is the first derivative of MV with respect to y; this is the second derivative.

$$\frac{\partial^2 MV}{\partial y^2} = \left(2 * \frac{\partial PV}{\partial y} * t/T * (1+y)^{t/T-1} \right) + \left(\frac{\partial^2 PV}{\partial y^2} * (1+y)^{t/T} \right)$$
$$+ (t/T * (t/T - 1) * PV * (1+y)^{t/T-2})$$

$$(A6.16)$$

At this point it is useful to define the Macaulay duration and convexity statistics as of the beginning of the period when $t/T = 0$ and there are N full periods to maturity.

$$\textit{Macaulay Duration}(t/T = 0) \equiv -\frac{\partial PV}{\partial y} * \frac{1+y}{PV} \qquad (A6.17)$$

$$\textit{Convexity}(t/T = 0) \equiv \frac{\partial^2 PV}{\partial y^2} * \frac{1}{PV} \qquad (A6.18)$$

Divide A6.16 by MV, using A6.3.

$$\frac{\partial^2 MV}{\partial y^2} * \frac{1}{MV} = \left(2 * \frac{\partial PV}{\partial y} * \frac{1}{PV} * t/T * \frac{1}{1+y} \right) + \left(\frac{\partial^2 PV}{\partial y^2} * \frac{1}{PV} \right)$$
$$+ \left(t/T * (t/T - 1) * \frac{1}{(1+y)^2} \right)$$

$$(A6.19)$$

This is the general definition of convexity, equation 6.6 in the text. Substitute A6.17 and A6.18 and rearrange the terms algebraically. This produces equation 6.17.

$$Convexity = Convexity(t/T = 0) - \frac{t/T}{(1+y)^2}$$
$$* \ [(2 * MacDur(t/T = 0)) + (1 - t/T)] \tag{A6.20}$$

The closed-form equation for convexity on a coupon date is derived by taking the second partial derivative of PV with respect to y. The first derivative is A6.9. The second derivative is this expression.

$$\frac{\partial^2 PV}{\partial y^2} = \left\{ -\left[\frac{c}{y} * \frac{N*(N+1)}{(1+y)^{N+2}} \right] - \left[\frac{2*c}{y^2} * \left(\frac{N}{(1+y)^{N+1}} \right) \right] \right.$$
$$\left. + \frac{2*c}{y^3} * \left(1 - \frac{1}{(1+y)^N} \right) + \left[\frac{N*(N+1)}{(1+y)^{N+2}} \right] \right\} * FV \tag{A6.21}$$

Divide this by PV, as defined in A6.8, and then multiply the numerator and denominator by the quantity $[y^3 * (1 + y)^{N+2}]$ and rearrange terms to obtain this expression:

$$\frac{\partial^2 PV}{\partial y^2} * \frac{1}{PV} = \frac{\left[2*c*(1+y)^2 * \left((1+y)^N - \frac{1+y+(y*N)}{1+y} \right) \right]}{y^2 * (1+y)^2 * (c*[(1+y)^N - 1] + y)} \\ \frac{+[N*(N+1)*y^2*(y-c)]}{} \tag{A6.22}$$

This is equation 6.16 in Chapter 6.

CHAPTER 7 FLOATERS AND LINKERS

Equation 7.6 provides a general pricing formula for a floating-rate note. It is repeated here.

$$MV = \frac{INT + FV + PV_{ANN}}{(1+y)^{1-t/T}} \tag{A7.1}$$

MV is the market value of the floater, including accrued interest; INT is the next interest payment; FV is the face (or par) value; PV_{ANN} is the present value of the annuity representing the difference between the quoted margin (QM) and the discount margin (DM), y is the yield used to discount the future cash flows, and t/T is the fraction of the period that has gone by.

The Macaulay duration of the floater ($MacDurFRN$) follows the Chapter 6 equation 6.3.

$$MacDurFRN \equiv -\frac{dMV}{dy} * \frac{(1+y)}{MV} \qquad (A7.2)$$

Using A7.1, the first derivative of MV with respect to the yield y is:

$$\frac{dMV}{dy} = -\frac{(1-t/T) * [INT + FV + PV_{ANN}]}{(1+y)^{2-t/T}} + \frac{\dfrac{dPV_{ANN}}{dy}}{(1+y)^{1-t/T}} \qquad (A7.3)$$

Substitute A7.3 and A7.1 into A7.2 to simplify.

$$MacDurFRN = (1-t/T) - \frac{\dfrac{dPV_{ANN}}{dy} * (1+y)}{MV * (1+y)^{1-t/T}} \qquad (A7.4)$$

Here it is useful to define the Macaulay duration of the annuity term (DUR_{ANN}) to be:

$$DUR_{ANN} \equiv -\frac{dPV_{ANN}}{dy} * \frac{(1+y)}{PV_{ANN}} \qquad (A7.5)$$

Substitute A7.5 into A7.4.

$$MacDurFRN = (1-t/T) + (\frac{PV_{ANN} * DUR_{ANN}}{MV * (1+y)^{1-t/T}}) \qquad (A7.6)$$

Equation 7.5 provides an expression for PV_{ANN}, repeated here.

$$PV_{ANN} = \left(\frac{(QM - DM) * FV}{PER * y} \right) * \left(1 - \frac{1}{(1+y)^{PER * Z-1}} \right) \quad \text{(A7.7)}$$

The first derivative of PV_{ANN} with respect to y is:

$$\frac{dPV_{ANN}}{dy} = \left(\frac{(QM - DM) * FV}{PER} \right)$$
$$* \left[-\frac{1}{y^2} * \left(1 - \frac{1}{(1+y)^{PER * Z-1}} \right) + \frac{1}{y} * \left(\frac{PER * Z - 1}{(1+y)^{PER * Z}} \right) \right] \quad \text{(A7.8)}$$

Substitute A7.7 and A7.8 into A7.5 and rearrange terms.

$$DUR_{ANN} = \frac{1+y}{y} - \frac{PER * Z - 1}{(1+y)^{PER * Z-1} - 1} \quad \text{(A7.9)}$$

Finally, substitute A7.9 into A7.6 and use A7.1 to get equation 7.9 in the text.

$$MacDurFRN = (1 - t/T) + \left(1 - \frac{INT + FV}{MV * (1+y)^{1-t/T}} \right)$$
$$* \left(\frac{1+y}{y} - \frac{PER * Z - 1}{(1+y)^{PER * Z-1} - 1} \right) \quad \text{(A7.10)}$$

Equation 7.11 gives the threshold inflation rate, which indicates the point at which after-tax cash flows on a P-Linker become negative.

$$Threshold\ Inflation\ Rate = \frac{Fixed\ Rate * (1 - TaxRate)}{Tax\ Rate - Fixed\ Rate * (1 - TaxRate)}$$
$$\text{(A7.11)}$$

Fixed Rate is the coupon interest rate on the P-Linker, and *Tax Rate* is the ordinary income tax rate. To derive A7.11, let *AP* stand for the accrued principal on the P-Linker at the end of a given year. The accrued principal at the end of the previous year is $AP(-1)$. The inflation rate for the year is given by:

$$Inflation\ Rate = \frac{AP - AP(-1)}{AP(-1)} \qquad (A7.12)$$

The interest income for the year is AP * *Fixed Rate*. The tax obligation is *Tax Rate* * AP * *Fixed Rate*, the ordinary tax rate times the interest income, plus the tax owed on the phantom income, *Tax Rate* * $[AP - AP(-1)]$.

Set the interest income equal to the tax obligation so the after-tax cash flow is zero.

$$AP * Fixed\ Rate = Tax\ Rate * AP * Fixed\ Rate + Tax\ Rate * [AP - AP(-1)]$$
$$(A7.13)$$

Rearrange A7.13 algebraically to get:

$$\frac{AP - AP(-1)}{AP(-1)} = \frac{Fixed\ Rate * (1 - Tax\ Rate)}{Tax\ Rate - Fixed\ Rate * (1 - Tax\ Rate)} \qquad (A7.14)$$

The derivation of equation 7.15, the real rate Macaulay duration for the P-Linker (*RealMacDurPLINK*), follows the same pattern as the derivations for Chapter 6. We start with the pricing formula for the P-Linker given in equation 7.14, repeated here.

$$PV_{PLINK} = \frac{c * FV}{r} * \left(1 - \frac{1}{(1+r)^N}\right) + \frac{FV}{(1+r)^N} \qquad (A7.15)$$

The fixed coupon rate is c; the real rate is r, the face (or par) value is FV, and the number of periods to maturity is N.

The real rate Macaulay duration is defined to be:

$$RealMacDurPLINK \equiv -\frac{dPV_{PLINK}}{dr} * \frac{(1+r)}{PV_{PLINK}} \qquad (A7.16)$$

The first derivative of the market value of the P-Linker in A7.15 with respect to the real rate r is:

$$\frac{dPV_{PLINK}}{dr} = -\frac{c * FV}{r^2} * \left(1 - \frac{1}{(1+r)^N}\right) + \frac{c * FV}{r} * \left(\frac{N}{(1+r)^{N+1}}\right)$$
$$- \frac{N * FV}{(1+r)^{N+1}} \tag{A7.17}$$

Multiply this expression by $(1 + r)$, divide by PV_{PLINK}, as defined in A7.15, and rearrange the terms algebraically (as in equations A6.9 through A6.13) to get:

$$RealMacDurPLINK = \frac{1+r}{r} - \frac{1+r+[N * (c-r)]}{c * [(1+r)^N - 1] + r} \tag{A7.18}$$

The derivation for real rate Macaulay duration for the C-Linker, equation 7.18, is very similar. It starts with the pricing formula, equation 7.17, repeated here.

$$PV_{CLINK} = \frac{(i+c) * FV}{y} * \left(1 - \frac{1}{(1+y)^N}\right) + \frac{FV}{(1+y)^N} \tag{A7.19}$$

The nominal rate is y and the inflation rate is i—they are related to the real rate in the usual manner: $(1 + y) = (1 + r) * (1 + i)$.

The real rate Macaulay duration for the C-Linker is defined to be:

$$RealMacDurCLINK \equiv -\frac{dPV_{CLINK}}{dr} * \frac{(1+r)}{PV_{CLINK}} \tag{A7.20}$$

The first derivative of PV_{CLINK} with respect to the real rate r is:

$$\frac{dPV_{CLINK}}{dr} = -\frac{(1+i) * (c+i) * FV}{y^2} * \left(1 - \frac{1}{(1+y)^N}\right)$$
$$+ \frac{(c+i) * FV}{y} * \left(\frac{N * (1+i)}{(1+y)^{N+1}}\right) - \frac{N * (1+i) * FV}{(1+y)^{N+1}} \tag{A7.21}$$

Note that the changes in the real rate r work through the nominal rate y. Multiply this expression by $(1 + r)$, divide by PV_{CLINK} as defined in A7.19, and rearrange the terms algebraically to get equation 7.18 in the text.

$$RealMacDurCLINK = \frac{1+y}{y} - \frac{1+y+[N*(c-r*(1+i))]}{(c+i)*[(1+y)^N - 1] + y} \quad (A7.22)$$

The inflation rate Macaulay duration for the C-Linker is defined to be:

$$InflationMacDurCLINK \equiv \frac{dPV_{CLINK}}{di} * \frac{(1+i)}{PV_{CLINK}} \quad (A7.23)$$

Its derivation is a bit more complicated because changes in the inflation rate i in the C-Linker pricing equation A7.19 enter directly as well as indirectly via the nominal rate y. The derivative is:

$$\frac{dPV_{CLINK}}{di} = -\frac{(1+r)*(c+i)*FV}{y^2} * \left(1 - \frac{1}{(1+y)^N}\right) + \frac{(c+i)*FV}{y}$$

$$* \left(\frac{N*(1+r)}{(1+y)^{N+1}}\right) - \frac{N*(1+r)*FV}{(1+y)^{N+1}} + \frac{FV}{y} * \left(1 - \frac{1}{(1+y)^N}\right)$$

$$(A7.24)$$

Multiply this expression by $(1 + i)$, divide by PV_{CLINK}, and rearrange the terms to get equation 7.19 in the text.

$$InflationMacDurCLINK = \frac{1+y}{y} - \frac{1+y+[N*(c-r*(1+i))]}{(c+i)*[(1+y)^N - 1]+y}$$

$$- \frac{(1+i)*[(1+y)^N - 1]}{(c+i)*[(1+y)^N - 1]+y} \quad (A7.25)$$

CHAPTER 9 BOND PORTFOLIOS

Chapter 9 uses the simplifying assumption that all the bonds in the portfolio are valued on a coupon date so that the number of periods to final maturity, N, is an integer. To generalize, assume here that the valuation is between coupon payment dates. Let f be the fraction of the period that has gone by and $(1 - f)$ be the fraction remaining. Note that f is equivalent to t/T

in previous chapters. Here the day-count convention (i.e., actual/actual or 30/360) does not matter so simpler notation is used.

The market value for the portfolio is MV and now can include accrued interest. The future cash flows, which include coupon interest and principal redemptions, are summarized by CF_n for $n = 1$ to N. These n do not have to be semiannual periods; in general, they can be months, weeks, or even days until final maturity. The cash flow yield on the portfolio, $YieldPORT$ in the text and here just Y, is the internal rate of return, the solution to the following expression:

$$MV = \sum_{n=1}^{N} \frac{CF_n}{(1+Y)^{n-f}} \tag{A9.1}$$

Let W_n represent the weights—the shares of total market value MV corresponding to the cash flows (CF_n) received on dates 1 to N:

$$W_n = \frac{\dfrac{CF_n}{(1+Y)^{n-f}}}{MV} \tag{A9.2}$$

Note that the weights sum to one:

$$\sum_{n=1}^{N} W_n = 1 \tag{A9.3}$$

Equations for Macaulay duration (here denoted D) and cash flow dispersion (denoted S) for the portfolio, equations 9.3 and 9.4, can now be written compactly as:

$$MacDurPORT = D = \sum_{n=1}^{N} (n-f) * W_n \tag{A9.4}$$

$$DispPORT = S = \sum_{n=1}^{N} (n-f-D)^2 * W_n \tag{A9.5}$$

The portfolio convexity (here X) is the second derivative of A9.1 with respect to the cash flow yield Y, divided by the market value MV.

$$Convexity = X \equiv \frac{d^2 MV}{dY^2} * \frac{1}{MV} \tag{A9.6}$$

That second derivative is:

$$\frac{d^2 MV}{dY^2} = \sum_{n=1}^{N} \frac{(n-f) * (n-f+1) * CF_n}{(1+Y)^{n-f+2}} \tag{A9.7}$$

Substitute A9.10 into A9.6 to get a general formula for the portfolio convexity statistic as of date f:

$$X = \frac{1}{(1+Y)^2} * \left[\frac{\sum_{n=1}^{N} \dfrac{(n-f) * (n-f+1) * CF_n}{(1+Y)^{n-f}}}{MV} \right] \tag{A9.8}$$

This is the general expression for *ConvPORT*, equation 9.6 in the text (for which $f = 0$). Using the weights, the convexity can be written as:

$$X = \frac{1}{(1+Y)^2} * \sum_{n=1}^{N} \left[(n-f)^2 + (n-f) \right] * W_n \tag{A9.9}$$

The derivation of the general expression linking portfolio cash flow yield, Macaulay duration, dispersion, and convexity starts by adding and subtracting D^2 within the brackets in equation A9.9.

$$X = \frac{1}{(1+Y)^2} * \sum_{n=1}^{N} [(n-f)^2 - D^2 + D^2 + D^2 + (n-f)] * W_n \tag{A9.10}$$

Using A9.4, this simplifies to:

$$X = \frac{1}{(1+Y)^2} * \left[\left(\sum_{n=1}^{N} [(n-f)^2 - D^2] * W_n \right) + D^2 + D \right] \tag{A9.11}$$

The key step in the derivation is to demonstrate that the remaining summation term in A9.11 equals the dispersion statistic, S. To see this, expand the squared term in A9.5:

$$S = \sum_{n=1}^{N} (n-f)^2 * W_n - 2 * D * \sum_{n=1}^{N} (n-f) * W_n + D^2 * \sum_{n=1}^{N} W_n \tag{A9.12}$$

Using A9.4 this reduces to:

$$S = \sum_{n=1}^{N} (n-f)^2 * W_n - D^2 * \sum_{n=1}^{N} W_n \tag{A9.13}$$

This expression equals the summation term in A9.11.

$$S = \sum_{n=1}^{N} [(n-f)^2 - D^2] * W_n \tag{A9.14}$$

Substitute A9.14 into A9.11.

$$X = \frac{1}{(1+Y)^2} * [S + D^2 + D] \tag{A9.15}$$

This is the same as equation 9.7 in the text.

Acronyms

AI	Accrued Interest
AOR	Add-On Rate
APR	Annual Percentage Rate
APY	Annual Percentage Yield
BA	Bankers Acceptance
BPV	Basis-Point Value
CATS	Certificates of Accrual on Treasury Securities
CD	Certificate of Deposit
CMT	Constant Maturity Treasury
CP	Commercial Paper
CPI	Consumer Price Index
CRR	Constant Reinvestment Rate
CUSIP	Committee on Uniform Security Identification Procedures
DCF	Discounted Cash Flow
DR	Discount Rate
DV01	Dollar Value of an '01'
EAR	Effective Annual Rate
ETY	Equivalent Taxable Yield
FRA	Forward Rate Agreement
FRN	Floating-Rate Note
HPR	Holding-Period Return
IFR	Implied Forward Rate
IR	Investment Rate
IRA	Individual Retirement Account

IRR	Internal Rate of Return
IRS	Internal Revenue Service
LDI	Liability-Driven Investing
LIBOR	London Inter-Bank Offered Rate
LIONS	Lehman Investment Opportunity Notes
MMC	Money Market Certificate
OAS	Option-Adjusted Spread
OAY	Option-Adjusted Yield
OID	Original Issue Discount
OIS	Overnight Indexed Swap
OTC	Over-the-Counter
PV01	Present Value of an '01'
ROR	Rate of Return
SABB	Semi-Annual Bond Basis
SFR	Swap Fixed Rate
SPE	Special Purpose Entity
STRIPS	Separate Trading in Registered Interest and Principal Securities
TIGRS	Treasury Investment Growth Receipts
TIPS	Treasury Inflation-Protected Securities
VaR	Value at Risk
YTM	Yield to Maturity

Bibliographic Notes

I have used Frank J. Fabozzi's textbook, *Bond Markets, Analysis, and Strategies*, in my Boston University money and capital markets and fixed-income analysis courses since the first edition back in the 1980s. It is now in the eighth edition (Pearson Prentice-Hall, 2013). So, in wanting to cite properly sources for the ideas in this book, I encounter the problem of not always remembering what I got from Fabozzi and what I thought up on my own.

For instance, I know for sure that I first saw the approximation formulas for modified duration and convexity in the Fabozzi book. On the other hand, he makes a point of not focusing on duration as a measure of time. I agree wholeheartedly but recall that I talked about duration as the elasticity of the bond price with respect to a change in its yield to maturity early on, before seeing the book. Needless to say, I am indebted to Frank Fabozzi's prolific work on fixed-income securities and markets.

Much of the content of this book is covered in Fabozzi and in many investments textbooks. For example, bond price and yield calculations, forward rates, term structure theories, and yield duration and convexity are standard fare, so I do not attempt here to identify specific sources for well-known aspects of bond math. I try to provide proper references when appropriate. You see that much of this is self-citation. I've written a number of articles on bond math topics over the last 30 years, and one of my motives for writing this book is to integrate that collection of work.

CHAPTER 1 MONEY MARKET INTEREST RATES

The "Treasury Bill Auction Results" section is based on my article "Bias at the Short End of the Yield Curve," published in *Global Investor* (April 1991). I first saw the official Investment Rate for T-bills having more than six months to maturity (equation 1.12) and its derivation in *Money Market Calculations: Yields, Break-Evens, and Arbitrage*, by Marcia Stigum and John Mann (Dow-Jones Irwin, 1981).

The hourly interest rates example originated as a midterm question in my MBA course in the fall semester of 2003. The point about first converting a money market rate to a 365-day basis before the periodicity conversion to a semiannual bond basis is based on a short article Scott Lummer and I wrote titled "Accurate Compounding Conversions," *Global Investor* (May 1991).

CHAPTER 2 ZERO-COUPON BONDS

The calculation of the implied probability of default is based on an example in John C. Hull, *Options, Futures, and Other Derivatives*, 6th ed. (Pearson Prentice-Hall, 2006).

CHAPTER 3 PRICES AND YIELDS ON COUPON BONDS

I presented a paper titled "Two Common Textbook Misstatements about Bond Prices and Yields" at the annual meeting of the Financial Education Association in Orlando, September 2003. One of the misstatements is the between-coupon-payments bond pricing curiosity when the coupon rate equals the yield to maturity.

The "Implied Probability of Default on Coupon Bonds" section, as in Chapter 2, is based on an example in John C. Hull, *Options, Futures, and Other Derivatives*, 6th ed. (Pearson Prentice-Hall, 2006).

CHAPTER 4 BOND TAXATION

I extended the example in "A Real Market Discount Corporate Bond" from the first edition where I used a Ford bond into a paper entitled "Bad Bond Math: An Object Lesson Using Bloomberg's After-Tax Yields on Market Discount Bonds" using MBIA bonds. The paper was published in the *Journal of Wealth Management* (Spring 2013).

The section on the more theoretically correct and useful equivalent taxable yield for municipal bonds at the end of the chapter is based on unpublished work by Alan J. Daskin, a former colleague at Boston University who is now at NERA Economic Consulting.

CHAPTER 5 YIELD CURVES

The idea of relating the three classic theories of the term structure of interest rates to the "stylized facts" is based on similar treatment in Stephen G. Cecchetti, *Money, Banking, and Financial Markets* (McGraw-Hill Irwin, 2006).

The section "Money Market Implied Forward Rates" is from an article I wrote, "The Calculation and Use of Money Market Implied Forward Rates," published in the *Journal of Cash Management* (September/October 1989). A related paper, which I coauthored with Alan J. Daskin, is "Using Implied Forward Rates in the Selection of a CD Maturity," *Financial Practice and Education* (Fall/Winter 1991).

The discussion of static, or zero-volatility, spreads is based on coverage in Frank J. Fabozzi, *Bond Markets, Analysis, and Strategies*, 7th ed. (Pearson Prentice-Hall, 2010).

CHAPTER 6 DURATION AND CONVEXITY

The 20-year versus 30-year deep discount bond curiosity is the second example that I use in "Two Common Textbook Misstatements about Bond Prices and Yields," presented at the annual meeting of the Financial Education Association in Orlando, September 2003. I first wrote about that phenomenon in a paper titled "The Duration of a Bond as a Price Elasticity and a Fulcrum," published in *Journal of Financial Education* (Fall 1988).

Frederick R. Macaulay's classic book is *Some Theoretical Problems Suggested by the Movements of Interest Rates, Bond Yields and Stock Prices in the United States Since 1856* (National Bureau of Economic Research, 1938).

The general formulas for yield duration and convexity, equations 6.13, 6.16, 6.17, are from my paper, "A Note on the Derivation of Closed-Form Formulas for Duration and Convexity Statistics on and between Coupon Dates," *Journal of Financial Engineering* (June 1998).

I first saw and came to appreciate the value of the approximate modified duration and convexity calculations in an earlier edition of Frank J. Fabozzi, *Bond Markets, Analysis, and Strategies.*

In the conclusion I mention that value-at-risk analysis builds on and goes beyond standard duration. I wrote a paper to demonstrate this point, "A Primer on Bond Portfolio Value at Risk," which I presented at the annual meeting of the Financial Education Association in Hilton Head, September 2008. It was published in *Advances in Financial Education* (Summer/Winter 2009).

CHAPTER 7 FLOATERS AND LINKERS

This chapter is based entirely on two of my papers. The first is "Negative Duration: The Odd Case of GMAC's Floating-Rate Note," which appeared in the *Journal of Applied Finance* (Fall/Winter 2006). The second is "Alternative

Designs for Inflation-Indexed Bonds: P-Linkers and C-Linkers." I presented this paper at the annual meeting of the Financial Education Association in Fort Lauderdale (September 2009). It was published in *Journal of Financial Education* (Fall/Winter 2010).

CHAPTER 8 INTEREST RATE SWAPS

Much of this chapter is rooted in a 1995 monograph that Keith C. Brown and I wrote for the Research Foundation of the Institute of Chartered Financial Analysts, titled *Interest Rate and Currency Swaps: A Tutorial*. In 2001, I co-authored (with Gary L. Gastineau and Rebecca Todd) another monograph, *Risk Management, Derivatives, and Financial Analysis under SFAS No. 133*, for the Research Foundation. Both are available at the CFA Institute's website.

The example of the Ho-Lee adjustment factor for the difference between interest rate futures and forwards is from John C. Hull, *Options, Futures, and Other Derivatives*, 6th ed. (Pearson Prentice-Hall, 2006).

The sections starting with collateralized swaps are based on "A Teaching Note on Pricing and Valuing Interest Rate Swaps Using LIBOR and OIS Discounting," which I wrote in July 2012 to supplement Chapter 8 of the first edition of this book for my MBA students. I later published another version of the paper as "Valuing Interest Rate Swaps Using Overnight Indexed Swap (OIS) Discounting" in the *Journal of Derivatives* (Summer 2013).

The observation that collateralization should raise the fixed rate on an interest rate swap is based on "The Impact of Collateralization on Swap Rates" (*Journal of Finance*, February 2007) by Michael Johannes and Suresh Sundaresan.

CHAPTER 9 BOND PORTFOLIOS

I first saw the relationship linking Macaulay duration, convexity, cash flow dispersion, and the yield to maturity (i.e., equation 9.7) in Olivier de la Grandville, *Bond Pricing and Portfolio Analysis: Protecting Investors in the Long Run* (MIT Press, 2001).

The idea of using the basis-point-value-weighted average of the yields to maturity as a good approximation for the portfolio cash flow yield is from Kenneth D. Garbade, *Fixed Income Analytics* (MIT Press, 1996). The same point is made in a thorough collection of articles on fixed-income management, *Quantitative Management of Bond Portfolios* (Princeton University Press, 2007), by Lev Dynkin, Anthony Gould, Jay Hyman, Vadim Konstantinovsky, and Bruce Phelps.

In the first edition to this book I wrote: "I do not know the source for the example of using curve duration and convexity to improve the hedge ratio between the 30-year T-bond and the 30-year STRIPS, instead of yield duration and convexity. Seriously, even if I did know, I couldn't tell you. In academics, we use a double-blind system for reviewing articles for publication in journals, meaning the reviewer does not know the identity of the author and vice versa. I was the reviewer for an article that makes this point as well as the theoretical propriety of aggregating curve durations and convexities and the implicit violation of the no-arbitrage principle when averaging the yield risk statistics. I recommended 'revise and resubmit' to the editor, but so far the paper has not been published. I thought it is an important contribution but needed editorial improvement. So, if you wrote that article, thank you and I hope someday to give you proper citation." Now, in the second edition I finally can give credit to the authors of that paper. It is "What's Wrong with Those Duration Measures? Nothing" by Robin Grieves and J. Clay Singleton. It appeared in *Frontiers in Finance and Economics* (April 2013).

CHAPTER 10 BOND STRATEGIES

I once wrote an article on lottery strategy, the idea being to identify "unpopular" numbers and number patterns so that if you are fortunate enough to win, you share the grand prize with fewer other winners. "Risk-Efficient Lottery Bets?!" was published in the *Journal of Portfolio Management* (Fall 1987).

Equations 10.1 and 10.2 to determine the notional principal for the interest rate swap needed to change the average duration of a bond portfolio are from an article I coauthored with James Adams, "Mind the Gap: Using Derivatives Overlays to Hedge Pension Duration," which appeared in *Financial Analysts Journal* (July/August 2009).

The "Immunization Implementation Issues" section is based on an article I wrote, "Bond Portfolio Duration, Cash Flow Dispersion and Convexity," published in *Applied Economics Letters* (November-December 2010).

The classic 1952 article by F. M. Redington is titled "Review of the Principles of Life-Office Valuations" and was published in the *Journal of the Institute of Actuaries*. My interest in liability-driven investing was piqued by an article by Laurence B. Siegel and M. Barton Waring, "TIPS, the Dual Duration, and the Pension Plan," which appeared in *Financial Analysts Journal* (September/October 2004).

About the Author

Donald J. Smith is an associate professor of finance at the School of Management, Boston University. He received his MBA and PhD in economic analysis and policy at the School of Business Administration, University of California at Berkeley. Don specializes in teaching fixed-income markets and risk management courses. He has published widely in academic and trade journals, including the *Financial Analysts Journal; Journal of Finance; Journal of Money, Credit, and Banking; Journal of Fixed Income; Journal of Financial Engineering; Financial Management; Journal of Portfolio Management; Journal of Financial Education; Journal of Applied Corporate Finance; Journal of Applied Finance; Applied Economic Letters; GARP Risk Review; Derivatives Strategy; Derivatives Quarterly;* and the *Journal of Derivatives.* Don has coauthored chapters in the *Handbook of Financial Engineering, Interest Rate Swaps, and Cross-Currency Swaps,* and two monographs for the CFA Institute, *Interest Rate and Currency Swaps: A Tutorial* and *Derivatives, Risk Management, and Financial Analysis under SFAS 133.*

Don has been actively involved with executive education for more than 25 years, starting with Manufacturers Hanover Trust Company, where he was senior consultant to the Corporate Professional Development Department. He has developed and led training courses for many financial institutions, including Chemical Bank, Chase Manhattan Bank, Bank of Boston, Lehman Brothers, and the World Bank. He has been teaching fixed-income instruments and advanced interest rate risk management courses for Euromoney Training for over 20 years. Although most of his executive training work is in New York City, Don has taught many courses in London and Hong Kong as well as in Toronto, Mexico City, Caracas, Chennai, Sao Paulo, Buenos Aires, Quito, Cairo, Bahrain, Tokyo, Seoul, Sydney, Singapore, and Kuala Lumpur.

Don lives in Dover, Massachusetts with his wife, Lori Waresmith, and their rescue greyhound, Dolce. His hobbies are easy golf and hard Sudoku.

Acknowledgments

I thank Stephen Isaacs, my original editor at Bloomberg Press, for getting me started on this project and the team at Wiley, Tiffany Charbonier, Bill Falloon, Meg Freeborn, and Chris Gage, for bringing the first edition of *Bond Math* to fruition. I again thank the Wiley team—Tiffany, Bill, Meg, and now Steven Kyritz and Helen Cho—for this second edition.

Many students, colleagues, and coauthors were responsible for all the math errors, typos, and misstatements that didn't appear in the first edition of this book. They were James Adams, Matt Cicero, Jon Katz, Nick Madrid, Gaurav Nagpaul, Brendon Reay, Mark Roberts, Andy Shapiro, Yu Wang, Kenneth Yow, Ethan Yu, and Lu Zhou. For the second edition, Wenjing Cai, Thomas Cui, Sunjoon Park, Chris Sondej, and Zilong Zheng searched for and found some errors. I accept responsibility for all that remain.

I continue to thank my wife, Lori Waresmith, who is a talented botanical artist and master gardener, for her support and enduring marriage to a man who likes bond math.

About the Companion Website

*B*ond Math, Second Edition has a companion website, which can be accessed at www.wiley.com/go/bondmath2e (password: wiley14).

Contents include an extensive set of multiple-choice questions and answers for each chapter in the book. The intent of this companion website is to help readers who might be tested on this material. This book and these questions are appropriate for MBA or advanced undergraduate students, as well as those sitting for the Chartered Financial Analyst® (CFA) exams. I have been using *Bond Math* in my Fixed Income Analysis and Markets courses at Boston University. Feedback on the online materials is very welcome. Contact me at donsmith@bu.edu. I thank Wenjing Cai for her prodigious work at checking the first draft of the questions and answers.

The full Answer Key is available for instructors only on Wiley's Higher Education Website.

Index

Printed and bound by CPI Group (UK) Ltd, Croydon, CR0 4YY

23/04/2025

14660925-0001